The Major Operations
of the Navies in the
War of American Independence

REMAINS OF THE *Revenge*, ONE OF BENEDICT ARNOLD'S SCHOONERS ON LAKE CHAMPLAIN IN 1776

The Major Operations
of the Navies in the
War of American Independence

A.T. Mahan

NONSUCH

First published 1913
Copyright © in this edition 2006
Nonsuch Publishing Ltd

Nonsuch Publishing Limited
The Mill, Brimscombe Port, Stroud, Gloucestershire, GL5 2QG
www.nonsuch-publishing.com

Nonsuch Publishing Ltd is an imprint of Tempus Publishing Group

British Library Cataloguing in Publication Data.
A catalogue record for this book is available from the British Library.

ISBN 1-84588-035-8

Typesetting and origination by Nonsuch Publishing Limited
Printed in Great Britain by Oaklands Book Services Limited

CONTENTS

Introduction to the Modern Edition 7

Preface 9

Introduction 11

I The Naval Campaign on Lake Champlain, 1775–76 15

II Naval Action at Boston, Charleston, New York and Narragansett Bay 29

III The Decisive Period of the War 43

IV France enters the War 47

V The Battle of Ushant 61

VI Operations in the West Indies, Georgia and South Carolina 71

VII The Naval War in European Waters 85

VIII Rodney and De Guichen's Naval Campaigns 91

IX Naval Campaign in the West Indies, 1781 111

X Naval Operations Preceding and Determining the Fall of Yorktown 119

XI Naval Events of 1781 in Europe 131

XII The Final Naval Campaign in the West Indies 137

XIII The Final Relief of Gibraltar 159

XIV The Naval Operations in the East Indies 163

Glossary 179

Index 187

INTRODUCTION TO THE MODERN EDITION

> There shall be a firm and perpetual peace between his Britannic Majesty and
> the said states, and between the subjects of the one and the citizens of the other,
> wherefore all hostilities both by sea and land shall from henceforth cease.
>
> Article 7, Treaty of Paris, 1783

THE BATTLES OF BUNKER HILL, Lexington, Saratoga and Yorktown—these names evoke
the American War of Independence and the victorious campaign of the newly formed
United States to win their freedom from what they perceived as the tyranny of British
rule. Yet it is often overlooked that, while the land battles of the Continental Army were
undoubtedly crucial to the victory of the Americans, the contest for control of the seas was
equally, if not more, important to the final outcome of the quest for independence, a fact
that is clearly recognised in Article 7 of the peace treaty of 1783.

By the late eighteenth century Britain was widely acknowledged to be the world's
leading naval power, not really surprising for an island nation whose trade and security,
as well as the stability of its colonial structure, relied on its ability to navigate the oceans
and defend against maritime threats. The Royal Navy had developed as a permanent naval
service during the Protectorate of Oliver Cromwell in the seventeenth century and had not
been defeated in battle since 1692. In contrast, the first American navy was only approved
in the Continental Congress on 13 October 1775 and was to consist of no ships bigger than
frigate class (a smaller, manoeuvrable, lightly-armed ship used for scouting and raiding).
Unsurprisingly, the aim of this newly formed body was not to contest the might of the
British navy, whose smallest ships of the line carried three tiers of guns, but rather to raid
enemy commercial vessels and attack British transports when not accompanied by Royal
Navy warships. As long as this disparity of force remained, the British navy could supply
and support its army with relative impunity, effectively eliminating any likelihood of an
American victory in the war.

Ironically, it was a land-based event that was to become the catalyst for an alteration in
the maritime situation that would even the odds for the United States. Since the start of
the war America had been receiving covert help from Britain's European rivals, particularly
France. The comprehensive defeat of part of the British army at Saratoga in October 1777
led France to enter the war openly on the side of the Americans, and, crucially, to provide
not only troops, but also the support of her navy in the fight against the British. In 1779
Spain also entered the war as an ally of the French, adding her naval might to the contest.
What had started as a colonial rebellion on one continent quickly became a global war,
with each side attempting not only to aid their respective armies in America, but also
contesting the naval conflict as far away as the Indian Ocean.

Alfred Thayer Mahan, an officer in the United States Navy for over thirty years, is generally considered to be one of the best naval strategists and historians that America has ever produced. In *Major Operations of the Navies* he provides an unparalleled, fully comprehensive account of each of the naval battles, both in American waters and on the wider global canvas, relating to and affecting the final outcome of the War of Independence. An unbiased account of the strategy and actions of both sides, this perceptive history clearly demonstrates the vital importance of the naval contest to the Americans' fight for independence.

PREFACE

T HE CONTENTS OF THIS VOLUME were first contributed as a chapter, under the title of "Major Operations, 1762–1783," to the "History of the Royal Navy," in seven volumes, published by Messrs. Sampson Low, Marston, and Company, under the general editorship of the late Sir William Laird Clowes. For permission to republish now in this separate form, the author has to express his thanks to the publishers of that work.

In the Introduction following this Preface, the author has summarized the general lesson to be derived from the course of this War of American Independence, as distinct from the particular discussion and narration of the several events which constitute the body of the treatment. These lessons he conceives to carry admonition for the present and future based upon the surest foundations; namely, upon the experience of the past as applicable to present conditions. The essential similarity between the two is evident in a common dependence upon naval strength.

There has been a careful re-reading and revision of the whole text; but the changes found necessary to be made are much fewer than might have been anticipated after the lapse of fifteen years. Numerous footnotes in the History, specifying the names of ships in fleets, and of their commanders in various battles, have been omitted, as not necessary to the present purpose, though eminently proper and indeed indispensable to an extensive work of general reference and of encyclopaedic scope, such as the History is. Certain notes retained with the inititials W.L.C. are due to the editor of that work.

A.T. MAHAN
DECEMBER, 1912

INTRODUCTION

M ACAULAY, IN A STRIKING PASSAGE of his Essay on Frederick the Great, wrote, "The evils produced by his wickedness were felt in lands where the name of Prussia was unknown. In order that he might rob a neighbour whom he had promised to defend, black men fought on the coast of Coromandel, and red men scalped each other by the Great Lakes of North America."

Wars, like conflagrations, tend to spread; more than ever perhaps in these days of close international entanglements and rapid communications. Hence the anxiety aroused and the care exercised by the governments of Europe, the most closely associated and the most sensitive on the earth, to forestall the kindling of even the slightest flame in regions where all alike are interested, though with diverse objects; regions such as the Balkan group of States in their exasperating relations with the Turkish empire, under which the Balkan peoples see constantly the bitter oppression of men of their own blood and religious faith by the tyranny of a government which can neither assimilate nor protect. The condition of Turkish European provinces is a perpetual lesson to those disposed to ignore or to depreciate the immense difficulties of administering politically, under one government, peoples traditionally and racially distinct, yet living side by side; not that the situation is much better anywhere in the Turkish empire. This still survives, though in an advanced state of decay, simply because other States are not prepared to encounter the risks of a disturbance which might end in a general bonfire, extending its ravages to districts very far remote from the scene of the original trouble.

Since these words were written, actual war has broken out in the Balkans. The Powers, anxious each as to the effect upon its own ambitions of any disturbance in European Turkey, have steadily abstained from efficient interference in behalf of the downtrodden Christians of Macedonia, surrounded by sympathetic kinsfolk. Consequently, in thirty years past this underbrush has grown drier and drier, fit kindling for fuel. In the Treaty of Berlin, in 1877, stipulation was made for their betterment in governance, and we are now told that in 1880 Turkey framed a scheme for such,—and pigeonholed it. At last, under unendurable conditions, spontaneous combustion has followed. There can be no assured peace until it is recognised practically that Christianity, by the respect which it alone among religions inculcates for the welfare of the individual, is an essential factor in developing in nations the faculty of self-government, apart from which fitness to govern others does not exist. To keep Christian peoples under the rule of a non-Christian race, is, therefore, to perpetuate a state hopeless of reconcilement and pregnant of sure explosion. Explosions always happen inconveniently. *Obsta principiis* is the only safe rule; the application of which is not suppression of overt discontent but relief of grievances.

The War of American Independence was no exception to the general rule of propagation that has been noted. When our forefathers began to agitate against the Stamp Act and the other measures that succeeded it, they as little foresaw the spread of their action to the East and West Indies, to the English Channel and Gibraltar, as did the British ministry which in framing the Stamp Act struck the match from which these consequences followed. When Benedict Arnold on Lake Champlain by vigorous use of small means obtained a year's delay for the colonists, he compassed the surrender of Burgoyne in 1777. The surrender of Burgoyne, justly estimated as the decisive event of the war, was due to Arnold's previous action, gaining the delay which is a first object for all defence, and which to the unprepared colonists was a vital necessity. The surrender of Burgoyne determined the intervention of France, in 1778; the intervention of France the accession of Spain thereto, in 1779. The war with these two Powers led to the maritime occurrences, the interferences with neutral trade, that gave rise to the Armed Neutrality; the concurrence of Holland in which brought war between that country and Great Britain, in 1780. This extension of hostilities affected not only the West Indies but the East, through the possessions of the Dutch in both quarters and at the Cape of Good Hope. If not the occasion of Suffren being sent to India, the involvement of Holland in the general war had a powerful effect upon the brilliant operations which he conducted there; as well as at, and for, the Cape of Good Hope, then a Dutch possession, on his outward voyage.

In the separate publication of these pages, my intention and hope are to bring home incidentally to American readers this vast extent of the struggle to which our own Declaration of Independence was but the prelude; with perchance the further needed lesson for the future, that questions the most remote from our own shores may involve us in unforeseen difficulties, especially if we permit a train of communication to be laid by which the outside fire can leap step by step to the American continents. How great a matter a little fire kindleth! Our Monroe Doctrine is in final analysis merely the formulation of national precaution that, as far as in its power to prevent, there shall not lie scattered about the material which foreign possessions in these continents might supply for the extension of combustion originating elsewhere; and the objection to Asiatic immigration, however debased by less worthy feelings or motives, is on the part of thinking men simply a recognition of the same danger arising from the presence of an inassimilable mass of population, racially and traditionally distinct in characteristics, behind which would lie the sympathies and energy of a powerful military and naval Asiatic empire.

Conducive as each of these policies is to national safety and peace amid international conflagration, neither the one nor the other can be sustained without the creation and maintenance of a preponderant navy. In the struggle with which this book deals, Washington at the time said that the navies had the casting vote. To Arnold on Lake Champlain, to de Grasse at Yorktown, fell the privilege of exercising that prerogative at the two great decisive moments of the War. To the Navy also, beyond any other single instrumentality, was due eighty years later the successful suppression of the movement of Secession. The effect of the blockade of the Southern coasts upon the financial and military efficiency of the Confederate Government has never been closely calculated, and probably is incalculable. At these two principal national epochs control of the water was the most determinative factor. In the future, upon the Navy will depend the successful maintenance of the two leading national policies mentioned; the two most essential to the part this country is to play in the progress of the world.

For, while numerically great in population, the United States is not so in proportion to territory; nor, though wealthy, is she so in proportion to her exposure. That Japan at four thousand miles distance has a population of over three hundred to the square mile, while our three great Pacific States average less than twenty, is a portentous fact. The immense aggregate numbers resident elsewhere in the United States cannot be transfered thither to meet an emergency, nor contribute effectively to remedy this insufficiency; neither can a land force on the defensive protect, if the way of the sea is open. In such opposition of smaller numbers against larger, nowhere do organisation and development count as much as in navies. Nowhere so well as on the sea can a general numerical inferiority be compensated by specific numerical superiority, resulting from the correspondence between the force employed and the nature of the ground. It follows strictly, by logic and by inference, that by no other means can safety be insured as economically and as efficiently. Indeed, in matters of national security, economy and efficiency are equivalent terms. The question of the Pacific is probably the greatest world problem of the twentieth century, in which no great country is so largely and directly interested as is the United States. For the reason given it is essentially a naval question, the third in which the United States finds its well-being staked upon naval adequacy.

I

THE NAVAL CAMPAIGN ON
LAKE CHAMPLAIN, 1775–76

AT THE TIME WHEN HOSTILITIES began between Great Britain and her American Colonies, the fact was realised generally, being evident to reason and taught by experience, that control of the water, both ocean and inland, would have a preponderant effect upon the contest. It was clear to reason, for there was a long seaboard with numerous interior navigable watercourses, and at the same time scanty and indifferent communications by land. Critical portions of the territory involved were yet an unimproved wilderness. Experience, the rude but efficient schoolmaster of that large portion of mankind which gains knowledge only by hard knocks, had confirmed through the preceding French wars the inferences of the thoughtful. Therefore, conscious of the great superiority of the British Navy, which, however, had not then attained the unchallenged supremacy of a later day, the American leaders early sought the alliance of the Bourbon kingdoms, France and Spain, the hereditary enemies of Great Britain. There alone could be found the counterpoise to a power which, if unchecked, must ultimately prevail.

Nearly three years elapsed before the Colonists accomplished this object, by giving a demonstration of their strength in the enforced surrender of Burgoyne's army at Saratoga. This event has merited the epithet "decisive," because, and only because, it decided the intervention of France. It may be affirmed, with little hesitation, that this victory of the colonists was directly the result of naval force,—that of the colonists themselves. It was the cause that naval force from abroad, entering into the contest, transformed it from a local to a universal war, and assured the independence of the Colonies. That the Americans were strong enough to impose the capitulation of Saratoga, was due to the invaluable year of delay secured to them by their little navy on Lake Champlain, created by the indomitable energy, and handled with the indomitable courage, of the traitor, Benedict Arnold. That the war spread from America to Europe, from the English Channel to the Baltic, from the Bay of Biscay to the Mediterranean, from the West Indies to the Mississippi, and ultimately involved the waters of the remote peninsula of Hindustan, is traceable, through Saratoga, to the rude flotilla which in 1776 anticipated its enemy in the possession of Lake Champlain. The events which thus culminated merit therefore a clearer understanding, and a fuller treatment, than their intrinsic importance and petty scale would justify otherwise.

In 1775, only fifteen years had elapsed since the expulsion of the French from the North American continent. The concentration of their power, during its continuance, in the valley of the St. Lawrence, had given direction to the local conflict, and had impressed upon men's minds the importance of Lake Champlain, of its tributary Lake George, and of the Hudson River, as forming a consecutive, though not continuous, water line of communications from the St. Lawrence to New York. The strength of Canada against attack by land lay in its remoteness, in the wilderness to be traversed before it was reached, and in the strength of the line of the St. Lawrence, with the fortified posts of Montreal and Quebec on its northern bank. The wilderness, it is true, interposed its passive resistance to attacks from Canada as well as to attacks upon it; but when it had been traversed, there were to the southward no such strong natural positions confronting the assailant. Attacks from the south fell upon the front, or at best upon the flank, of the line of the St. Lawrence. Attacks from Canada took New York and its dependencies in the rear.

These elements of natural strength, in the military conditions of the North, were impressed upon the minds of the Americans by the prolonged resistance of Canada to the greatly superior numbers of the British Colonists in the previous wars. Regarded, therefore, as a base for attacks, of a kind with which they were painfully familiar, but to be undergone now under disadvantages of numbers and power never before experienced, it was desirable to gain possession of the St. Lawrence and its posts before they were strengthened and garrisoned. At this outset of hostilities, the American insurgents, knowing clearly their own minds, possessed the advantage of the initiative over the British government, which still hesitated to use against those whom it styled rebels the preventive measures it would have taken at once against a recognised enemy.

Under these circumstances, in May, 1775, a body of two hundred and seventy Americans, led by Ethan Allen and Benedict Arnold, seized the posts of Ticonderoga and Crown Point, which were inadequately garrisoned. These are on the upper waters of Lake Champlain, where it is less than a third of a mile wide; Ticonderoga being on a peninsula formed by the lake and the inlet from Lake George, Crown Point on a promontory twelve miles lower down.[1] They were positions of recognised importance, and had been advanced posts of the British in previous wars. A schooner being found there, Arnold, who had been a seaman, embarked in her and hurried to the foot of the lake. The wind failed him when still thirty miles from St. John's, another fortified post on the lower narrows, where the lake gradually tapers down to the Richelieu River, its outlet to the St. Lawrence. Unable to advance otherwise, Arnold took to his boats with thirty men, pulled through the night, and at six o'clock on the following morning surprised the post, in which were only a sergeant and a dozen men. He reaped the rewards of celerity. The prisoners informed him that a considerable body of troops was expected from Canada, on its way to Ticonderoga; and this force in fact reached St. John's on the next day. When it arrived, Arnold was gone, having carried off a sloop which he found there and destroyed everything else that could float. By such trifling means two active officers had secured the temporary control of the lake itself and of the approaches to it from the south. There being no roads, the British, debarred from the water line, were unable to advance. Sir Guy Carleton, Governor and Commander-in-Chief in Canada, strengthened the works at St. John's, and built a schooner; but his force was inadequate to meet that of the Americans.

The seizure of the two posts, being an act of offensive war, was not at once pleasing to the American Congress, which still clung to the hope of reconciliation; but events were marching rapidly, and ere summer was over the invasion of Canada was ordered. General Montgomery, appointed to that enterprise, embarked at Crown Point with two thousand men on September 4th, and soon afterwards appeared before St. John's, which after prolonged operations capitulated on the 3d of November. On the 13th Montgomery entered Montreal, and thence pressed down the St. Lawrence to Pointe aux Trembles, twenty miles above Quebec. There he joined Arnold, who in the month of October had

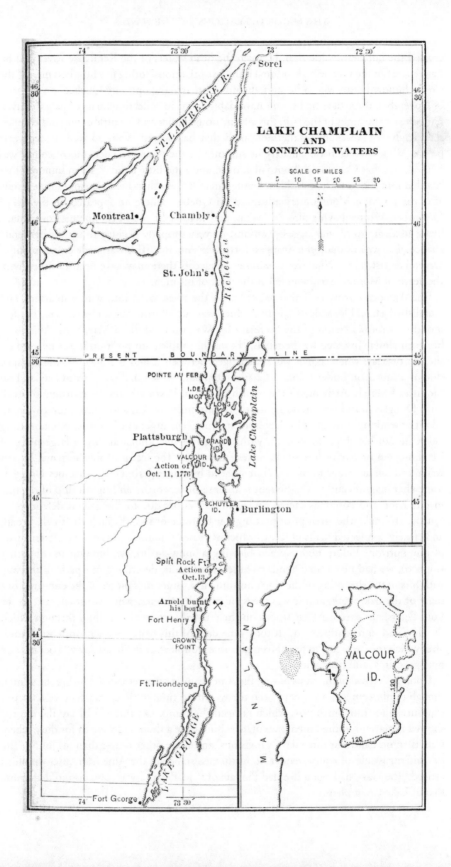

LAKE CHAMPLAIN
AND
CONNECTED WATERS

SCALE OF MILES
0   5   10   15   20   25   30

N

Sorel

Montreal

Chambly

St. John's

St. Lawrence R.

Richelieu R.

PRESENT   BOUNDARY   LINE

POINTE AU FER

I. DE LA MOTTE

LONG ID.

Lake Champlain

Plattsburgh

GRAND ID.

VALCOUR ID.
Action of
Oct. 11, 1776

SCHUYLER ID.   Burlington

Split Rock Pt.
Action of
Oct. 13

Arnold burnt
his boats

Fort Henry

CROWN POINT

Ft. Ticonderoga

LAKE GEORGE

Fort George

MAINLAND

VALCOUR
ID.

120

120

120

crossed the northern wilderness, between the head waters of the Kennebec River and St. Lawrence. On the way he had endured immense privations, losing five hundred men of the twelve hundred with whom he started; and upon arriving opposite Quebec, on the 10th of November, three days had been unavoidably spent in collecting boats to pass the river. Crossing on the night of the 13th, this adventurous soldier and his little command climbed the Heights of Abraham by the same path that had served Wolfe so well sixteen years before. With characteristic audacity he summoned the place. The demand of course was refused; but that Carleton did not fall at once upon the little band of seven hundred that bearded him shows by how feeble a tenure Great Britain then held Canada. Immediately after the junction Montgomery advanced on Quebec, where he appeared on the 5th of December. Winter having already begun, and neither his numbers nor his equipments being adequate to regular siege operations, he very properly decided to try the desperate chance of an assault upon the strongest fortress in America. This was made on the night of December 31st, 1775. Whatever possibility of success there may have been vanished with the death of Montgomery, who fell at the head of his men.

The American army retired three miles up the river, went into winter-quarters, and established a land blockade of Quebec, which was cut off from the sea by the ice. "For five months," wrote Carleton to the Secretary for War, on the 14th of May, 1776, "this town has been closely invested by the rebels." From this unpleasant position it was relieved on the 6th of May, when signals were exchanged between it and the *Surprise*, the advance ship of a squadron under Captain Charles Douglas,[2] which had sailed from England on the 11th of March. Arriving off the mouth of the St. Lawrence, on the morning of April 12th, Douglas found ice extending nearly twenty miles to sea, and packed too closely to admit of working through it by dexterous steering. The urgency of the case not admitting delay, he ran his ship, the *Isis*, 50, with a speed of five knots, against a large piece of ice about ten or twelve feet thick, to test the effect. The ice, probably softened by salt water and salt air, went to pieces. "Encouraged by this experiment," continues Douglas, somewhat magnificently, "we thought it an enterprise worthy an English ship of the line in our King and country's sacred cause, and an effort due to the gallant defenders of Quebec, to make the attempt of pressing her by force of sail, through the thick, broad, and closely connected fields of ice, to which we saw no bounds towards the western part of our horizon. Before night (when blowing a snow-storm, we brought-to, or rather stopped), we had penetrated about eight leagues into it, describing our path all the way with bits of the sheathing of the ship's bottom, and sometimes pieces of the cutwater, but none of the oak plank; and it was pleasant enough at times, when we stuck fast, to see Lord Petersham exercising his troops on the crusted surface of that fluid through which the ship had so recently sailed." It took nine days of this work to reach Anticosti Island, after which the ice seems to have given no more trouble; but further delay was occasioned by fogs, calms, and head winds.

Upon the arrival of the ships of war, the Americans at once retreated. During the winter, though reinforcements must have been received from time to time, they had wasted from exposure, and from small-pox, which ravaged the camp. On the 1st of May the returns showed nineteen hundred men present, of whom only a thousand were fit for duty. There were then on hand but three days' provisions, and none other nearer than St. John's. The inhabitants would of course render no further assistance to the Americans after the ships arrived. The Navy had again decided the fate of Canada, and was soon also to determine that of Lake Champlain.

When two hundred troops had landed from the ships, Carleton marched out, "to see," he said, "what these mighty boasters were about." The sneer was unworthy a man of his generous character, for the boasters had endured much for faint chances of success; and the smallness of the reinforcement which encouraged him to act shows either an extreme prudence on his part, or the narrow margin by which Quebec escaped. He found the enemy busy with preparations for retreat, and upon his appearance they abandoned their camp. Their forces on the two sides of the river being now separated by the enemy's shipping, the Americans retired first to Sorel, where the Richelieu enters the St. Lawrence, and thence continued to fall back by gradual stages. It was not until June 15th that Arnold quitted Montreal; and at the end of June the united force was still on the Canadian side of the present border line. On the 3d of July it reached Crown Point, in a pitiable state from small-pox and destitution.

Both parties began at once to prepare for a contest upon Lake Champlain. The Americans, small as their flotilla was, still kept the superiority obtained for them by Arnold's promptitude a year before. On the 25th of June the American General Schuyler, commanding the Northern Department, wrote: "We have happily such a naval superiority on Lake Champlain, that I have a confident hope the enemy will not appear upon it this campaign, especially as our force is increasing by the addition of gondolas, two nearly finished. Arnold, however,"—whose technical knowledge caused him to be intrusted with the naval preparations,—"says that 300 carpenters should be employed and a large number of gondolas, row-galleys, etc., be built, twenty or thirty at least. There is great difficulty in getting the carpenters needed." Arnold's ideas were indeed on a scale worthy of the momentous issues at stake. "To augment our navy on the lake appears to me of the utmost importance. There is water between Crown Point and Pointe au Fer for vessels of the largest size. I am of opinion that row-galleys are the best construction and cheapest for this

MAJOR-GENERAL
PHILIP SCHUYLER

EDWARD PELLEW, AFTERWARDS
ADMIRAL LORD EXMOUTH

lake. Perhaps it may be well to have one frigate of 36 guns. She may carry 18-pounders on the Lake, and be superior to any vessel that can be built or floated from St. John's."

Unfortunately for the Americans, their resources in men and means were far inferior to those of their opponents, who were able eventually to carry out, though on a somewhat smaller scale, Arnold's idea of a sailing ship, strictly so called, of force as yet unknown in inland waters. Such a ship, aided as she was by two consorts of somewhat similar character, dominated the Lake as soon as she was afloat, reversing all the conditions. To place and equip her, however, required time, invaluable time, during which Arnold's two schooners exercised control. Baron Riedesel, the commander of the German contingent with Carleton, after examining the American position at Ticonderoga, wrote, "If we could have begun our expedition four weeks earlier, I am satisfied that everything would have been ended this year (1776); but, not having shelter nor other necessary things, we were unable to remain at the other [southern] end of Champlain." So delay favors the defence, and changes issues. What would have been the effect upon the American cause if, simultaneously with the loss of New York, August 20th–September 15th, had come news of the fall of Ticonderoga, the repute of which for strength stood high? Nor was this all; for in that event, the plan which was wrecked in 1777 by Sir William Howe's ill-conceived expedition to the Chesapeake would doubtless have been carried out in 1776. In a contemporary English paper occurs the following significant item: "London, September 26th, 1776. Advices have been received here from Canada, dated August 12th, that General Burgoyne's army has found it impracticable to get across the lakes this season. The naval force of the Provincials is too great for them to contend with at present. They must build larger vessels for this purpose, and these cannot be ready before next summer. The design *was*[3] that the two armies commanded by Generals Howe and Burgoyne should cooperate; that they should both be on the Hudson River at the same time; that they should join about Albany, and thereby cut off all communication between the northern and southern Colonies."[4]

As Arnold's more ambitious scheme could not be realised, he had to content himself with gondolas and galleys, for the force he was to command as well as to build. The precise difference between the two kinds of rowing vessels thus distinguished by name, the writer has not been able to ascertain. The gondola was a flat-bottomed boat, and inferior in nautical qualities—speed, handiness, and seaworthiness—to the galleys, which probably were keeled. The latter certainly carried sails, and may have been capable of beating to windward. Arnold preferred them, and stopped the building of gondolas. "The galleys," he wrote, "are quick moving, which will give us a great advantage in the open lake." The complements of the galleys were eighty men, of the gondolas forty-five; from which, and from their batteries, it may be inferred that the latter were between one third and one half the size of the former. The armaments of the two were alike in character, but those of the gondolas much lighter. American accounts agree with Captain Douglas's report of one galley captured by the British. In the bows, an 18 and a 12-pounder; in the stern, two 9s; in broadside, from four to six 6s. There is in this a somewhat droll reminder of the disputed merits of bow, stern, and broadside fire, in a modern iron-clad; and the practical conclusion is much the same. The gondolas had one 12-pounder and two 6s. All the vessels of both parties carried a number of swivel guns.

Amid the many difficulties which lack of resources imposed upon all American undertakings, Arnold succeeded in getting afloat with three schooners, a sloop, and five gondolas, on the 20th of August. He cruised at the upper end of Champlain till the 1st of September, when he moved rapidly north, and on the 3d anchored in the lower narrows, twenty-five miles above St. John's, stretching his line from shore to shore. Scouts had kept him informed of the progress of the British naval preparations, so that he knew that there was no immediate danger; while an advanced position, maintained with a bold front, would certainly prevent reconnoissances by water, and possibly might impose somewhat upon the enemy. The latter, however, erected batteries on each side of the anchorage, compelling Arnold to fall back to the broader lake. He then had soundings taken about Valcour Island, and between it and the western shore; that being the position in which he intended to make a stand. He retired thither on the 23d of September.

The British on their side had contended with no less obstacles than their adversaries, though of a somewhat different character. To get carpenters and materials to build, and seamen to man, were the chief difficulties of the Americans, the necessities of the seaboard conceding but partially the demands made upon it; but their vessels were built upon the shores of the Lake, and launched into navigable waters. A large fleet of transports and ships of war in the St. Lawrence supplied the British with adequate resources, which were utilized judiciously and energetically by Captain Douglas; but to get these to the Lake was a long and arduous task. A great part of the Richelieu River was shoal, and obstructed by rapids. The point where lake navigation began was at St. John's, to which the nearest approach, by a hundred-ton schooner, from the St. Lawrence, was Chambly, ten miles below. Flat-boats and long-boats could be dragged up stream, but vessels of any size had to be transported by land; and the engineers found the roadbed too soft in places to bear the weight of a hundred tons. Under Douglas's directions, the planking and frames of two schooners were taken down at Chambly, and carried round by road to St. John's, where they were again put together. At Quebec he found building a new hull, of one hundred and eighty tons. This he took apart nearly to the keel, shipping the frames in thirty long-boats, which the transport captains consented to surrender, together with their carpenters, for service on the Lake. Drafts from the ships of war, and volunteers from the transports, furnished a body of seven hundred seamen for the same employment,—a force to which the Americans could oppose nothing equal, commanded as it was by regular naval officers. The largest vessel was ship-rigged, and had a battery of eighteen 12-pounders; she was called the *Inflexible*, and was commanded by Lieutenant John Schanck. The two schooners, *Maria*, Lieutenant Starke, and *Carleton*, Lieutenant James Richard Dacres, carried respectively fourteen and twelve 6-pounders. These were the backbone of the British flotilla. There were also a radeau, the *Thunderer*, and a large gondola, the *Loyal Convert*, both heavily armed; but, being equally heavy of movement, they do not appear to have played any important part. Besides these, when the expedition started, there were twenty gunboats, each carrying one fieldpiece, from 24s to 9-pounders; or, in some cases, howitzers.[5]

"By all these means," wrote Douglas on July 21st, "our acquiring an absolute dominion over Lake Champlain is not doubted of." The expectation was perfectly sound. With a working breeze, the *Inflexible* alone could sweep the Lake clear of all that floated on it. But the element of time remained. From the day of this writing till that on which he saw the *Inflexible* leave St. John's, October 4th, was over ten weeks; and it was not until the 9th that Carleton was ready to advance with the squadron. By that time the American troops at the head of the Lake had increased to eight or ten thousand. The British land force is reported[6] as thirteen thousand, of which six thousand were in garrison at St. John's and elsewhere.

Arnold's last reinforcements reached him at Valcour on the 6th of October. On that day, and in the action of the 11th, he had with him all the American vessels on the Lake, except one schooner and one galley. His force, thus, was two schooners and a sloop, broadside vessels, besides four galleys and eight gondolas, which may be assumed reasonably to have depended on their bow guns; there, at least, was their heaviest fire. Thus reckoned, his flotilla, disposed to the best advantage, could bring into action at one time, two 18s, thirteen 12s, one 9, two 6s, twelve 4s, and two 2-pounders, independent of swivels; total thirty-two guns, out of eighty-four that were mounted in fifteen vessels. To this the British had to oppose, in three broadside vessels, nine 12s and thirteen 6s, and in twenty gunboats, twenty other brass guns, "from twenty-four to nines, some with howitzers;"[7] total forty-two guns. In this statement the radeau and gondola have not been included, because of their unmanageableness. Included as broadside vessels, they would raise the British armament—by three 24s, three 12s, four 9s, and a howitzer—to a total of fifty-three guns. Actually, they could be brought into action only under exceptional circumstances, and are more properly omitted.

These minutiae are necessary for the proper appreciation of what Captain Douglas justly called "a momentous event." It was a strife of pigmies for the prize of a continent, and the leaders are entitled to full credit both for their antecedent energy and for their dispositions in the contest; not least the unhappy man who, having done so much to save his country, afterwards blasted his name by a treason unsurpassed in modern war. Energy and audacity had so far preserved the Lake to the Americans; Arnold determined to have one more try of the chances. He did not know the full force of the enemy, but he expected that "it would be very formidable, if not equal to ours."[8] The season, however, was so near its end that a severe check would equal a defeat, and would postpone Carleton's further advance to the next spring. Besides, what was the worth of such a force as the American, such a flotilla, under the guns of Ticonderoga, the Lake being lost? It was eminently a case for taking chances, even if the detachment should be sacrificed, as it was.

Arnold's original purpose had been to fight under way; and it was from this point of view that he valued the galleys, because of their mobility. It is uncertain when he first learned of the rig and battery of the *Inflexible*; but a good look-out was kept, and the British squadron was sighted from Valcour when it quitted the narrows. It may have been seen even earlier; for Carleton had been informed, erroneously, that the Americans were near Grand Island, which led him to incline to that side, and so open out Valcour sooner. The British anchored for the night of October 10th, between Grand and Long⁹ Islands. Getting under way next morning, they stood up the Lake with a strong north-east wind, keeping along Grand Island, upon which their attention doubtless was fastened by the intelligence which they had received; but it was a singular negligence thus to run to leeward with a fair wind, without thorough scouting on both hands. The consequence was that the American flotilla was not discovered until Valcour Island, which is from one hundred and twenty to one hundred and eighty feet high throughout its two miles of length, was so far passed that the attack had to be made from the south,—from leeward.

When the British were first made out, Arnold's second in command, Waterbury, urged that in view of the enemy's superiority the flotilla should get under way at once, and fight them "on a retreat in the main lake;" the harbour being disadvantageous "to fight a number so much superior, and the enemy being able to surround us on every side, we lying between an island and the main." Waterbury's advice evidently found its origin in that fruitful source of military errors of design, which reckons the preservation of a force first of objects, making the results of its action secondary. With sounder judgment, Arnold decided to hold on. A retreat before square-rigged sailing vessels having a fair wind, by a heterogeneous force like his own, of unequal speeds and batteries, could result only in disaster. Concerted fire and successful escape were alike improbable; and besides, escape, if feasible, was but throwing up the game. Better trust to a steady, well-ordered position, developing the utmost fire. If the enemy discovered him, and came in by the northern entrance, there was a five-foot knoll in mid-channel which might fetch the biggest of them up; if, as proved to be the case, the island should be passed, and the attack should be made from leeward, it probably would be partial and in disorder, as also happened. The correctness of Arnold's decision not to chance a retreat was shown in the retreat of two days later.

Valcour is on the west side of the Lake, about three quarters of a mile from the main; but a peninsula projecting from the island at mid-length narrows this interval to a half-mile. From the accounts, it is clear that the American flotilla lay south of this peninsula. Arnold therefore had a reasonable hope that it might be passed undetected. Writing to Gates, the Commander-in-Chief at Ticonderoga, he said: "There is a good harbour, and if the enemy venture up the Lake it will be impossible for them to take advantage of our situation. If we succeed in our attack upon them, it will be impossible for any to escape. If we are worsted, our retreat is open and free. In case of wind, which generally blows fresh at this season, our craft will make good weather, while theirs cannot keep the Lake." It is apparent from this, written three weeks before the battle, that he then was not expecting a force materially different from his own. Later, he describes his position as being "in a small bay on the west side of the island, as near together as possible, and in such a form that few vessels can attack us at the same time, and those will be exposed to the fire of the whole fleet." Though he unfortunately gives no details, he evidently had sound tactical ideas. The formation of the anchored vessels' is described by the British officers as a half-moon.

When the British discovered the enemy, they hauled up for them. Arnold ordered one of his schooners, the *Royal Savage*, and the four galleys, to get under way; the two other schooners and the eight gondolas remaining at their anchors. *The Royal Savage*, dropping to leeward,—by bad mangement, Arnold says,—came, apparently unsupported, under the distant fire of the *Inflexible*, as she drew under the lee of Valcour at 11 A.M., followed by the *Carleton*, and at greater distance by the *Maria* and the gunboats. Three shots from the ship's 12-pounders struck the *Royal Savage*, which then ran ashore on the southern point of the island. The *Inflexible*, followed closely by the *Carleton*, continued on, but fired only occasionally; showing that Arnold was keeping his galleys in hand, at long bowls,—as small vessels with one eighteen should be kept, when confronted with a broadside of nine guns. Between the island and the main the north-east wind doubtless drew more northerly, adverse to the ship's approach; but, a flaw off the cliffs taking the fore and aft sails of the *Carleton*, she fetched "nearly into the middle of the rebel half-moon, where Lieutenant J.R. Dacres intrepidly anchored with a spring on her cable." The *Maria*, on board which was Carleton, together with Commander Thomas Pringle, commanding the flotilla, was to leeward when the chase began, and could not get into close action that day. By this time, seventeen of the twenty gunboats had come up, and, after silencing the *Royal Savage*, pulled up to within point-blank range of the American flotilla. "The cannonade was tremendous," wrote Baron Riedesel. Lieutenant Edward Longcroft, of the radeau *Thunderer*, not being able to get his raft into action, went with a boat's crew on board the *Royal Savage*, and for a time turned her guns upon her former friends; but the fire of the latter forced him again to abandon her, and it seemed so likely that she might be retaken that she was set on fire by Lieutenant Starke of the *Maria*, when already "two rebel boats were very near her. She soon after blew up." The American guns converging on the *Carleton* in her central position, she suffered severely. Her commander, Lieutenant Dacres, was knocked senseless; another officer lost an arm; only Mr. Edward Pellew, afterwards Lord Exmouth, remained fit for duty. The spring being shot away, she swung bows on to the enemy, and her fire was thus silenced. Captain Pringle signalled to her to withdraw; but she was unable to obey. To pay her head off the right way, Pellew himself had to get out on the bowsprit under a heavy fire of musketry, to bear the jib over to windward; but to make sail seems to have been impossible. Two artillery boats were sent to her assistance, "which towed her off through a very thick fire, until out of farther reach, much to the honour of Mr. John Curling and Mr. Patrick Carnegy, master's mate and midshipman of the *Isis*, who conducted them; and of Mr. Edward Pellew, mate of the *Blonde*, who threw the tow-rope from the *Carleton's* bowsprit."[10] This service on board the *Carleton* started Pellew on his road to fortune; but, singularly enough, the lieutenancy promised him in consequence, by both the First Lord and Lord Howe, was delayed by the fact that he stayed at the front, instead of going to the rear, where he would have been "within their jurisdiction."[11] The *Carleton* had two feet of water in the hold, and had lost eight killed and six wounded,—about half her crew,—when she anchored out of fire. In this small but stirring business, the Americans, in addition to the *Royal Savage*, had lost one gondola. Besides the injuries to the *Carleton*, a British artillery boat, commanded by a German lieutenant, was sunk. Towards evening the *Inflexible* got within point-blank shot of the Americans, "when five broadsides," wrote Douglas, "silenced their whole line." One fresh ship, with scantling for sea-going, and a concentrated battery, has an unquestioned advantage over a dozen light-built craft, carrying one or two guns each, and already several hours engaged.

At nightfall the *Inflexible* dropped out of range, and the British squadron anchored in line of battle across the southern end of the passage between the island and the main; some vessels were extended also to the eastward, into the open Lake. "The best part of my intelligence," wrote Burgoyne next day from St. John's, to Douglas at Quebec, "is that our whole fleet was formed in line above the enemy, and consequently they must have surrendered this morning, or given us battle on our own terms. The Indians and light troops are abreast with the fleet; they cannot, therefore, escape by land." The British squadron sharing this confidence, a proper look-out was not kept. The American leader immediately held a conference with his officers, and decided to attempt a retreat, "which was done with such secrecy," writes Waterbury, "that we went through them entirely undiscovered." The movement began at 7 P.M., a galley leading, the gondolas and schooners following, and Arnold and his second bringing up the rear in the two heaviest galleys. This delicate operation was favoured by a heavy fog, which did not clear till next morning at eight. As the Americans stole by, they could not see any of the hostile ships. By daylight they were out of sight of the British. Riedesel, speaking of this event, says, "The ships anchored, secure of the enemy, who stole off during the night, and sailing round the left wing, aided by a favourable wind, escaped under darkness." The astonishment next morning, he continues, was great, as was Carleton's rage. The latter started to pursue in such a hurry that he forgot to leave orders for the troops which had been landed; but, failing to discover the fugitives, he returned and remained at Valcour till nightfall, when scouts brought word that the enemy were at Schuyler's Island, eight miles above.

The retreat of the Americans had been embarrassed by their injuries, and by the wind coming out ahead. They were obliged to anchor on the 12th to repair damages, both hulls and sails having suffered severely. Arnold took the precaution to write to Crown Point for bateaux, to tow in case of a southerly wind; but time did not allow these to arrive. Two gondolas had to be sunk on account of their injuries, making three of that class so far lost. The retreat was resumed at 2 P.M., but the breeze was fresh from the southward, and the gondolas made very little way. At evening the British chased again. That night the wind moderated, and at daybreak the American flotilla was twenty-eight miles from Crown Point,—fourteen from Valcour,—having still five miles' start. Later, however, by Arnold's report, "the wind again breezed up to the southward, so that we gained very little either by beating or rowing. At the same time the enemy took a fresh breeze from northeast, and, by the time we had reached Split Rock, were alongside of us." The galleys of Arnold and Waterbury, the *Congress* and the *Washington*, had throughout kept in the rear, and now received the brunt of the attack, made by the *Inflexible* and the two schooners, which had entirely distanced their sluggish consorts. This fight was in the upper narrows, where the Lake is from one to three miles wide; and it lasted, by Arnold's report, for five glasses (two hours and a half),[12] the Americans continually retreating, until about ten miles from Crown Point. There, the *Washington* having struck some time before, and final escape being impossible, Arnold ran the *Congress* and four gondolas ashore in a small creek on the east side; pulling to windward, with the cool judgment that had marked all his conduct, so that the enemy could not follow him—except in small boats with which he could deal. There he set his vessels on fire, and stood by them until assured that they would blow up with their flags flying. He then retreated to Crown Point through the woods, "despite the savages;" a phrase which concludes this singular aquatic contest with a quaint touch of local colour.

In three days of fighting and retreating the Americans had lost one schooner, two galleys, and seven gondolas,—in all, ten vessels out of fifteen. The killed and wounded amounted to over eighty, twenty odd of whom were in Arnold's galley. The original force, numbering seven hundred, had been decimated. Considering its raw material and the recency of its organisation, words can scarcely exaggerate the heroism of the resistance, which undoubtedly depended chiefly upon the personal military qualities of the leader. The British loss in killed and wounded did not exceed forty.

The little American navy on Champlain was wiped out; but never had any force, big or small, lived to better purpose or died more gloriously, for it had saved the Lake for that year. Whatever deductions may be made for blunders, and for circumstances of every character which made the British campaign of 1777 abortive and disastrous, thus leading directly to the American alliance with France in 1778, the delay, with all that it involved, was obtained by the Lake campaign of 1776. On October 15th, two days after Arnold's final defeat, Carleton dated a letter to Douglas from before Crown Point, whence the American garrison was withdrawn. A week later Riedesel arrived, and wrote that, "were our whole army here it would be an easy matter to drive the enemy from their entrenchments," at Ticonderoga, and—as has been quoted already—four weeks sooner would have insured its fall. It is but a coincidence that just four weeks had been required to set up the *Inflexible* at St. John's; but it typifies the whole story. Save for Arnold's flotilla, the two British schooners would have settled the business. "Upon the whole, Sir," wrote Douglas in his final letter from Quebec before sailing for England, "I scruple not to say, that had not General Carleton authorized me to take the extraordinary measure of sending up the *Inflexible* from Quebec, things could not this year have been brought to so glorious a conclusion on Lake Champlain." Douglas further showed the importance attached to this success by men of that day, by sending a special message to the British ambassador at Madrid, "presuming that the early knowledge of this great event in the southern parts of Europe may be of advantage to His Majesty's service." That the opinion of the government was similar may be inferred from the numerous rewards bestowed. Carleton was made a Knight of the Bath, and Douglas a baronet.

The gallantry shown by both sides upon Lake Champlain in 1776 is evident from the foregoing narrative. With regard to the direction of movements,—the skill of the two leaders,—the same equal credit cannot be assigned. It was a very serious blunder, on October 11th, to run to leeward, passing a concealed enemy, undetected, upon waters so perfectly well known as those of Champlain were; it having been the scene of frequent British operations in previous wars. Owing to this, "the *Maria*, because of her distant situation (from which the *Inflexible* and *Carleton* had chased by signal) when the rebels were first discovered, and baffling winds, could not get into close action."[13] For the same reason the *Inflexible* could not support the *Carleton*. The Americans, in the aggregate distinctly inferior, were thus permitted a concentration of superior force upon part of their enemies. It is needless to enlarge upon the mortifying incident of Arnold's escape that evening. To liken small things to great,—always profitable in military analysis,—it resembled Hood's slipping away from de Grasse at St. Kitts.[14]

In conduct and courage, Arnold's behavior was excellent throughout. Without enlarging upon the energy which created the flotilla, and the breadth of view which suggested preparations that he could not enforce, admiration is due to his recognition of the fact—

BENEDICT ARNOLD

implicit in deed, if unexpressed in word—that the one use of the Navy was to contest the control of the water; to impose delay, even if it could not secure ultimate victory. No words could say more clearly than do his actions that, under the existing conditions, the navy was useless, except as it contributed to that end; valueless, if buried in port. Upon this rests the merit of his bold advance into the lower narrows; upon this his choice of the strong defensive position of Valcour; upon this his refusal to retreat, as urged by Waterbury, when the full force of the enemy was disclosed,—a decision justified, or rather, illustrated, by the advantages which the accidents of the day threw into his hands. His personal gallantry was conspicuous there as at all times of his life. "His countrymen," said a generous enemy of that day, "chiefly gloried in the dangerous attention which he paid to a nice point of honour, in keeping his flag flying, and not quitting his galley till she was in flames, lest the enemy should have boarded, and struck it." It is not the least of the injuries done to his nation in after years, that he should have silenced this boast and effaced this glorious record by so black an infamy.

With the destruction of the flotilla ends the naval story of the Lakes during the War of the American Revolution. Satisfied that it was too late to proceed against Ticonderoga that year, Carleton withdrew to St. John's and went into winter-quarters. The following year the enterprise was resumed under General Burgoyne; but Sir William Howe, instead of cooperating by an advance up the Hudson, which was the plan of 1776, carried his army to Chesapeake Bay, to act thence against Philadelphia. Burgoyne took Ticonderoga and forced his way as far as Saratoga, sixty miles from Ticonderoga and thirty from Albany, where Howe should have met him. There he was brought to a stand by the army which the Americans had collected, found himself unable to advance or to retreat, and was forced to lay down his arms on October 17th, 1777. The garrisons left by him at Ticonderoga and Crown Point retired to Canada, and the posts were re-occupied by the Americans. No further contest took place on the Lake, though the British vessels remained in control of it, and showed themselves from time to time up to 1781. With the outbreak of war between Great Britain and France, in 1778, the scene of maritime interest shifted to salt water, and there remained till the end.

1. In customary representation of maps, North is upper, and movement northward is commonly spoken of as up. It is necessary therefore to bear in mind that the flow of water from Lake George to the St. Lawrence, though northward, is *down*.

2. Afterwards Captain of the Fleet (Chief of Staff) to Rodney in his great campaign of 1782. He died a Rear-Admiral and Baronet in 1789.

3. Author's italics.

4. *Remembrancer*, iv. 291.

5. The radeau had six 24-pounders, six 12s, and two howitzers; the gondola, seven 9 pounders. The particulars of armament are from Douglas's letters.

6. By American reports. Beatson gives the force sent out, in the spring of 1776, as 13,357. ("Mil. and Nav. Memoirs," vi. 44.)

7. Douglas's letters.

8. Douglas thought that the appearance of the *Inflexible* was a complete surprise; but Arnold had been informed that a third vessel, larger than the schooners, was being set up. With a man of his character, it is impossible to be sure, from his letters to his superior, how much he knew, or what he withheld.

9. Now called North Hero.

10. Douglas's letter. The *Isis* and the *Blonde* were vessels of the British squadron under Douglas, then lying in the St. Lawrence. The officers named were temporarily on the lake service.

11. Sandwich, First Lord of the Admiralty, to Pellew.

12. Beatson, "Nav. and Mil. Memoirs," says two hours.

13. Douglas's letters. The sentence is awkward, but carefully compared with the copy in the author's hands. Douglas says, of the details he gives, that "they have been collected with the most scrupulous circumspection."

14. *Post*, p. 143.

II

NAVAL ACTION AT BOSTON, CHARLESTON, NEW YORK AND NARRAGANSETT BAY

T HE OPENING CONFLICT BETWEEN GREAT Britain and her North American Colonies teaches clearly the necessity, too rarely recognised in practice, that when a State has decided to use force, the force provided should be adequate from the first. This applies with equal weight to national policies when it is the intention of the nation to maintain them at all costs. The Monroe Doctrine for instance is such a policy; but unless constant adequate preparation is maintained also, the policy itself is but a vain form of words. It is in preparation beforehand, chiefly if not uniformly, that the United States has failed. It is better to be much too strong than a little too weak. Seeing the evident temper of the Massachusets Colonists, force would be needed to execute the Boston Port Bill and its companion measures of 1774; for the Port Bill especially, naval force. The supplies for 1775 granted only 18,000 seamen,—2000 less than for the previous year. For 1776, 28,000 seamen were voted, and the total appropriations rose from £5,556,000 to £10,154,000; but it was then too late. Boston was evacuated by the British army, 8000 strong on the 17th of March, 1776; but already, for more than half a year, the spreading spirit of revolt in the thirteen Colonies had been encouraged by the sight of the British army cooped up in the town, suffering from want of necessaries, while the colonial army blockading it was able to maintain its position, because ships laden with stores for the one were captured, and the cargoes diverted to the use of the other. To secure free and ample communications for one's self, and to interrupt those of the opponent, are among the first requirements of war. To carry out the measures of the British government a naval force was needed, which not only should protect the approach of its own transports to Boston Bay, but should prevent access to all coast ports whence supplies could be carried to the blockading army. So far from this, the squadron was not equal, in either number or quality, to the work to be done about Boston; and it was not until October, 1775, that the Admiral was authorized to capture colonial merchant vessels, which therefore went and came unmolested, outside of Boston, carrying often provisions which found their way to Washington's army.

After evacuating Boston, General Howe retired to Halifax, there to await the coming of reinforcements, both military and naval, and of his brother, Vice-Admiral Lord Howe, appointed to command the North American Station. General Howe was commander-in-chief of the forces throughout the territory extending from Nova Scotia to West Florida; from Halifax to Pensacola. The first operation of the campaign was to be the reduction of New York.

The British government, however, had several objects in view, and permitted itself to be distracted from the single-minded prosecution of one great undertaking to other subsidiary operations, not always concentric. Whether the control of the line of the Hudson and Lake

Champlain ought to have been sought through operations beginning at both ends, is open to argument; the facts that the Americans were back in Crown Point in the beginning of July, 1776, and that Carleton's 13,000 men got no farther than St. John's that year, suggest that the greater part of the latter force would have been better employed in New York and New Jersey than about Champlain. However that may be, the diversion to the Carolinas of a third body, respectable in point of numbers, is scarcely to be defended on military grounds. The government was induced to it by the expectation of local support from royalists. That there were many of these in both Carolinas is certain; but while military operations must take account of political conditions, the latter should not be allowed to overbalance elementary principles of the military art. It is said that General Howe disapproved of this ex-centric movement.

The force destined for the Southern coasts assembled at Cork towards the end of 1775, and sailed thence in January, 1776. The troops were commanded by Lord Cornwallis, the squadron by Nelson's early patron, Commodore Sir Peter Parker, whose broad pennant was hoisted on board the *Bristol*, 50. After a boisterous passage, the expedition arrived in May off Cape Fear in North Carolina, where it was joined by two thousand men under Sir Henry Clinton, Cornwallis's senior, whom Howe by the government's orders had detached to the southward in January. Upon Clinton's appearance, the royalists in North Carolina had risen, headed by the husband of Flora Macdonald, whose name thirty years before had been associated romantically with the escape of the young Pretender from Scotland. She had afterwards emigrated to America. The rising, however, had been put down, and Clinton had not thought it expedient to try a serious invasion, in face of the large force assembled to resist him. Upon Parker's coming, it was decided to make an attempt upon Charleston, South Carolina. The fleet therefore sailed from Cape Fear on the 1st of June, and on the 4th anchored off Charleston Bar.

Charleston Harbour opens between two of the sea-islands which fringe the coasts of South Carolina and Georgia. On the north is Sullivan's Island, on the south James Island. The bar of the main entrance was not abreast the mouth of the port, but some distance south of it. Inside the bar, the channel turned to the northward, and thence led near Sullivan's Island, the southern end of which was therefore chosen as the site of the rude fort hastily thrown up to meet this attack, and afterwards called Fort Moultrie, from the name of the commander. From these conditions, a southerly wind was needed to bring ships into action. After sounding and buoying the bar, the transports and frigates crossed on the 7th and anchored inside; but as it was necessary to remove some of the *Bristol's* guns, she could not follow until the 10th. On the 9th Clinton had landed in person with five hundred men, and by the 15th all the troops had disembarked upon Long Island, next north of Sullivan's. It was understood that the inlet between the two was fordable, allowing the troops to cooperate with the naval attack, by diversion or otherwise; but this proved to be a mistake. The passage was seven feet deep at low water, and there were no means for crossing; consequently a small American detachment in the scrub wood of the island sufficed to check any movement in that quarter. The fighting therefore was confined to the cannonading of the fort by the ships.

Circumstances not fully explained caused the attack to be fixed for the 23d; an inopportune delay, during which Americans were strengthening their still very imperfect defences. On the 23d the wind was unfavourable. On the 25th the *Experiment*, 50, arrived, crossed the bar, and, after taking in her guns again, was ready to join in the assault. On the 27th, at 10 A.M., the ships got under way with a southeast breeze,

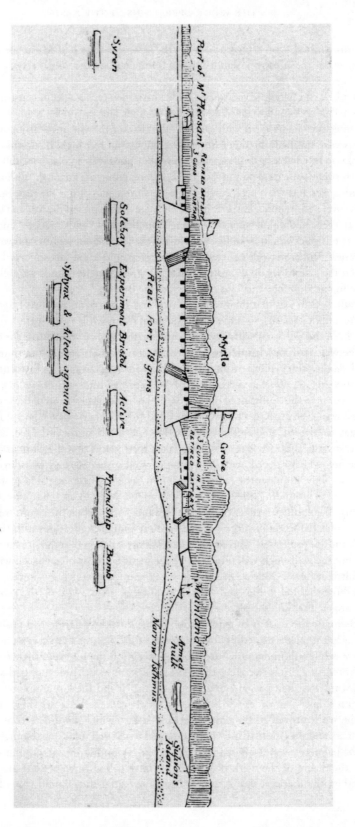

ATTACK ON FORT MOULTRIE, 28TH JUNE 1776
(From a sketch by a British officer on the spot)

but this shifted soon afterwards to north-west, and they had to anchor again, about a mile nearer to Sullivan's Island. On the following day the wind served, and the attack was made.

In plan, Fort Moultrie was square, with a bastion at each angle. In construction, the sides were palmetto logs, dovetailed and bolted together, laid in parallel rows, sixteen feet apart; the interspace being filled with sand. At the time of the engagement, the south and west fronts were finished; the other fronts were only seven feet high, but surmounted by thick planks, to be tenable against escalade. Thirty-one guns were in place, 18- and 9-pounders, of which twenty-one were on the south face, commanding the channel. Within was a traverse running east and west, protecting the gunners from shots from the rear; but there was no such cover against enfilading fire, in case an enemy's ship passed the fort and anchored above it. "The general opinion before the action," Moultrie says, "and especially among sailors, was that two frigates would be sufficient to knock the town about our ears, notwithstanding our batteries." Parker may have shared this impression, and it may account for his leisureliness. When the action began, the garrison had but twenty-eight rounds for each of twenty-six cannon, but this deficiency was unknown to the British.

Parker's plan was that the two 50s, *Bristol* and *Experiment*, and two 28-gun frigates, the *Active* and the *Solebay*, should engage the main front; while two frigates of the same class, the *Actæn* and the *Syren*, with a 20-gun corvette, the *Sphinx*, should pass the fort, anchoring to the westward, up channel, to protect the heavy vessels against fire-ships, as well as to enfilade the principal American battery. The main attack was to be further supported by a bomb-vessel, the *Thunder*, accompanied by the armed transport *Friendship*, which were to take station to the southeast of the east bastion of the engaged front of the fort. The order to weigh was given at 10.30 A.M., when the flood-tide had fairly made; and at 11.15 the *Active*, *Bristol*, *Experiment*, and *Solebay*, anchored in line ahead, in the order named, the *Active* to the eastward. These ships seem to have taken their places skilfully without confusion, and their fire, which opened at once, was rapid, well-sustained, and well-directed; but their position suffered under the radical defect that, whether from actual lack of water, or only from fear of grounding, they were too far from the works to use grape effectively. The sides of ships being much weaker than those of shore works, while their guns were much more numerous, the secret of success was to get near enough to beat down the hostile fire by a multitude of projectiles. The bomb-vessel *Thunder* anchored in the situation assigned her; but her shells, though well aimed, were ineffective. "Most of them fell within the fort," Moultrie reported, "but we had a morass in the middle, which swallowed them instantly, and those that fell in the sand were immediately buried." During the action the mortar bed broke, disabling the piece.

Owing to the scarcity of ammunition in the fort, the garrison had positive orders not to engage at ranges exceeding four hundred yards. Four or five shots were thrown at the *Active*, while still under sail, but with this exception the fort kept silence until the ships anchored, at a distance estimated by the Americans to be three hundred and fifty yards. The word was then passed along the platform, "Mind the Commodore; mind the two 50-gun ships,"—an order which was strictly obeyed, as the losses show. The protection of the work proved to be almost perfect—a fact which doubtless contributed to the coolness and precision of fire vitally essential with such deficient resources. The texture of the palmetto wood suffered the balls to sink smoothly into it without splintering, so that the facing of the work held well. At times, when three or four broadsides struck together, the merlons shook so that Moultrie feared they would come bodily in; but they withstood, and the small loss inflicted was chiefly through the embrasures. The flagstaff being shot away, falling outside into the ditch, a young sergeant, named Jasper, distinguished himself by jumping after it, fetching back and rehoisting the colours under a heavy fire.

In the squadron an equal gallantry was shown under circumstances which made severe demands upon endurance. Whatever Parker's estimate of the worth of the defences, no trace of vain-confidence appears in his dispositions, which were thorough and careful, as the execution of the main attack was skilful and vigorous; but the ships' companies, expecting an easy victory, had found themselves confronted with a resistance and a punishment as severe as were endured by the leading ships at Trafalgar, and far more prolonged. Such conditions impose upon men's tenacity the additional test of surprise and discomfiture. The *Experiment*, though very small for a ship of the line, lost 23 killed and 56 wounded, out of a total probably not much exceeding 300; while the *Bristol*, having the spring shot away, swung with her head to the southward and her stern to the fort, undergoing for a long time a raking fire to which she could make little reply. Three several attempts to replace the spring were made by Mr. James Saumarez,—afterwards the distinguished admiral, Lord de Saumarez, then a midshipman,—before the ship was relieved from this grave disadvantage. Her loss was 40 killed and 71 wounded; not a man escaping of those stationed on the quarter-deck at the beginning of the action. Among the injured was the Commodore himself, whose cool heroism must have been singularly conspicuous, from the notice it attracted in a service where such bearing was not rare. At one time when the quarter-deck was cleared and he stood alone upon the poop-ladder, Saumarez suggested to him to come down; but he replied, smiling, "You want to get rid of me, do you?" and refused to move. The captain of the ship, John Morris, was mortally wounded. With commendable modesty Parker only reported himself as slightly bruised; but deserters stated that for some days he needed the assistance of two men to walk, and that his trousers had been torn off him by shot or splinters. The loss in the other ships was only one killed, 14 wounded. The Americans had 37 killed and wounded.

The three vessels assigned to enfilade the main front of the fort did not get into position. They ran on the middle ground, owing, Parker reported, to the ignorance of the pilots. Two had fouled each other before striking. Having taken the bottom on a rising tide, two floated in a few hours, and retreated; but the third, the *Actæon*, 28, sticking fast, was set on fire and abandoned by her officers. Before she blew up, the Americans boarded her, securing her colours, bell, and some other trophies. "Had these ships effected their purpose," Moultrie reported, "they would have driven us from our guns."

The main division held its ground until long after nightfall, firing much of the time, but stopping at intervals. After two hours it had been noted that the fort replied very slowly, which was attributed to its being overborne, instead of to the real cause, the necessity for sparing ammunition. For the same reason it was entirely silent from 3.30 P.M. to 6, when fire was resumed from only two or three guns, whence Parker surmised that the rest had been dismounted. The Americans were restrained throughout the engagement by the fear of exhausting entirely their scanty store.

"About 9 P.M.," Parker reported, "being very dark, great part of our ammunition expended, the people fatigued, the tide of ebb almost done, no prospect from the eastward (that is, from the army), and no possibility of our being of any further service, I ordered the ships to withdraw to their former moorings." Besides the casualties among the crew, and severe damage to the hull, the *Bristol's* mainmast, with nine cannon-balls in it, had to be shortened, while the mizzenmast was condemned. The injury to the frigates was immaterial, owing to the garrison's neglecting them.

The fight in Charleston Harbour, the first serious contest in which ships took part in this war, resembles generically the battle of Bunker's Hill, with which the regular land warfare had opened a year before. Both illustrate the difficulty and danger of a front attack, without cover, upon a fortified position, and the advantage conferred even upon untrained men, if naturally cool, resolute, and intelligent, not only by the protection of a work, but also, it may be urged, by the recognition of a tangible line up to which to hold, and to abandon which means defeat, dishonour, and disaster. It is much for untried men to recognise in their surroundings something which gives the unity of a common purpose, and thus the coherence which discipline imparts. Although there was in Barker's dispositions nothing open to serious criticism,—nothing that can be ascribed to undervaluing his opponent,—and although, also, he had good reason to expect from the army active cooperation which he did not get, it is probable that he was very much surprised, not only at the tenacity of the Americans' resistance, but at the efficacy of their fire. He felt, doubtless, the traditional and natural distrust—and, for the most part, the justified distrust—with which experience and practice regard inexperience. Some seamen of American birth, who had been serving in the *Bristol*, deserted after the fight. They reported that her crew said, "We were told the Yankees would not stand two fires, but we never saw better fellows;" and when the fire of the fort slackened and some cried, "They have done fighting," others replied, "By God, we are glad of it, for we never had such a drubbing in our lives." "All the common men of the fleet spoke loudly in praise of the garrison,"—a note of admiration so frequent in generous enemies that we may be assured that it was echoed on the quarter-deck also. They could afford it well, for there was no stain upon their own record beyond the natural mortification of defeat; no flinching under the severity of their losses, although a number of their men were comparatively raw, volunteers from the transports, whose crews had come forward almost as one man when they knew that the complements of the ships were short through sickness. Edmund Burke, a friend to both sides, was justified in saying that "never did British valour shine more conspicuously, nor did our ships in an engagement of the same nature experience so serious an encounter." There were several death-vacancies for lieutenants; and, as the battle of Lake Champlain gave Pellew his first commission, so did that of Charleston Harbour give his to Saumarez, who was made lieutenant of the *Bristol* by Parker. Two years later, when the ship had gone to Jamaica, he was followed on her quarter-deck by Nelson and Collingwood, who also received promotion in her from the same hand.

The attack on Fort Moultrie was not resumed. After necessary repairs, the ships of war with the troops went to New York, where they arrived on the 4th of August, and took part in the operations for the reduction of that place under the direction of the two Howes.

The occupation of New York Harbour, and the capture of the city were the most conspicuous British successes of the summer and fall of 1776. While Parker and Clinton were meeting with defeat at Charleston, and Arnold was hurrying the preparation of his flotilla on Champlain, the two brothers, General Sir William Howe and the Admiral, Lord Howe, were arriving in New York Bay, invested not only with the powers proper to the commanders of great fleets and armies, but also with authority as peace commissioners, to negotiate an amicable arrangement with the revolted Colonies.

Sir William Howe had awaited for some time at Halifax the arrival of the expected reinforcements, but wearying at last he sailed thence on the 10th of June, 1776, with the army then in hand. On the 25th he himself reached Sandy Hook, the entrance to New York Bay, having preceded the transports in a frigate. On the 29th, the day after Parker's repulse at Fort Moultrie, the troops arrived; and on July 3d, the date on which Arnold, retreating from Canada, reached Crown Point, the British landed on Staten Island, which is on the west side of the lower Bay. On the 12th came in the *Eagle*, 64, carrying the flag of Lord Howe. This officer was much esteemed by the Americans for his own personal qualities, and for his attitude towards them in the present dispute, as well as for the memory of his brother, who had endeared himself greatly to them in the campaign of 1758, when he had fallen near Lake Champlain; but the decisive step of declaring their independence had been taken already, on July 4th, eight days before the Admiral's arrival. A month was spent in fruitless attempts to negotiate with the new government, without recognising any official character in its representatives. During that time, however, while abstaining from decisive operations, cruisers were kept at sea to intercept American traders, and the Admiral, immediately upon arriving, sent four vessels of war twenty-five miles up the Hudson River, as far as Tarrytown. This squadron was commanded by Hyde Parker, afterwards, in 1801, Nelson's commander-in-chief at Copenhagen. The service was performed under a tremendous cannonade from all the batteries on both shores, but the ships could not be stopped. Towards the middle of August it was evident that the Americans would not accept any terms in the power of the Howes to offer, and it became necessary to attempt coercion by arms.

In the reduction of New York in 1776, the part played by the British Navy, owing to the nature of the campaign in general and of the enemy's force in particular, was of that inconspicuous character which obscures the fact that without the Navy the operations could not have been undertaken at all, and that the Navy played to them the part of the base of operations and line of communications. Like the foundations of a building, these lie outside the range of superficial attention, and therefore are less generally appreciated than the brilliant fighting going on at the front, to the maintenance of which they are all the time indispensable. Consequently, whatever of interest may attach to any, or to all, of the minor affairs, which in the aggregate constitute the action of the naval force in such circumstances, the historian of the major operations is confined perforce to indicating the broad general effect of naval power upon the issue. This will be best done by tracing in outline the scene of action, the combined movements, and the Navy's influence in both.

The harbour of New York divides into two parts—the upper and lower Bays—connected by a passage called the Narrows, between Long and Staten Islands, upon the latter of which the British troops were encamped. Long Island, which forms the eastern shore of the Narrows, extends to the east-north-east a hundred and ten miles, enclosing between itself and the continent a broad sheet of water called Long Island Sound, that reaches nearly to Narragansett Bay. The latter, being a fine anchorage, entered also into the British scheme of operations, as an essential feature in a coastwise maritime campaign. Long Island Sound and the upper Bay of New York are connected by a crooked and difficult passage, known as the East River, eight or ten miles in length, and at that time nearly a mile wide[1] abreast the city of New York. At the point where the East River joins New York Bay, the Hudson River, an estuary there nearly two miles wide, also enters from the north,—a circumstance which has procured for it the alternative name of the North River. Near their confluence is Governor's Island, half a mile below the town, centrally situated to command the entrances to both. Between the East and North rivers, with their general directions from north and east-north-east, is embraced a long strip of land gradually narrowing to the southward. The end of this peninsula, as it would otherwise be, is converted into an island, of a mean length of about eight miles, by the Harlem River,—a narrow and partially navigable stream connecting the East and North rivers. To the southern extreme of this island, called Manhattan, the city of New York was then confined.

As both the East and North rivers were navigable for large ships, the former throughout, the latter for over a hundred miles above its mouth, it was evident that control of the water must play a large part in warlike operations throughout the district described. With the limited force at Washington's disposal, he had been unable to push the defences of the city as far to the front as was desirable. The lower Bay was held by the British Navy, and Staten Island had been abandoned, necessarily, without resistance, thereby giving up the strong defensive position of the Narrows. The lines were contracted thus to the immediate neighbourhood of New York itself. Small detached works skirted the shores of Manhattan Island, and a line of redoubts extended across it, following the course of a small stream which then partly divided it, a mile from the southern end. Governor's Island was also occupied as an outpost. Of more intrinsic strength, but not at first concerned, strong works had been thrown up on either side of the North River, upon commanding heights eight miles above New York, to dispute the passage of ships.

The crucial weakness in this scheme of defence was that the shore of Long Island opposite the city was much higher than that of Manhattan. If this height were seized, the city, and all below it, became untenable. Here, therefore, was the key of the position and the chief station for the American troops. For its protection a line of works was thrown up, the flanks of which rested upon Wallabout Bay and Gowanus Cove, two indentations in the shores of Long Island. These Washington manned with nine thousand of the eighteen thousand men under his command. By the arrival of three divisions of Hessian troops, Howe's army now numbered over thirty-four thousand men, to which Clinton brought three thousand more from before Charleston.[2]

On the 22d of August the British crossed from Staten Island to Gravesend Bay, on the Long Island shore of the Narrows. The Navy covered the landing, and the transportation of the troops was under the charge of Commodore William Hotham, who, nineteen years later, was Nelson's commander-in-chief in the Mediterranean. By noon fifteen thousand men and forty field-guns had been carried over and placed on shore. The force of the Americans permitted little opposition to the British advance; but General Howe was cautious and easy-going, and it was not till the 27th that the army, now increased to twenty-five thousand, was fairly in front of the American lines, having killed, wounded, and taken about 1,500 men. Hoping that Howe would be tempted to storm the position, Washington replaced these with two thousand drawn from his meagre numbers; but his opponent, who had borne a distinguished part at Bunker's Hill, held back his troops, who were eager for the assault. The Americans now stood with their backs to a swift tidal stream, nearly a mile wide, with only a feeble line of works between them and an enemy more than double their number.

On the morning of the 27th, Sir Peter Parker, with a 64 gun ship, two 50s, and two frigates, attempted to work up to New York, with a view of supporting the left flank of the army; but the wind came out from the north, and, the ebb-tide making, the ships got no nearer than three miles from the city. Fortunately for the Americans, they either could not or would not go farther on the following two days. After dark of the 28th, Howe broke ground for regular approaches. Washington, seeing this, and knowing that there

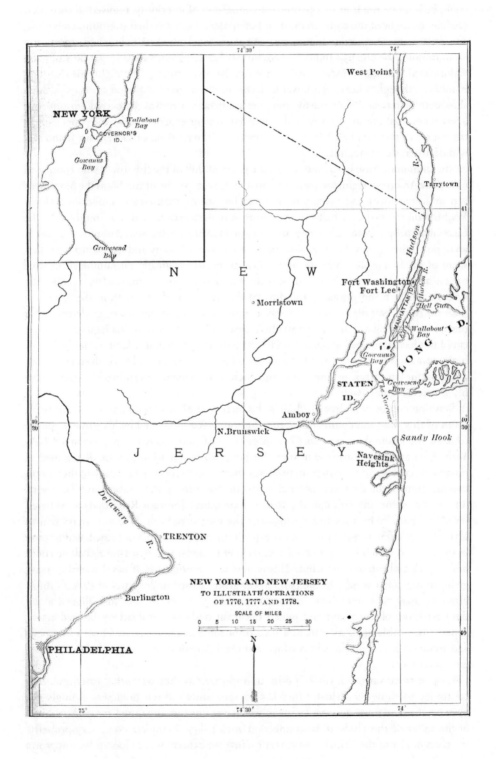

NEW YORK

Wallabout Bay

GOVERNOR'S ID.

Gowanus Bay

Gravesend Bay

74°30'

74°

West Point

Tarrytown

41

N   E   W

Hudson R.

Morristown

Fort Washington

Fort Lee

Harlem R.

Hell Gate

Wallabout Bay

LONG ID.

MANHATTAN ID.

Gowanus Bay

Gravesend Bay

STATEN ID.

The Narrows

Amboy

40 30

N. Brunswick

Sandy Hook

40 30

J   E   R   S   E   Y

Navesink Heights

Delaware R.

TRENTON

Burlington

NEW YORK AND NEW JERSEY

TO ILLUSTRATE OPERATIONS

OF 1776, 1777 AND 1778.

SCALE OF MILES

0   5   10   15   20   25   30

N

75°

74°30'

74°

PHILADELPHIA

40

could be but one result to a siege under his condition of inferiority, resolved to withdraw. During the night of the 29th ten thousand men silently quitted their positions, embarked, and crossed to Manhattan Island, carrying with them all their belongings, arms, and ammunition. The enemy's trenches were but six hundred yards distant, yet no suspicion was aroused, nor did a single deserter give treacherous warning. The night was clear and moonlit, although a heavy fog towards daybreak prolonged the period of secrecy which shrouded the retreat. When the fog rose, the last detachment was discovered crossing, but a few ineffectual cannon-shot were the only harassment experienced by the Americans in the course of this rapid and dexterous retirement. The garrison of Governor's Island was withdrawn at the same time.

The unmolested use of the water, and the nautical skill of the fishermen who composed one of the American regiments, were essential to this escape; for admirable as the movement was in arrangement and execution, no word less strong than escape applies to it. By it Washington rescued over half his army from sure destruction, and, not improbably, the cause of his people from immediate collapse. An opportunity thus seized implies necessarily an opportunity lost on the other side. For that failure both army and navy must bear their share of the blame. It is obvious that when an enemy is greatly outnumbered his line of retreat should be watched. This was the business of both commanders-in-chief, the execution of it being primarily the duty of the navy as withdrawal from the American position could be only by water. It was a simple question of look-out, of detection, of prevention by that means. To arrest the retreat sailing ships were inadequate, for they could not have remained at anchor under the guns of Manhattan Island, either by day or night; but a few boats with muffled oars could have watched, could have given the alarm, precipitating an attack by the army, and such a movement interrupted in mid-course brings irretrievable disaster.

Washington now withdrew the bulk of his force to the line of the Harlem. On his right, south of that river and commanding the Hudson, was a fort called by his name; opposite to it on the Jersey shore was Fort Lee. A garrison of four thousand men occupied New York. After amusing himself with some further peace negotiations, Howe determined to possess the city. As a diversion from the main effort, and to cover the crossing of the troops, two detachments of ships were ordered to pass the batteries on the Hudson and East rivers. This was done on the 13th and the 15th of September. The East River division suffered severely, especially in spars and rigging;[3] but the success of both, following upon that of Hyde Parker a few weeks earlier, in his expedition to Tarrytown, confirmed Washington in the opinion which he expressed five years later to de Grasse, that batteries alone could not stop ships having a fair wind. This is now a commonplace of naval warfare; steam giving always a fair wind. On the 15th Howe's army crossed under cover of Parker's ships, Hotham again superintending the boat work. The garrison of New York slipped along the west shore of the island and joined the main body on the Harlem; favored again, apparently, in this flank movement a mile from the enemy's front, by Howe's inertness, and fondness for a good meal, to which a shrewd American woman invited him at the critical moment.

Despite these various losses of position, important as they were, the American army continued to elude the British general, who apparently did not hold very strongly the opinion that the most decisive factor in war is the enemy's organised force. As control of the valley of the Hudson, in connection with Lake Champlain, was, very properly, the chief object of the British government, Howe's next aim was to loosen Washington's grip on the peninsula north of the Harlem. The position seeming to him too strong for a front attack, he decided to strike for its left flank and rear by way of Long Island Sound. In this, which involved the passage of the tortuous and dangerous channel called Hell Gate, with its swift conflicting currents, the Navy again bore an essential part. The movement began on October 12th, the day after Arnold was defeated at Valcour. So far as its leading object went it was successful, Washington feeling obliged to let go the line of the Harlem, and change front to the left. As the result of the various moments and encounters of the two armies, he fell back across the Hudson into New Jersey, ordering the evacuation of Fort Washington, and deciding to rest his control of the Hudson Valley upon West Point, fifty miles above New York, a position of peculiar natural strength, on the west bank of the river. To these decisions he was compelled by his inferiority in numbers, and also by the very isolated and hazardous situation in which he was operating, between two navigable waters, absolutely controlled by the enemy's shipping. This conclusion was further forced upon him by another successful passage before the guns of Forts Washington and Lee by Hyde Parker, with three ships, on the 9th of October. On this occasion the vessels, two of which were frigates of the heaviest class, suffered very severely, losing nine killed and eighteen wounded; but the menace to the communications of the Americans could not be disregarded, for their supplies came mostly from the west of the Hudson.

It was early in November that Washington crossed into New Jersey with five thousand men; and soon afterwards he directed the remainder of his force to follow. At that moment the blunder of one subordinate, and the disobedience of another, brought upon him two serious blows. Fort Washington not being evacuated when ordered, Howe carried it by storm, capturing not only it but its garrison of twenty-seven hundred men; a very heavy loss to the Americans. On the other hand, the most explicit orders failed to bring the officer left in command on the east of the Hudson, General Charles Lee, to rejoin the commander-in-chief. This criminal perverseness left Washington with only six thousand men in New Jersey, seven thousand being in New York. Under these conditions nothing remained but to put the Delaware also between himself and the enemy. He therefore retreated rapidly through New Jersey, and on the 8th of December crossed into Pennsylvania with an army reduced to three thousand by expiry of enlistments. The detachment beyond the Hudson, diminishing daily by the same cause, gradually worked its way to him; its commander luckily being captured on the road. At the time it joined, a few battalions also arrived from Ticonderoga, released by Carleton's retirement to the foot of Champlain. Washington's force on the west bank of the Delaware was thus increased to six thousand men.

In this series of operations, extending from August 22d to December 14th, when Howe went into winter-quarters in New Jersey, the British had met with no serious mishaps, beyond the inevitable losses undergone by the assailants of well-chosen positions. Nevertheless, having in view the superiority of numbers, of equipment, and of discipline, and the command of the water, the mere existence of the enemy's army as an organised body, its mere escape, deprives the campaign of the claim to be considered successful. The red ribbon of the Bath probably never was earned more cheaply than by Sir William Howe that year. Had he displayed anything like the energy of his two elder brothers, Washington, with all his vigilance, firmness, and enterprise, could scarcely have brought off the force, vastly diminished but still a living organism, around which American resistance again crystallised and hardened. As it was, within a month he took the offensive, and recovered a great part of New Jersey.

Whatever verdict may be passed upon the merit of the military conduct of affairs, there is no doubt of the value, or of the unflagging energy, of the naval support given. Sir William Howe alludes to it frequently, both in general and specifically; while the Admiral sums up his always guarded and often cumbrous expressions of opinion in these words: "It is incumbent upon me to represent to your Lordships, and I cannot too pointedly express, the unabating perseverance and alacrity with which the several classes of officers and seamen have supported a long attendance and unusual degree of fatigue, consequent of these different movements of the army."

The final achievement of the campaign, and a very important one, was the occupation of Rhode Island and Narragansett Bay by a combined expedition, which left New York on the 1st of December, and on the 8th landed at Newport without opposition. The naval force, consisting of five 50-gun ships and eight smaller vessels, was commanded by Sir Peter Parker; the troops, seven thousand in number, by Lieutenant-General Sir Henry Clinton. The immediate effect was to close a haven of privateers, who centred in great numbers around an anchorage which flanked the route of all vessels bound from Europe to New York. The possession of the bay facilitated the control of the neighbouring waters by British ships of war, besides giving them a base central for coastwise operations and independent of tidal considerations for entrance or exit. The position was abandoned somewhat precipitately three years later. Rodney then deplored its loss in the following terms: "The evacuating Rhode Island was the most fatal measure that could possibly have been adopted. It gave up the best and noblest harbor in America, capable of containing the whole Navy of Britain, and where they could in all seasons lie in perfect security; and from whence squadrons, in forty-eight hours, could blockade the three capital cities of America; namely, Boston, New York, and Philadelphia."

At the end of 1776 began the series of British reverses which characterised the year 1777, making this the decisive period of the war, because of the effect thus produced upon general public opinion abroad; especially upon the governments of France and Spain. On the 20th of December, Howe, announcing to the Ministry that he had gone into winter-quarters, wrote: "The chain, I own, is rather too extensive, but I was induced to occupy Burlington to cover the county of Monmouth; and trusting to the loyalty of the inhabitants, and the strength of the corps placed in the advanced posts, I conclude the troops will be in perfect security." Of this unwarranted security Washington took prompt advantage. On Christmas night a sudden descent, in a blinding snow-storm, upon a British outpost at Trenton, swept off a thousand prisoners; and although for the moment the American leader again retired behind the Delaware, it was but to resume the offensive four days later. Cornwallis, who was in New York on the point of sailing for England, hurried back to the front, but in vain. A series of quick and well-directed movements recovered the State of New Jersey; and by the 5th of January the American headquarters, and main body of the army, were established at Morristown in the Jersey hills, the left resting upon the Hudson, thus recovering touch with the strategic centre of interest. This menacing position of the Americans, upon the flank of the line of communications from New York to the Delaware, compelled Howe to contract abruptly the lines he had extended so lightly; and the campaign he was forced thus reluctantly to reopen closed under a gloom of retreat and disaster, which profoundly and justly impressed not only the generality of men but military critics as well. "Of all the great conquests which his Majesty's troops had made in the Jersies," writes Beatson, "Brunswick and Amboy were the only two places of any note which they retained; and however brilliant their successes had been in the beginning of the campaign, they reaped little advantage from them when the winter advanced, and the contiguity of so vigilant an enemy forced them to perform the severest duty." With deliberate or unconscious humour he then immediately concludes/ the chronicle of the year with this announcement: "His Majesty was so well pleased with the abilities and activity which General Howe had displayed this campaign, that on the 25th of October he conferred upon him the Most Honourable Order of the Bath."

1. At the present day reduced by reclaimed land.

2. Beatson's "Military and Naval Memoirs," vi. 44, give 34,614 as the strength of Howe's army. Clinton's division is not included in this. vi. 45.

3. Admiral James's Journal, p. 30. (Navy Records Society.)

III

THE DECISIVE PERIOD OF THE WAR

THE LEADING PURPOSE OF THE British government in the campaign of 1777 was the same as that with which it had begun in 1776,—the control of the line of the Hudson and Lake Champlain, to be mastered by two expeditions, one starting from each end, and both working towards a common centre at Albany, near the head of navigation of the River. Preliminary difficulties had been cleared away in the previous year, by the destruction of the American flotilla on the Lake, and by the reduction of New York. To both these objects the Navy had contributed conspicuously. It remained to complete the work by resuming the advance from the two bases of operations secured. In 1777 the fortifications on the Hudson were inadequate to stop the progress of a combined naval and military expedition, as was shown in the course of the campaign.

The northern enterprise was intrusted to General Burgoyne. The impossibility of creating a new naval force, able to contend with that put afloat by Carleton, had prevented the Americans from further building. Burgoyne therefore moved by the Lake without opposition to Ticonderoga, before which he appeared on the 2d of July. A position commanding the works was discovered, which the Americans had neglected to occupy. It being seized, and a battery established, the fort had to be evacuated. The retreat being made by water, the British Lake Navy, under Captain Skeffington Lutwidge, with whom Nelson had served a few years before in the Arctic seas, had a conspicuous part in the pursuit; severing the boom blockading the narrow upper lake and joining impetuously in an attack upon the floating material, the flat-boat transports, and the few relics of Arnold's flotilla which had escaped the destruction of the previous year. This affair took place on the 6th of July. From that time forward the progress of the army was mainly by land. The Navy, however, found occupation upon Lake George, where Burgoyne established a depôt of supplies, although he did not utilise its waterway for the march of the army. A party of seamen under Edward Pellew, still a midshipman, accompanied the advance, and shared the misfortunes of the expedition. It is told that Burgoyne used afterwards to chaff the young naval officer with being the cause of their disaster, because he and his men, by rebuilding a bridge at a critical moment, had made it possible to cross the upper Hudson. Impeded in its progress by immense difficulties, both natural and imposed by the enemy, the army took twenty days to make twenty miles. On the 30th of July it reached Fort Edward, forty miles from Albany, and there was compelled to stay till the middle of September.

Owing to neglect at the War Office, the peremptory orders to Sir William Howe, to move up the Hudson and make a junction with Burgoyne, were not sent forward. Consequently, Howe, acting upon the discretionary powers which he possessed already, and swayed by political reasons into which it is not necessary to enter, determined to renew his attempt upon Philadelphia. A tentative advance into New Jersey, and the consequent manœuvres of

Washington, satisfied him that the enterprise by this route was too hazardous. He therefore embarked fourteen thousand men, leaving eight thousand with Sir Henry Clinton to hold New York and make diversions in favor of Burgoyne; and on the 23d of July sailed from Sandy Hook, escorted by five 64-gun ships, a 50, and ten smaller vessels, under Lord Howe's immediate command. The entire expedition numbered about 280 sail. Elaborate pains were taken to deceive Washington as to the destination of the armament; but little craft was needed to prevent a competent opponent from imagining a design so contrary to sound military principle, having regard to Burgoyne's movements and to the well-understood general purpose of the British ministry. Accordingly Washington wrote, "Howe's in a manner abandoning Burgoyne is so unaccountable a matter, that till I am fully assured of it, I cannot help casting my eyes continually behind me." He suspected an intention to return upon New York.

On the 31st of July, just as Burgoyne reached Fort Edward, where he stuck fast for six weeks, Howe's armament was off the Capes of the Delaware. The prevailing summer wind on the American coast is south-south-west, fair for ascending the river; but information was received that the enemy had obstructed the channel, which lends itself to such defences for some distance below Philadelphia. Therefore, although after occupying the city the free navigation of the river to the sea would be essential to maintaining the position,—for trial had shown that the whole army could not assure communications by land with New York, the other sea base,—Howe decided to prosecute his enterprise by way of the Chesapeake, the ascent of which, under all the conditions, could not be seriously impeded. A fortnight more was consumed in contending against the south-west winds and calms, before the fleet anchored on the 15th of August within the Capes of the Chesapeake; and yet another week passed before the head of the Bay was reached. On the 25th the troops landed. Washington, though so long in doubt, was on hand to dispute the road, but in inferior force; and Howe had no great difficulty in fighting his way to Philadelphia, which was occupied on the 26th of September. A week earlier Burgoyne had reached Stillwater, on the west bank of the Hudson, the utmost point of his progress, where he was still twenty miles from Albany. Three weeks later, confronted by overwhelming numbers, he was forced to capitulate at Saratoga, whither he had retreated.

Lord Howe held on at the head of the Chesapeake until satisfied that his brother no longer needed him. On the 14th of September he started down the Bay with the squadron and convoy, sending ahead to the Delaware a small division, to aid the army, if necessary. The winds holding southerly, ten days were required to get to sea; and outside further delay was caused by very heavy weather. The Admiral there quitted the convoy and hastened up river. On the 6th of October he was off Chester, ten miles below Philadelphia. The navy had already been at work for a week, clearing away obstructions, of which there were two lines; both commanded by batteries on the farther, or Jersey, shore of the Delaware. The lower battery had been carried by troops; and when Howe arrived, the ships, though meeting lively opposition from the American galleys and fire-rafts, had freed the channel for large vessels to approach the upper obstructions. These were defended not only by a work at Red Bank on the Jersey shore, but also, on the other side of the stream, by a fort called Fort Mifflin, on Mud Island.[1] As the channel at this point, for a distance of half a mile, was only two hundred yards wide, and troops could not reach the island, the position was very strong, and it detained the British for six weeks. Fort Mifflin was supported by two floating batteries and a number of galleys. The latter not only fought, offensively and defensively, but maintained the supplies and ammunition of the garrison.

On the 22d of October, a concerted attack, by the army on the works at Red Bank, and by the Navy on Fort Mifflin, resulted disastrously. The former was repulsed with considerable loss, the officer commanding being killed. The squadron, consisting of a 64, three frigates, and a sloop, went into action with Mud Island at the same time; but, the channel having shifted, owing possibly to the obstructions, the sixty-four and the sloop grounded, and could not be floated that day. On the 23d the Americans concentrated their batteries, galleys, and fire-rafts upon the two; and the larger ship took fire and blew up in the midst of the preparations for lightening her. The sloop was then set on fire and abandoned.

So long as this obstacle remained, all supplies for the British army in Philadelphia had to be carried by boats to the shore, and transported considerable distances by land. As direct attacks had proved unavailing, more deliberate measures were adopted. The army built batteries, and the navy sent ashore guns to mount in them; but the decisive blow to Mud Island was given by a small armed ship, the *Vigilant*, 20, which was successfully piloted through a channel on the west side of the river, and reached the rear of the work, towing with her a floating battery with three 24-pounders. This was on the 15th of November. That night the Americans abandoned Fort Mifflin. Their loss, Beatson says, amounted to near 400 killed and wounded; that of the British to 43. If this be correct, it should have established the invincibility of men who under such prodigious disparity of suffering could maintain their position so tenaciously. After the loss of Mud Island, Red Bank could not be held to advantage, and it was evacuated on the 21st, when an attack was imminent. The American vessels retreated up the river; but they were cornered, and of course ultimately were destroyed. The obstructions being now removed, the British water communications by the line of the Delaware were established,—eight weeks after the occupation of the city, which was to be evacuated necessarily six months later.

While these things were passing, Howe's triumph was marred by the news of Burgoyne's surrender on the 17th of October. For this he could not but feel that the home government must consider him largely responsible; for in the Chesapeake, too late to retrieve his false step, he had received a letter from the minister of war saying that, whatever else he undertook, support to Burgoyne was the great object to be kept in view.

During the operations round Philadelphia, Sir Henry Clinton in New York had done enough to show what strong probabilities of success would have attended an advance up the Hudson, by the twenty thousand men whom Howe could have taken with him. Starting on the 3d of October with three thousand troops, accompanied by a small naval division of frigates, Clinton in a week had reached West Point, fifty miles up the river. The American fortifications along the way were captured, defences levelled, stores and shipping burned; while an insignificant detachment, with the light vessels, went fifty miles further up, and there destroyed more military stores without encountering any resistance worth mentioning. Certainly, had Howe taken the same line of operations, he would have had to reckon with Washington's ten thousand men which confronted him on the march from the Chesapeake to Philadelphia; but his flank would have been covered, up to Albany, by a navigable stream on either side of which he could operate by that flying bridge which the presence and control of the navy continually constituted. Save the fortifications, which Clinton easily carried, there was no threat to his communications or to his flank, such as the hill country of New Jersey had offered and Washington had skilfully utilised.

The campaign of 1777 thus ended for the British with a conspicuous disaster, and with an apparent success which was as disastrous as a failure. At its close they held Narragansett

Bay, the city and harbour of New York, and the city of Philadelphia. The first was an admirable naval base, especially for sailing ships, for the reasons given by Rodney. The second was then, as it is now, the greatest military position on the Atlantic coast of the United States; and although the two could not communicate by land, they did support each other as naval stations in a war essentially dependent upon maritime power. Philadelphia served no purpose but to divide and distract British enterprise. Absolutely dependent for maintenance upon the sea, the forces in it and in New York could not cooperate; they could not even unite except by sea. When Clinton relieved Howe as commander-in-chief, though less than a hundred miles away by land, he had to take a voyage of over two hundred miles, from New York to Philadelphia, half of it up a difficult river, to reach his station; and troops were transferred by the same tedious process. In consequence of these conditions, the place had to be abandoned the instant that war with France made control of the sea even doubtful. The British held it for less than nine months in all.

During 1777 a number of raids were made by British combined land and sea forces, for the purpose of destroying American depôts and other resources. Taken together, such operations are subsidiary to, and aid, the great object of interrupting or harassing the communications of an enemy. In so far, they have a standing place among the major operations of war; but taken singly they cannot be so reckoned, and the fact, therefore, is simply noted, without going into details. It may be remarked, however, that in them, although the scale was smaller, the Navy played the same part that it now does in the many expeditions and small wars undertaken by Great Britain in various parts of the world; the same that it did in Wellington's campaigns in the Spanish peninsula, 1808–1812. The land force depended upon the water, and the water was controlled by the Navy.

1. This was just below the mouth of the Schuylkill, a short distance below the present League Island navy yard.

IV

FRANCE ENTERS THE WAR

THE EVENTS OF 1777 SATISFIED the French goverament that the Americans had strength and skill sufficient to embarrass Great Britain seriously, and that the moment, therefore, was opportune for taking steps which scarcely could fail to cause war. On the 6th of February, 1778, France concluded with the United States an open treaty of amity and commerce; and at the same time a second secret treaty, acknowledging the independence of the late Colonies, and contracting with them a defensive alliance. On the 13th of March, the French Ambassador in London communicated the open treaty to the British government, with the remark that "the United States were in full possession of the independence proclaimed by their declaration of July 4th, 1776." Great Britain at once recalled her Ambassador, and both countries prepared for war, although no declaration was issued. On the 13th of April, a French fleet of twelve ships of the line and five frigates, under the command of the Count d'Estaing,[1] sailed from Toulon for the American coast. It was destined to Delaware Bay, hoping to intercept Howe's squadron. D'Estaing was directed to begin hostilities when forty leagues west of Gibraltar.

The British ministry was not insensible of the danger, the imminence of which had been felt during the previous year; but it had not got ready betimes, owing possibly to confident expectations of success from the campaign of 1777. The ships, in point of numbers and equipment, were not as far forward as the Admiralty had represented; and difficulty, amounting for the moment to impossibility, was experienced in manning them. The vessels of the Channel fleet had to be robbed of both crews and stores to compose a proper reinforcement for America. Moreover, the destination of the Toulon squadron was unknown, the French government having given out that it was bound to Brest, where over twenty other ships of the line were in an advanced state of preparation. Not until the 5th of June, when d'Estaing was already eight weeks out, was certain news brought by a frigate, which had watched his fleet after it had passed Gibraltar, and which had accompanied it into the Atlantic ninety leagues west of the Straits. The reinforcement for America was then permitted to depart. On the 9th of June, thirteen ships of the line sailed for New York under the command of Vice-Admiral John Byron.[2]

These delays occasioned a singular and striking illustration of the ill effects upon commerce of inadequate preparation for manning the fleet. A considerable number of West India ships, with stores absolutely necessary for the preservation of the islands, waited at Portsmouth for convoy for upwards of three months, while the whole fleet, of eighty sail, was detained for five weeks after it had assembled; "and, although the wind came fair on the 19th of May, it did not sail till the 26th, owing to the convoying ships, the *Boyne* and the *Ruby*, not being ready." Forty-five owners and masters signed a letter to the Admiralty, stating these facts. "The convoy," they said, "was appointed to sail April 10th." Many ships had been ready as early as February. "Is not this shameful usage, my Lords, thus to deceive the public in general? There are two hundred ships loaded with provisions, etc., waiting at Spithead these three months. The average expense of each ship amounts to £150 monthly, so that the expense of the whole West India fleet since February amounts to £90,000."

The West Indies before the war had depended chiefly upon their fellow colonies on the American continent for provisions, as well as for other prime necessaries. Not only were these cut off as an incident of the war, entailing great embarrassment and suffering, which elicited vehement appeals from the planter community to the home government, but the American privateers preyed heavily upon the commerce of the islands, whose industries were thus smitten root and branch, import and export. In 1776, salt food for whites and negroes had risen from 50 to 100 per cent, and corn, the chief support of the slaves,—the laboring class,—by 400 per cent. At the same time sugar had fallen from 25 to 40 per cent in price, rum over 37 per cent. The words "starvation" and "famine" were freely used in these representations, which were repeated in 1778. Insurance rose to 23 per cent; and this, with actual losses by capture,[3] and by cessation of American trade, with consequent fall of prices, was estimated to give a total loss of £66 upon every £100 earned before the war. Yet, with all this, the outward West India fleet in 1778 waited six weeks, April 10th-May 26th, for convoy. Immediately after it got away, a rigorous embargo was laid upon all shipping in British ports, that their crews might be impressed to man the Channel fleet. Market-boats, even, were not allowed to pass between Portsmouth and the Isle of Wight.

Three days after Byron had sailed, Admiral Augustus Keppel also put to sea with twenty-one ships of the line, to cruise off Brest. His instructions were to prevent the junction of the Toulon and Brest divisions, attacking either that he might meet. On the 17th of June, two French frigates were sighted. In order that they might not report his force or his movements, the British Admiral sent two of his own frigates, with the request that they would speak him. One, the *Belle Poule*, 36, refused; and an engagement followed between her and the British ship, the *Arethusa*, 32. The King of France subsequently declared that this occurrence fixed the date of the war's beginning. Although both Keppel's and d'Estaing's orders prescribed acts of hostility, no formal war yet existed.

Byron had a very tempestuous passage, with adverse winds, by which his vessels were scattered and damaged. On the 18th of August, sixty-seven days from Plymouth, the flagship arrived off the south coast of Long Island, ninety miles east of New York, without one of the fleet in company. There twelve ships were seen at anchor to leeward (north), nine or ten miles distant, having jury masts, and showing other signs of disability. The British vessel approached near enough to recognise them as French. They were d'Estaing's squadron, crippled by a very heavy gale, in which Howe's force had also suffered, though to a less extent. Being alone, and ignorant of existing conditions, Byron thought it inexpedient to continue on for either New York or Narragansett Bay. The wind being southerly, he steered for Halifax, which he reached August 26th. Some of his ships also entered there. A very few had already succeeded in joining Howe in New York, being fortunate enough to escape the enemy.

So far as help from England went, Lord Howe would have been crushed long before this. He owed his safety partly to his own celerity, partly to the delays of his opponent. Early in May he received advices from home, which convinced him that a sudden and rapid abandonment of Philadelphia and of Delaware Bay might become necessary. He therefore withdrew his ships of the line from New York and Narragansett, concentrating them at the mouth of Delaware Bay, while the transports embarked all stores, except those needed for a fortnight's supply of the army in a hostile country. The threatening contingency of a superior enemy's appearing off the coast might, and did, make it imperative not to risk the troops at sea, but to choose instead the alternative of a ninety-mile march through New Jersey, which a year before had been rejected as too hazardous for an even larger force. Thus prepared, no time was lost when the evacuation became necessary. Sir William Howe, who had been relieved on the 24th of May by Sir Henry Clinton, and had returned to England, escaped the humiliation of giving up his dearly bought conquest. On the 18th of June the British troops, twelve thousand in number, were ferried across the Delaware, under the supervision of the Navy, and began their hazardous march to New York. The next day the transports began to move down the river; but, owing to the intricate navigation, head winds, and calms, they did not get to sea until the 28th of June. On the 8th of July, ten days too late, d'Estaing anchored in the mouth of the Delaware. "Had a passage of even ordinary length taken place," wrote Washington, "Lord Howe with the British ships of war and all the transports in the river Delaware must inevitably have fallen; and Sir Henry Clinton must have had better luck than is commonly dispensed to men of his profession under such circumstances, if he and his troops had not shared at least the fate of Burgoyne."

Had Howe's fleet been intercepted, there would have been no naval defence for New York; the French fleet would have surmounted the difficulties of the harbour bar at its ease; and Clinton, caught between it and the American army, must have surrendered. Howe's arrival obviated this immediate danger; but much still needed to be done, or the end would be postponed only, not averted. A fair wind carried the fleet and the whole convoy from the Delaware to Sandy Hook in forty-eight hours. On the morning of the 29th, as Howe was approaching his port, he spoke a packet from England, which not only brought definite news of d'Estaing's sailing, but also reported that she herself had fallen in with him to the southward, not very far from the American coast, and had been chased by his ships. His appearance off New York, therefore, was imminent.

Howe's measures were prompt and thorough, as became his great reputation. To watch for d'Estaing's approach, a body of cruisers was despatched, numerous enough for some to bring frequent word of his movements, while others kept touch with him. The ships at New York were ordered down to Sandy Hook, where the defence of the entrance was to be made. Clinton, who had been hard pressed by Washington throughout his march, arrived on the 30th of June—the day after Howe himself—on the heights of Navesink, on the seacoast, just south of Sandy Hook. During the previous winter the sea had made a breach between the heights and the Hook, converting the latter into an island. Across this inlet the Navy threw a bridge of boats, by which the army on the 5th of July passed to the Hook, and thence was conveyed to the city.

On the same day the French fleet was sighted off the coast of Virginia by a cruiser, which reached Howe on the 7th; and two days later another brought word that the enemy had anchored on the 8th off the Delaware. There d'Estaing again tarried for two days, which were diligently improved by the British Admiral, who at the same time sent off despatches to warn Byron, of whose coming he now had heard. Despite all his energy, his preparations still were far from complete, when on the morning of the 11th a third vessel arrived, announcing that the French were approaching. That evening they anchored outside, four miles south of Sandy Hook. Howe, who during all these days was indefatigable, not only in planning but also in personal supervision of details, hastened at once to place his vessels according to the disposition which he had determined, and which he had carefully explained to his captains, thus insuring an intelligent cooperation on their part.

The narrow arm of land called Sandy Hook projects in a northerly direction from the New Jersey coast, and covers the lower bay of New York on the south side. The main ship-channel, then as now, ran nearly east and west, at right angles to the Hook and close to its northern end. Beyond the channel, to the north, there was no solid ground for fortification within the cannon range of that day. Therefore such guns as could be mounted on shore, five in number, were placed in battery at the end of the Hook. These formed the right flank of the defence, which was continued thence to the westward by a line of seven ships, skirting the southern edge of the channel. As the approach of the French, if they attacked, must be with an easterly wind and a rising tide, the ships were placed with that expectation; and in such wise that, riding with their heads to the eastward, each successive one, from van to rear, lay a little outside—north—of her next ahead. The object of this indented formation was that each ship might bring her broadside to bear east, and yet fire clear of those to the east of her. In order to effect this concentration of all the batteries in an easterly direction, which would rake the approach of the enemy, a spring[4] was run from the outer, or port quarter of every ship, except the leader.[5] These springs were not taken to the bow cable or anchor, as was often done, but to anchors of their own, placed broad off the port bows. If, then, the enemy attacked, the ships, by simply keeping fast the springs and veering the cables, would swing with their broadsides facing east. If the enemy, which had no bow fire, survived his punishment, and succeeded in advancing till abreast the British line, it was necessary only to keep fast the cables and let go the springs; the ships would swing head to the east wind, and the broadsides would once more bear north, across the channel instead of along it. These careful arrangements were subject, of course, to the mischance of shot cutting away cables or springs; but this was more than offset by the probable injury to the enemy's spars and rigging, as well as hulls, before he could use his batteries at all.

Such was the main defence arranged by Howe; with which New York stood or fell. In the line were five 64s, one 50, and an armed storeship. An advanced line, of one fifty with two smaller vessels, was placed just inside the bar—two or three miles outside the Hook—to rake the enemy as he crossed, retiring as he approached; and four galleys, forming a second line, were also stationed for the same purpose, across the channel, abreast of the Hook.[6] The retreat of these was secure into the shoal water, where they could not be followed. One 64 and some frigates were held as a reserve, inside the main line, to act as occasion might require. The total available force was, six 64s, three 50s, and six frigates. D'Estaing's fleet, in detail, consisted of one 90-gun ship, one 80, six 74s and one 50. Great as was this discrepancy between the opponents, it was counterbalanced largely by Howe's skilful dispositions, which his enemy could not circumvent. If the latter once got alongside, there was little hope for the British; but it was impossible for the French to evade the primary necessity of undergoing a raking fire, without reply, from the extreme range of their enemies' cannon up to the moment of closing. The stake, however, was great, and the apparent odds stirred to the bottom the fighting blood of the British seamen. The ships of war being shorthanded, Howe called for volunteers from the transports. Such numbers came forward that the agents of the vessels scarcely could keep a watch on board; and many whose names were not on the lists concealed themselves in the boats which carried their companions to the fighting ships. The masters and mates of merchantmen in the harbour in like manner offered their services, taking their stations at the guns. Others cruised off the coast in small boats, to warn off approaching vessels; many of which nevertheless fell into the enemy's hands.

Meanwhile d'Estaing was in communication with Washington, one of whose aides-de-camp visited his flagship. A number of New York pilots also were sent. When these learned the draught of the heavier French ships, they declared that it was impossible to take them in; that there was on the bar only twenty-three feet at high water. Had that been really the case, Howe would not have needed to make the preparations for defence that were visible to thousands of eyes on sea and on shore; but d'Estaing, though personally brave as a lion, was timid in his profession, which he had entered at the age of thirty, without serving in the lower grades. The assurances of the pilots were accepted after an examination by a lieutenant of the flagship, who could find nothing deeper than twenty-two feet. Fortune's favors are thrown away, as though in mockery, on the incompetent or the irresolute. On the 22d of July a fresh north-east wind concurred with a spring tide to give the highest possible water on the bar.[7]

> "At eight o'clock," wrote an eye-witness in the British fleet, "d'Estaing with all his squadron appeared under way. He kept working to windward, as if to gain a proper position for crossing the bar by the time the tide should serve. The wind could not be more favourable for such a design; it blew from the exact point from which he could attack us to the greatest advantage. The spring tides were at the highest, and that afternoon thirty feet on the bar. We consequently expected the hottest day that had ever been fought between the two nations. On our side all was at stake. Had the men-of-war been defeated, the fleet of transports and victuallers must have been destroyed, and the army, of course, have fallen with us. D'Estaing, however, had not spirit equal to the risk; at three o'clock we saw him bear off to the southward, and in a few hours he was out of sight."

Four days later, Howe, reporting these occurrences, wrote: "The weather having been favourable the last three days for forcing entrance to this port, I conclude the French commander has desisted." It is clear that the experienced British admiral did not recognise the impossibility of success for the enemy.

After the demonstration of the 22d, d'Estaing stood to the southward, with the wind at east. The British advice-boats brought back word that they had kept company with him as far south as the Capes of the Delaware, and there had left him ninety miles from land. When their leaving freed him from observation, he turned, and made for Narragansett Bay, an attack on which, in support of an American land force, had been concerted between him and Washington. On the 29th he anchored three miles south of Rhode Island, and there awaited a suitable moment for forcing the entrance.

Narragansett Bay contains several islands, the two largest, near the sea, are Rhode Island and Conanicut, the latter being the more westerly. Their general direction, as that of the Bay itself, is north and south; and by them the entrance is divided into three passages. Of these the eastern, called Seakonnet, is not navigable above Rhode Island. The central, which is the main channel, is joined by the western above Conanicut, and thus the two lead to the upper Bay. The town of Newport is on the west side of Rhode Island, four miles from the main entrance.

On the 30th of July, the day after the French fleet had arrived, two of its ships of the line, under command of the afterwards celebrated Suffren, went up the western channel, anchoring within it near the south end of Conanicut. One of them, as she passed, was hulled twice by the British batteries. At the same time, two frigates and a corvette entered Seakonnet; whereupon the British abandoned and burned a sloop of war, the *Kingfisher*, 16, and some galleys there stationed. The British general, Sir Robert Pigot, now withdrew his detachments from Conanicut, after disabling the guns, and concentrated the bulk of his force in the southern part of Rhode Island and about Newport. Goat Island, which covers the inner harbour of the town, was still occupied, the main channel being commanded by its batteries, as well as by those to the north and south of it upon Rhode Island. On the 5th of August, Suffren's two ships again got under way, sailed through the western passage, and anchored in the main channel, north of Conanicut; their former positions being taken by two other ships of the line.[8] The senior British naval officer, seeing retreat cut off both north and south, now destroyed those ships of war[9] which could not enter the inner harbour, sinking two between Goat and Rhode Islands, to prevent any enemy passing there. Five transports also were sunk north of Goat Island, between it and Coaster's Harbour, to protect the inside anchorage in that direction. These preliminary operations cost the British five frigates and two sloops, besides some galleys. Guns and ammunition taken from them went to increase the defences; and their officers and crews, over a thousand in number, served in the fortifications.

On the 8th of August the eight remaining French ships of the line ran the batteries on Rhode and Goat Islands, anchoring above the latter, between it and Conanicut, and were rejoined there by the four previously detached to the western passage. Ten thousand American troops having by this time crossed from the mainland to the northern part of Rhode Island, d'Estaing immediately landed four thousand soldiers and seamen from the fleet upon Conanicut, for a preliminary organisation; after which they also were to pass to Rhode Island and join in the operations. For the moment, therefore, the British garrison, numbering probably six thousand men,[10] was hemmed in by vastly superior forces, by land and by water. Its embarrassment, however, did not last long. On the following morning Lord Howe appeared and anchored off Point Judith, seven miles from the entrance to the Bay, and twelve from the position then occupied by the French fleet. He brought a stronger force than he had been able to gather for the defence of New York, having now one 74, seven 64s, and five 50s, in all thirteen of the line, besides several smaller vessels; but he still was greatly inferior to opponent, by any rational mode of naval reckoning.

Howe's energies in New York had not been confined to preparations for resisting the entrance of the enemy, nor did they cease with the latter's departure. When he first arrived there from Philadelphia, he had hastened to get his ships ready for sea, a pre-occupation which somewhat, but not unduly, delayed their taking their positions at Sandy Hook. Two, for instance, had been at the watering-place when the approach of the French was signalled. Owing to this diligence, no time was lost by his fault when the new destination of the enemy was made known to him, on the 28th or 29th of July, by the arrival of the *Raisonnable*, 64,[11] from Halifax. This ship narrowly escaped the French fleet, having passed it on the evening of the 27th, steering for Rhode Island. The *Renown*, 50, which on the 26th had reached New York from the West Indies, had a similar close shave, having sailed unnoticed through the rear of the enemy the night before. Besides these two, Howe was joined also by the *Centurion*, 50, from Halifax, and by the *Cornwall*, 74; the latter, which

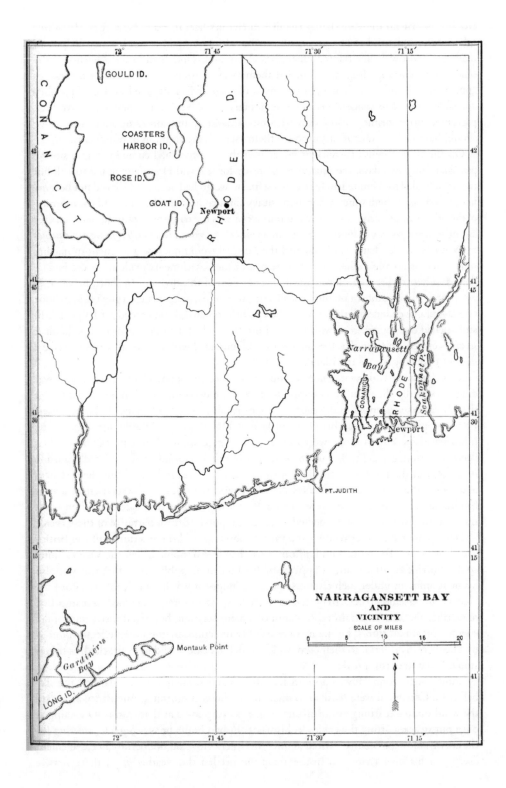

GOULD ID.

C O N A N I C U T

COASTERS
HARBOR ID.

ROSE ID.

GOAT ID

Newport

R H O D E ID.

Narragansett
Bay

CONANICUT

RHODE ID.

Seakonnet R.

Newport

PT. JUDITH

NARRAGANSETT BAY
AND
VICINITY

SCALE OF MILES

0   5   10   15   20

N

Gardiner's
Bay

Montauk Point

LONG ID.

crossed the bar on the 30th, being the first of Byron's fleet to reach New York. The three others belonged to Howe's own squadron. For the two Halifax ships which helped to make this most welcome reinforcement, the Admiral was indebted to the diligence of the officer there commanding, who hurried them away as soon as he learned of d'Estaing's appearance on the coast. The opportuneness of their arrival attracted notice. "Had they appeared a few days sooner," says a contemporary narrative, "either they must have been prevented from forming a junction with our squadron, and forced again to sea, or we should have had the mortification to see them increase the triumph of our enemy."

On the 1st of August, forty-eight hours after the *Cornwall* had come in from a stormy passage of fifty-two days, the squadron was ready for sea, and Howe attempted to sail; but the wind hauled foul immediately after the signal to weigh had been made. It did not become fair at the hour of high water, when alone heavy ships could cross the bar, until the morning of the 6th. "Rhode Island was of such importance," says the narrator already quoted, "*and the fate of so large a portion of the British army as formed the garrison was of such infinite consequence to the general cause*, that it was imagined the Admiral would not lose a moment in making some attempt for their relief." He had learned of the detachments made from the French fleet, and hoped that some advantage might be taken of this division. In short, he went, as was proper and incumbent on him in such critical circumstances, to take a great risk, in hope of a favourable chance offering. On the 9th, as before stated, he anchored off Point Judith, and opened communications with the garrison, from which he learned the events that had so far occurred, and also that the enemy was well provided with craft of all kinds to make a descent upon any part of the Island.

As de Grasse at Yorktown, when rumour announced the approach of a British fleet, was deterred only by the most urgent appeals of Washington from abandoning his control of the Chesapeake, essential to the capture of Cornwallis, so now d'Estaing, in Narragansett Bay, was unwilling to keep his place, in face of Howe's greatly inferior squadron.[12] The influence exerted upon these two admirals by the mere approach of a hostile fleet, when decisive advantages depended upon their holding their ground, may be cited plausibly in support of the most extreme view of the effect of a "fleet in being;" but the instances also, when the conditions are analysed, will suggest the question: Is such effect always legitimate, inherent in the existence of the fleet itself, or does it not depend often upon the characteristics of the man affected? The contemporary British narrative of these events in Narragansett Bay, after reciting the various obstacles and the inferiority of the British squadron, says: "The most skilful officers were therefore of opinion that the Vice-Admiral could not risk an attack; and it appears by his Lordship's public letter that this was also his own opinion: under such circumstances, he judged it was impracticable to afford the General any essential relief." In both these instances, the admirals concerned were impelled to sacrifice the almost certain capture, not of a mere position, but of a decisive part of the enemy's organised forces, by the mere possibility of action; by the moral effect produced by a fleet greatly inferior to their own, which in neither case would have attacked, as things stood. What does this prove?

Immediately upon Howe's appearance, the French seamen who had landed the day before on Conanicut were recalled to their ships. The next morning, August 10, at 7 A.M., the wind came out strong at north-east, which is exceptional at that season. D'Estaing at once put to sea, cutting the cables in his haste. In two hours he was outside, steering for the enemy. Howe, of course, retired at once; his inferiority[13] did not permit an engagement except on his own terms. To insure these, he needed the weather-gage, the offensive position of that day, which by keeping south he expected to gain, when the usual wind from that quarter should set in. The French Admiral had the same object, hoping to crush his agile opponent; and, as the sea breeze from south-west did not make that day, he succeeded in keeping the advantage with which he had started, despite Howe's skill. At nightfall both fleets were still steering to the southward, on the port tack, the French five or six miles in the rear of the British, with the wind variable at east. The same course was maintained throughout the night, the French gradually overhauling the British, and becoming visible at 3 A.M. of the 11th. By Howe's dispatch, they bore in the morning, at an hour not specified, east-north-east, which would be nearly abeam, but somewhat more distant than the night before, having apparently kept closer to the wind, which by this had steadied at east-north-east.

In the course of the day Howe shifted his flag from the *Eagle*, 64, to the *Apollo*, 32, and placed himself between the two fleets, the better to decide the movements of his own. Finding it impossible to gain the weather-gage, and unwilling, probably, to be drawn too far from Rhode Island, he now made a wide circle with the fleet by a succession of changes of course: at 8 A.M. to south, then to south-west and west, until finally, at 1.30 P.M., the ships were steering north-west; always in line of battle. The French Admiral seems to have followed this movement cautiously, on an outer circle but with a higher speed, so that from east-north-east in the morning, which, as the fleets were then heading, would be on the starboard side of the British, abreast and to windward, at 4 P.M. the French bore south-south-east, which would be somewhat on the port quarter, or nearly astern but to leeward. At this time their van was estimated by Howe to be two or three miles from the British rear, and, according to his reading of their manœuvres, d'Estaing was forming his line for the same tack as the British, with a view of "engaging the British squadron to leeward," whereby he would obtain over it the advantage of using the lower-deck guns, the wind and sea having become much heavier. As the French Admiral, in this new disposition, had put his heaviest ships in the van, and his line was nearly in the wake of the British, Howe inferred an attack upon his rear. He therefore ordered his heaviest ship, the *Cornwall*, 74, to go there from the centre, exchanging places with the *Centurion*, 50, and at the same time signalled the fleet to close *to the centre*,—a detail worth remembering in view of Rodney's frustrated manœuvre of April 17th, 1780. It now remained simply to await firmly the moment when the French should have covered the intervening ground, and brought to action so much of his rear as d'Estaing saw fit to engage; the conditions of the sea favoring the speed of the bulkier ships that composed the hostile fleet. The latter, however, soon abandoned the attempt, and "bore away to the southward, apparently from the state of the weather, which, by the wind freshening much, with frequent rain, was now rendered very unfavorable for engaging." It may be added that the hour was very late for beginning an action. At sundown the British were under close-reefed topsails, and the sea such that Howe was unable to return to the *Eagle*.[14]

The wind now increased to great violence, and a severe storm raged on the coast until the evening of the 13th, throwing the two fleets into confusion, scattering the ships, and causing numerous disasters. The *Apollo* lost her foremast, and sprung the mainmast, on the night of the 12th. The next day only two British ships of the line and three smaller vessels were in sight of their Admiral. When the weather moderated, Howe went on board the *Phoenix*, 44, and thence to the *Centurion*, 50, with which he "proceeded to the southward, and on the 15th discovered ten sail of the French squadron, some at anchor in the sea, about twenty-five leagues east from Cape May."[15] Leaving there the *Centurion*, to direct to New York any of Byron's ships that might come on the coast, he departed thither himself also, and on the evening of the 17th rejoined the squadron off Sandy Hook, the appointed rendezvous. Many injuries had been received by the various ships, but they were mostly of a minor character; and on the 22d the fleet again put to sea in search of the enemy.

The French had suffered much more severely. The flagship *Languedoc*, 90, had carried away her bowsprit, all her lower masts followed it overboard, and her tiller also was broken, rendering the rudder unserviceable. The *Marseillais*, 74, lost her foremast and bowsprit. In the dispersal of the two fleets that followed the gale, each of these crippled vessels, on the evening of the 13th, encountered singly a British 50-gun ship; the *Languedoc* being attacked by the *Renown*, and the *Marseillais* by the *Preston*. The conditions in each instance were distinctly favourable to the smaller combatant; but both unfortunately withdrew at nightfall, making the mistake of postponing to to-morrow a chance which they had no certainty would exist after to-day. When morning dawned, other French ships appeared, and the opportunity passed away. The British *Isis*, 50, also was chased and overtaken by the *César*, 74. In the action which ensued, the French ship's wheel was shot away, and she retired;—two other British vessels, one of the line, being in sight. The latter are not mentioned in the British accounts, and both sides claimed the advantage in this drawn action. The French captain lost an arm.

After making temporary repairs, at the anchorage where Howe saw them on the 15th of August, the French fleet had proceeded again towards Newport. It was in the course of this passage that they were seen by Byron's flagship[16] on the 18th, to the southward of Long Island. The *Experiment*, 50, which Howe had sent to reconnoitre Narragansett Bay, was chased by them into Long Island Sound, and only reached New York by the East River;

RICHARD, EARL HOWE

CHARLES HENRI,
COMTE D'ESTAING

being the first ship of the line or 50-gun ship that ever passed through Hell Gate. On the
20th d'Estaing communicated with General Sullivan, the commander of the American
land forces on Rhode Island; but it was only to tell him that in his own opinion, and in
that of a council of war, the condition of the squadron necessitated going to Boston to
refit. Whatever may be thought of the propriety of this decision, its seriousness can be
best understood from the report sent by Pigot to Howe. "The rebels had advanced their
batteries within fifteen hundred yards of the British works. He was under no apprehensions
from any of their attempts in front; but, should the French fleet come in, it would make
an alarming change. Troops might be landed and advanced in his rear; and in that case he
could not answer for the consequences." Disregarding Sullivan's entreaties that he would
remain, d'Estaing sailed next day for Boston, which he reached on August 28th. On the
31st the indefatigable Howe came in sight; but the French had worked actively in the three
days. Forty-nine guns, 18 and 24-pounders, with six mortars, were already in position
covering the anchorage; and "the French squadron, far from fearing an attack, desired it
eagerly."[17] The withdrawal of the French fleet from Rhode Island was followed by that of
the American troops from before Newport.

Howe had quitted New York the instant he heard of d'Estaing's reappearance off
Rhode Island. He took with him the same number of vessels as before,—thirteen of the
line,—the *Monmouth*, 64, of Byron's squadron, having arrived and taken the place of the
Isis, crippled in her late action. Before reaching Newport, he learned that the French had
started for Boston. He hoped that they would find it necessary to go outside George's
Bank, and that he might intercept them by following the shorter road inside. In this
he was disappointed, as has been seen, and the enemy's position was now too strong

for attack. The French retreat to Boston closed the naval campaign of 1778 in North American waters.

The inability or unwillingness of d'Estaing to renew the enterprise against Rhode Island accords the indisputable triumph in this campaign to Howe,—an honour he must share, and doubtless would have shared gladly, with his supporters in general. That his fleet, for the most part two years from home, in a country without dockyards, should have been able to take the sea within ten days after the gale, while their opponents, just from France, yet with three months' sea practice, were so damaged that they had to abandon the field and all the splendid prospects of Rhode Island,—as they already had allowed to slip the chance at New York,—shows a decisive superiority in the British officers and crews. The incontestable merits of the rank and file, however, must not be permitted to divert attention from the great qualities of the leader, but for which the best material would have been unavailing. The conditions were such as to elicit to the utmost Howe's strongest qualities,—firmness, endurance, uninterrupted persistence rather than celerity, great professional skill, ripened by constant reflection and ready at an instant's call. Not brilliant in intellect, perhaps, but absolutely clear, and replete with expedients to meet every probable contingency, Howe exhibited an equable, unflagging energy, which was his greatest characteristic, and which eminently fitted him for the task of checkmating an enemy's every move—for a purely defensive campaign. He was always on hand and always ready; for he never wearied, and he knew his business. To great combinations he was perhaps unequal. At all events, such are not associated with his name. The distant scene he did not see; but step by step he saw his way with absolute precision, and followed it with unhesitating resolution. With a force inferior throughout, to have saved, in one campaign, the British fleet, New York, and Rhode Island, with the entire British army, which was divided between those two stations and dependent upon the sea, is an achievement unsurpassed in the annals of naval defensive warfare. It may be added that his accomplishment is the measure of his adversary's deficiencies.

Howe's squadron had been constituted in 1776 with reference to the colonial struggle only, and to shallow water, and therefore was composed, very properly, of cruisers, and of ships of the line of the smaller classes; there being several fifties, and nothing larger than a sixty-four. When war with France threatened, the Ministry, having long warning, committed an unpardonable fault in allowing such a force to be confronted by one so superior as that which sailed from Toulon, in April, 1778. This should have been stopped on its way, or, failing that, its arrival in America should have been preceded by a British reinforcement. As it was, the government was saved from a tremendous disaster only by the efficiency of its Admiral and the inefficiency of his antagonist. As is not too uncommon, gratitude was swamped by the instinct of self-preservation from the national wrath, excited by this, and by other simultaneous evidences of neglect. An attempt was made to disparage Howe's conduct, and to prove that his force was even superior to that of the French, by adding together the guns in all his ships, disregarding their classes, or by combining groups of his small vessels against d'Estaing's larger units. The instrument of the attack was a naval officer, of some rank but slender professional credit, who at this most opportune moment underwent a political conversion, which earned him employment on the one hand, and the charge of apostasy on the other. For this kind of professional arithmetic, Howe felt and expressed just and utter contempt. Two and two make four in a primer, but in the field they may make three, or they may make five. Not to speak of the greater defensive power of heavy ships, nor of the concentration of their fire, the unity of direction under one captain possesses here also that importance which has caused unity of command and of effort to be recognised as the prime element in military efficiency, from the greatest things to the smallest. Taken together, the three elements—greater defensive power, concentration of fire, and unity of direction—constitute a decisive and permanent argument in favor of big ships, in Howe's days as in our own. Doubtless, now, as then, there is a limit; most arguments can be pushed to an absurdum, intellectual or practical. To draw a line is always hard; but, if we cannot tell just where the line has been passed we can recognise that one ship is much too big, while another certainly is not. Between the two an approximation to an exact result can be made.

On his return to New York on September 11th, Howe found there Rear-Admiral Hyde Parker[18] with six ships of the line of Byron's squadron. Considering his task now accomplished, Howe decided to return to England, in virtue of a permission granted some time before at his own request. The duty against the Americans, lately his fellow-countrymen, had been always distasteful to him, although he did not absolutely refuse to undertake it, as did Admiral Keppel. The entrance of France into the quarrel, and the coming of d'Estaing, refreshed the spirits of the veteran, who moreover scorned to abandon his command in the face of such odds. Now, with the British positions secure, and superiority of force insured for the time being, he gladly turned over his charge and sailed for home; burning against the Admiralty with a wrath common to most of the distinguished seamen of that war. He was not employed afloat again until a change of Ministry took place, in 1782.

1. Charles H., Comte d'Estaing. Born, 1729. Served in India under Lally Tollendal, 1758. After having been taken prisoner at Madras in 1759, exchanged into the navy. Commanded in North America, 1778-80. Guillotined, 1794. W.L.C.

2. Grandfather of the poet.

3. The Secretary of Lloyd's, for the purposes of this work, has been so good as to cause to be specially compiled a summary of the losses and captures during the period 1775–1783. This so far as it deals with merchantmen and privateers, gives the following results. W.L.C.

| | British Vessels | | | | Enemy's Vessels | | | |
| | Merchantmen | | Privateers | | Merchantmen | | Privateers | |
	Taken*	Re-taken or Ransomed	Taken*	Re-taken or Ransomed	Taken*	Re-taken or Ransomed	Taken*	Re-taken or Ransomed
1775	—	—	—	—	—	—	—	—
1776	229	51	—	—	19	—	6	—
1777	331	52	—	—	51	1	18	—
1778	359	87	5	—	232	5	16	—
1779	487	106	29	5	238	5	31	—
1780	581	260	15	2	203	3	34	1
1781	587	211	38	6	277	10	40	—
1782	415	99	1	—	104	1	68	—
1783	98	13	1	1	11	2	3	—

*Including those re-taken or ransomed

4. A spring is a rope taken usually from the quarter (one side of the stern) of a ship, to the anchor. By hauling upon it the battery is turned in the direction desired.

5. The leader, the *Leviathan*, was excepted, evidently because she lay under the Hook, and her guns could not bear down channel. She was not a fighting ship of the squadron, but an armed storeship, although originally a ship of war, and therefore by her thickness of side better fitted for defence than an ordinary merchant vessel. Placing her seems to have been an afterthought, to close the gap in the line, and prevent even the possibility of the enemy's ships turning in there and doubling on the van. Thus Howe avoided the fatal oversight made by Brueys twenty years later, in Aboukir Bay.

6. It may be recalled that a similar disposition was made by the Confederates at Mobile against Farragut's attack in 1864, and that it was from these small vessels that his flagship *Hartford* underwent her severest loss. To sailing ships the odds were greater, as injury to spars might involve stoppage. Moreover, Howe's arrangements brought into such fire all his heavier ships.

7. A letter to the Admiralty, dated October 8th, 1779, from Vice-Admiral Marriot Arbuthnot, then commander-in-chief at New York, states that "at spring tides there is generally thirty feet of water on the bar at high water."

8. These four ships were among the smallest of the fleet, being one 74, two 64s, and a 50. D'Estaing very properly reserved his heaviest ships to force the main channel.

9. *Flora*, 32 ; *Juno*, 32; *Lark*, 32 ; *Orpheus*, 32; *Falcon*, 16.

10. I have not been able to find an exact statement of the number; Beatson gives eight regiments, with a reinforcement of five battalions.

11. It may be interesting to recall that this was the ship on the books of which Nelson's name was first borne in the navy, in 1771.

12. Troude attributes d'Estaing's sortie to a sense of the insecurity of his position; Lapeyrouse Bonfils, to a desire for contest. Chevalier dwells upon the exposure of the situation.

13. For the respective force of the two fleets see pp. 66, 67, 71.

14. This account of the manœuvres of the two fleets is based upon Lord Howe's dispatch, and amplified from the journal of Captain Henry Duncan of the flagship *Eagle* which has been published (1902) since the first publication of this work. See "Navy Records Society, Naval Miscellany." Vol. i, p. 161.

15. At the mouth of Delaware Bay.

16. *Ante*, p. 48.

17. Chevalier: "Marine Française," 1778.

18. Later Vice-Admiral Sir Hyde Parker, Bart., who perished in the *Cato* in 1783. He was father of that Admiral Sir Hyde Parker, who in 1801 was Nelson's commander-in-chief at Copenhagen, and who in 1778 commanded the *Phoenix*, 44, in Howe's fleet. (*Ante*, pp. 35, 39.)

V

THE BATTLE OF USHANT

DURING THE SAME TWO MONTHS that saw the contest between d'Estaing and Howe in America the only encounter between nearly equal fleets in 1778 took place in European waters. Admiral Keppel, having returned to Spithead after the affair between the *Belle Poule* and the *Arethusa*,[1] again put to sea on the 9th of July, with a force increased to thirty ships of the line. He had been mortified by the necessity of avoiding action, and of even retiring into port, with the inadequate numbers before under his command, and his mind was fixed now to compel an engagement, if he met the French.

The Brest fleet also put to sea, the day before Keppel, under the command of Admiral the Comte d'Orvilliers. It contained thirty-two ships of the line. Of these, three—a 64, a 60, and a 50—were not considered fit for the line of battle, which was thus reduced to twenty-nine sail, carrying 2098 guns. To these the British opposed an aggregate of 2278; but comparison by this means only is very rough. Not only the sizes of the guns, but the classes and weight of the vessels need to be considered. In the particular instance the matter is of little importance; the action being indecisive, and credit depending upon manœuvres rather than upon fighting.

The French admiral was hampered by vacillating instructions, reflections of the unstable impulses which swayed the Ministry. Whatever his personal wishes, he felt that he was expected to avoid action, unless under very favourable circumstances. At the moment of sailing he wrote: "Since you leave me free to continue my cruise, I will not bring the fleet back to Brest, unless by positive orders, until I have fulfilled the month at sea mentioned in my instructions, and known to all the captains. Till then I will not fly before Admiral Keppel, whatever his strength; only, if I know him to be too superior, I will avoid a disproportionate action as well as I can; but if the enemy really seeks to force it, it will be very hard to shun." These words explain his conduct through the next few days.

On the afternoon of July 23d the two fleets sighted each other, about a hundred miles west of Ushant, the French being then to leeward. Towards sunset, they were standing south-west, with the wind at west-north-west, and bore north-east from the enemy, who were lying-to, heads to the northward. The British remaining nearly motionless throughout the night, and the wind shifting, d'Orvilliers availed himself of the conditions to press to windward, and in the morning was found to bear north-west from his opponent.[2] Their relative positions satisfied both admirals for the moment; for Keppel found himself interposed between Brest and the French, while d'Orvilliers, though surrendering the advantage of open retreat to his port, had made it possible, by getting the weather-gage, to fulfil his promise to keep the sea and yet to avoid action. Two of his ships, however, the *Duc de Bourgogne*, 80, and a 74, were still to leeward, not only of their own main body, but also of the British. Keppel sent chasers after them, for the expressed purpose of compelling d'Orvilliers to action in their support,[3] and it was believed by the British that they were forced to return to Brest, to avoid being cut off. They certainly quitted their fleet, which was thus reduced to twenty-seven effective sail. From this time until July 27th the wind continued to the westward, and the wariness of the French admiral baffled all his antagonist's efforts to get within range. Keppel, having no doubts as to what was expected of him, pursued vigorously, watching his chance.

On the morning of July 27th the two fleets (Fig. 1, AA, AA) were from six to ten miles apart, wind south-west, both on the port tack,[4] steering north-west; the French dead to windward, in line ahead. The British were in bow-and-quarter line. In this formation, when exact, the ships of a fleet were nearly abreast each other; so ranged, however, that if they tacked all at the same time they would be at once in line of battle ahead close to the wind,—the fighting order.[5] Both fleets were irregularly formed, the British especially so; for Keppel rightly considered that he would not accomplish his purpose, if he were pedantic concerning the order of his going. He had therefore signalled a "General Chase," which, by permitting much individual freedom of movement, facilitated the progress of the whole body. At daylight, the division commanded by Sir Hugh Palliser—the right wing, as then heading—had dropped astern (R); and at 5.30 A.M. the signal was made to seven of its fastest sailers to chase to windward, to get farther to windward by pressing sail, the object being so to place them relatively to the main body, as to support the latter, if an opportunity for action should offer.

At 9 A.M. the French admiral, wishing to approach the enemy and to see more clearly, ordered his fleet to wear in succession,—to countermarch. As the van ships went round (b) under this signal, they had to steer off the wind (bc), parallel to their former line, on which those following them still were, until they reached the point to which the rear ship meantime had advanced (c), when they could again haul to the wind. This caused a loss of ground to leeward, but not more than d'Orvilliers could afford, as things stood. Just after he had fairly committed himself to the manœuvre, the wind hauled to the southward two points,[6] from south-west to south-south-west, which favoured the British, allowing them to head more nearly towards the enemy. The shift also threw the bows of the French off the line they were following, deranging their order. Keppel therefore continued on the port tack, until all the French (BB), were on the starboard, and at 10.15, being nearly in their wake, he ordered his own ships to tack together (dd), which would bring them into line ahead on the same tack as the French; that is, having the wind on the same side. This put the British in column,[7] still to leeward, but nearly astern of the enemy and following (CC). At this moment a thick rain-squall came up, concealing the fleets one from another for three quarters of an hour. With the squall the wind shifted back to southwest, favouring the British on this tack, as it had on the other, and enabling them to lay up for the enemy's rear after which (French BB) they were standing and could now bring to action. When the weather cleared, at 11, the French were seen to have gone about again, all the ships together, and were still in the confusion of a partly executed manœuvre (CC). Their admiral had doubtless recognised, from the change of wind, and from the direction of the enemy when last visible, that an encounter could not be avoided. If he continued on the starboard tack, the van of the pursuing enemy, whose resolve to force battle could not be misunderstood, would overtake his rear ships, engaging as many of them as he might choose. By resuming the port tack, the heads of the columns would meet, and the fleets pass in opposite directions, on equal terms as regarded position; because all the French would engage, and not only a part of their rear. Therefore he had ordered his ships to go

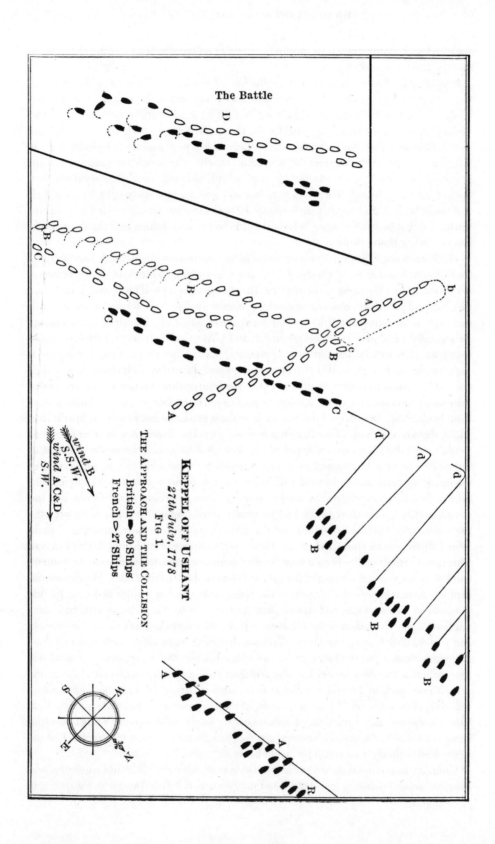

The Battle

KEPPEL OFF USHANT
27th July, 1778
Fig 1.
THE APPROACH AND THE COLLISION
British ▶ 30 Ships
French ▷ 27 Ships

wind B
S.S.W.
wind A C & D
S.W.

about, all at the same time; thus forming column again rapidly, but reversing the order so that the rear became the van.

Keppel so far had made no signal for the line of battle, nor did he now. Recognising from the four days' chase that his enemy was avoiding action, he judged correctly that he should force it, even at some risk. It was not the time for a drill-master, nor a parade. Besides, thanks to the morning signal for the leewardly ships to chase, these, forming the rear of the disorderly column in which he was advancing, were now well to windward, able therefore to support their comrades, if needful, as well as to attack the enemy. In short, practically the whole force was coming into action, although much less regularly than might have been desired. What was to follow was a rough-and-ready fight, but it was all that could be had, and better than nothing. Keppel therefore simply made the signal for battle, and that just as the firing began. The collision was so sudden that the ships at first had not their colours flying.

The French also, although their manœuvres had been more methodical, were in some confusion. It is not given to a body of thirty ships, of varying qualities, to attain perfection of movement in a fortnight of sea practice. The change of wind had precipitated an action, which one admiral had been seeking, and the other shunning; but each had to meet it with such shift as he could. The British (CC) being close-hauled, the French (CC), advancing on a parallel line, were four points[8] off the wind. Most of their ships, therefore, could have gone clear to windward of their opponents, but the fact that the latter could reach some of the leaders compelled the others to support them. As d'Orvilliers had said, it was hard to avoid an enemy resolute to fight. The leading three French vessels[9] (e) hauled their wind, in obedience to the admiral's signal to form the line of battle, which means a close-hauled line. The effect of this was to draw them gradually away from the hostile line, taking them out of range of the British centre and rear. This, if imitated by their followers, would render the affair even more partial and indecisive than such passing by usually was. The fourth French ship began the action, opening fire soon after eleven. The vessels of the opposing fleets surged by under short canvas (D), firing as opportunity offered, but necessarily much handicapped by smoke, which prevented the clear sight of an enemy, and caused anxiety lest an unseen friend might receive a broadside. "The distance between the *Formidable*, 90, (Palliser's flagship) and the *Egmont*, 74, was so short," testified Captain John Laforey, whose three-decker, the *Ocean*, 90, was abreast and outside this interval, "that it was with difficulty I could keep betwixt them to engage, without firing upon them, and I was once very near on board the *Egmont*,"—next ahead of the *Ocean*. The *Formidable* kept her mizzen topsail aback much of the time, to deaden her way, to make the needed room ahead for the *Ocean*, and also to allow the rear ships to close. "At a quarter past one," testified Captain Maitland of the *Elizabeth*, 74, "we were very close behind the *Formidable*, and a midshipman upon the poop called out that there was a ship coming on board on the weatherbow. I put the helm up, . . . and found, when the smoke cleared away, I was shot up under the *Formidable's* lee. She was then engaged with the two last ships in the French fleet, and, as I could not fire at them without firing through the *Formidable*, I was obliged to shoot on."[10] Captain Bazely, of the *Formidable*, says of the same incident, "The *Formidable* did at the time of action bear up to one of the enemy's ships, to avoid being aboard of her, whose jib boom nearly touched the main topsail weather leech of the *Formidable*. I thought we could not avoid being on board."

Contrary to the usual result, the loss of the rear division, in killed and wounded, was heaviest, nearly equalling the aggregate of the two others.[11] This was due to the morning signal to chase to windward, which brought these ships closer than their leaders. As soon as the British van, ten ships, had passed the French rear, its commander, Vice-Admiral Sir Robert Harland, anticipating Keppel's wishes, signalled it to go about and follow the enemy (Fig. 2, V). As the French column was running free, these ships, when about, fetched to windward of its wake. When the *Victory* drew out of the fire, at 1 P.M., Keppel also made a similar signal, and attempted to wear, (c), the injuries to his rigging not permitting tacking; but caution was needed in manœuvring across the bows of the following ships, and it was not till 2 P.M., that the *Victory* was about on the other tack (C), heading after the French. At this time, 2 P.M., just before or just after wearing, the signal for battle was hauled down, and that for the line of battle was hoisted. The object of the latter was to re-form the order, and the first was discontinued, partly because no longer needed, chiefly that it might not seem to contradict the urgent call for a re-formation.

At this time six or seven of Harland's division were on the weather bow of the *Victory*, to windward (westward), but a little ahead, and standing like her after the French; all on the port tack (Fig. 2). None of the centre division succeeded in joining the flagship at once. At 2.30 Palliser's ship, the *Formidable* (R), on the starboard tack, passed the *Victory* to leeward, apparently the last of the fleet out of action. A half-hour after this the *Victory* had been joined by three of the centre, which were following her in close order, the van remaining in the same relative position. Astern of these two groups from van and centre were a number of other ships in various degrees of confusion,—some going about, some trying to come up, others completely disabled. Especially, there was in the south-south-east, therefore well to leeward, a cluster of four or five British vessels, evidently temporarily incapable of manœuvring.

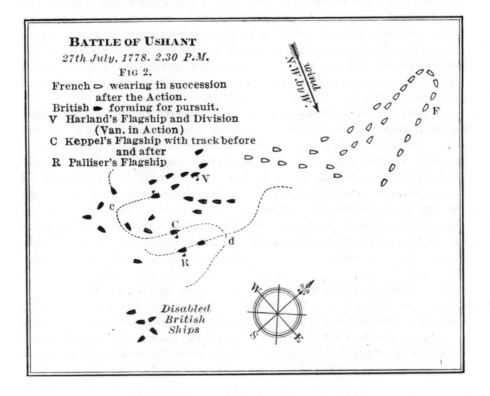

BATTLE OF USHANT

27th July, 1778. 2.30 P.M.

FIG 2.

French ▷ wearing in succession
after the Action.
British ▶ forming for pursuit.
V Harland's Flagship and Division
(Van. in Action)
C Keppel's Flagship with track before
and after
R Palliser's Flagship

*Disabled
British
Ships*

This was the situation which met the eye of the French admiral, scanning the field as the smoke drove away. The disorder of the British, which originated in the general chase, had increased through the hurry of the manœuvres succeeding the squall, and culminated in the conditions just described. It was an inevitable result of a military exigency confronted by a fleet only recently equipped. The French, starting from a better formation, had come out in better shape. But, after all, it seems difficult wholly to remedy the disadvantage of a policy essentially defensive; and d'Orvilliers' next order, though well conceived, was resultless. At 1 P.M.[12] he signalled his fleet to wear in succession, and form the line of battle on the starboard tack (F). This signal was not seen by the leading ship, which should have begun the movement. The junior French admiral, in the fourth ship from the van, at length went about, and spoke the flagship, to know what was the Commander-in-Chief's desire. D'Orvilliers explained that he wished to pass along the enemy's fleet from end to end, to leeward, because in its disordered state there was a fair promise of advantage, and by going to leeward—presenting his weather side to the enemy—he could use the weather lower-deck guns, whereas, in the then state of the sea, the lee lower ports could not be opened. Thus explained, the movement was executed, but the favourable moment had passed. It was not till 2.30 that the manœuvre was evident to the British.

As soon as Keppel recognised his opponent's intention, he wore the *Victory* again (d), a few minutes after 3 P.M., and stood slowly down, on the starboard tack off the wind, towards his crippled ships in the south-south-east, keeping aloft the signal for the line of battle, which commanded every manageable ship to get to her station (Fig. 3, C). As this deliberate movement was away from the enemy (F), Palliser tried afterwards to fix upon it the stigma of flight,—a preposterous extravagancy. Harland put his division about at once and joined the Admiral. On this tack his station was ahead of the *Victory*, but in consequence of a message from Keppel he fell in behind her, to cover the rear until Palliser's division could repair damage and take their places. At 4 P.M. Harland's division was in the line. Palliser's ships, as they completed refitting, ranged themselves before or behind his flagship; their captains considering, as they testified, that they took station from their divisional commander, and not from the ship of the Commander-in-Chief. There was formed thus, on the weather quarter of the *Victory*, and a mile or two distant, a separate line of ships, constituting on this tack the proper rear of the fleet, and dependent for initiative on Palliser's flagship (Fig. 3, R). At 5 P.M. Keppel sent word by a frigate to Palliser to hasten into the line, as he was only waiting for him to renew the action, the French now having completed their manœuvre. They had not attacked, as they might have done, but had drawn up under the lee of the British, their van abreast the latter's centre. At the same time Harland was directed to move to his proper position in the van, which he at once did (Fig. 3, V). Palliser made no movement, and Keppel with extraordinary—if not culpable—forbearance refrained from summoning the rear ships into line by their individual pennants. This he at last did about 7 P.M., signalling specifically to each of the vessels then grouped with Palliser, (except his own flagship), to leave the latter and take their posts in the line. This was accordingly done, but it was thought then to be too late to renew the action. At daylight the next morning, only three French ships were in sight from the decks; but the main body could be seen in the south-east from some of the mastheads, and was thought to be from fifteen to twenty miles distant.

Though absolutely indecisive, this was a pretty smart skirmish; the British loss being 133 killed and 373 wounded, that of the French 161 killed and 513 wounded. The general result would appear to indicate that the French, in accordance with their usual policy, had fired to cripple their enemy's spars and rigging, the motive-power. This would be consistent with

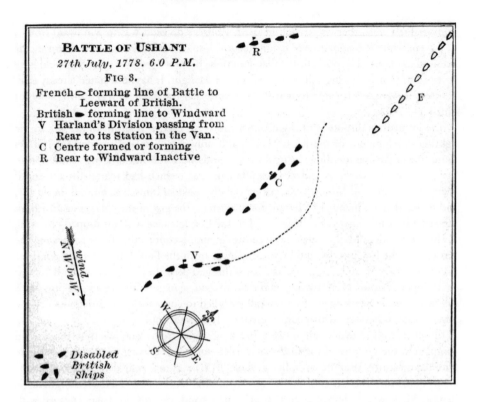

BATTLE OF USHANT
27th July, 1778. 6.0 P.M.
FIG 3.
French ○ forming line of Battle to
Leeward of British.
British ● forming line to Windward
V Harland's Division passing from
Rear to its Station in the Van.
C Centre formed or forming
R Rear to Windward Inactive

Disabled
British
Ships

d'Orvilliers' avowed purpose of avoiding action except under favourable circumstances. As the smoke thickened and confusion increased, the fleets had got closer together, and, whatever the intention, many shot found their way to the British hulls. Nevertheless, as the returns show, the number of men hit among the French was to the British nearly as 7 to 5. On the other hand, it is certain that the manœuvring power of the French after the action was greater than that of the British.

Both sides claimed the advantage. This was simply a point of honour, or of credit, for material advantage accrued to neither. Keppel had succeeded in forcing d'Orvilliers to action against his will; d'Orvilliers, by a well-judged evolution, had retained a superiority of manœuvring power after the engagement. Had his next signal been promptly obeyed, he might have passed again by the British fleet, in fairly good order, before it re-formed, and concentrated his fire on the more leewardly of its vessels. Even under the delay, it was distinctly in his power to renew the fight; and that he did not do so forfeits all claim to victory. Not to speak of the better condition of the French ships, Keppel, by running off the wind, had given his opponent full opportunity to reach his fleet and to attack. Instead of so doing, d'Orvilliers drew up under the British lee, out of range, and offered battle; a gallant defiance, but to a crippled foe.

Time was thus given to the British to refit their ships sufficiently to bear down again. This the French admiral should not have permitted. He should have attacked promptly, or else have retreated; to windward, or to leeward, as seemed most expedient. Under the conditions, it was not good generalship to give the enemy time, and to await his pleasure. Keppel, on the other hand, being granted this chance, should have renewed the fight; and here arose the controversy which set all England by the ears, and may be said to have immortalised this otherwise trivial incident. Palliser's division was to windward from 4 to 7 P.M., while the signals were flying to form line of battle, and to bear down in the Admiral's wake; and Keppel alleged that, had these been obeyed by 6 P.M., he would have renewed the battle, having still over two hours of daylight. It has been stated already that, besides the signals, a frigate brought Palliser word that the Admiral was waiting only for him.

The immediate dispute is of slight present interest, except as an historical link in the fighting development of the British Navy; and only this historical significance justifies more than a passing mention. In 1778 men's minds were still full of Byng's execution in 1757, and of the Mathews and Lestock affair in 1744, which had materially influenced Byng in his action off Minorca. Keppel repeatedly spoke of himself as on trial for his life; and he had been a member of Byng's court-martial. The gist of the charges against him, preferred by Palliser, was that he attacked in the first instance without properly forming his line, for which, Mathews had been censured; and, secondly, that by not renewing the action after the first pass-by, and by wearing away from the French fleet, he had not done his utmost to "take, sink, burn, and destroy." This had been the charge on which Byng was shot. Keppel, besides his justifying reasons for his course in general, alleged and proved his full intention to attack again, had not Palliser failed to come into line, a delinquency the same as that of Lestock, which contributed to Mathew's ruin.

In other words, men's minds were breaking away from, but had not thrown off completely, the tyranny of the Order of Battle,—one of the worst of tyrannies, because founded on truth. Absolute error, like a whole lie, is open to speedy detection; half-truths are troublesome. The Order of Battle[13] was an admirable servant and a most objectionable despot. Mathews, in despair over a recalcitrant second, cast off the yoke, engaged with part of his force, was ill supported and censured; Lestock escaping. Byng, considering this, and being a pedant by nature, would not break his line; the enemy slipped away, Minorca surrendered, and he was shot. In Keppel's court-martial, twenty-eight out of the thirty captains who had been in the line were summoned as witnesses. Most of them swore that if Keppel had chased in line of battle that day, there could have been no action, and the majority of them cordially approved his course; but there was evidently an undercurrent still of dissent, and especially in the rear ships, where there had been some of the straggling inevitable in such movements. Their commanders therefore had uncomfortable experience of the lack of mutual support, which the line of battle was meant to insure.

Another indication of still surviving pedantry was the obligation felt in the rear ships to take post about their own admiral, and to remain there when the signals for the line of battle, and to bear down in the admiral's wake, were flying. Thus Palliser's own inaction, to whatever cause due, paralysed the six or eight sail with him; but it appears to the writer that Keppel was seriously remiss in not summoning those ships by their own pennants, as soon as he began to distrust the purposes of the Vice-Admiral, instead of delaying doing so till 7 P.M., as he did. It is a curious picture presented to us by the evidence. The Commander-in-Chief, with his staff and the captain of the ship, fretting and fuming on the *Victory*'s quarter-deck; the signals flying which have been mentioned; Harland's division getting into line ahead; and four points on the weather quarter, only two miles distant, so that "every gun and port could be counted," a group of seven or eight sail, among them the flag of the third in command, apparently indifferent spectators. The *Formidable*'s only sign of disability was the foretopsail unbent for four hours,—a delay which, being unexplained, rather increased than relieved suspicion, rife then throughout the Navy. Palliser was a Tory, and had left the Board of Admiralty to take his command. Keppel was so strong a Whig that he would not serve against the Americans; and he evidently feared that he was to be betrayed to his ruin.

Palliser's defence rested upon three principal points: (1), that the signal for the line of battle was not seen on board the *Formidable*; (2), that the signal to get into the Admiral's wake was repeated by himself; (3), that his foremast was wounded, and, moreover, found to be in such bad condition that he feared to carry sail on it. As regards the first, the signal was seen on board the *Ocean*, next astern of and "not far from"[14] the *Formidable*; for the second, the Admiral should have been informed of a disability by which a single ship was neutralizing a division. The frigate that brought Keppel's message could have carried back this. Thirdly, the most damaging feature to Palliser's case was that he asserted that, after coming out from under fire, he wore at once towards the enemy; afterwards he wore back again. A ship that thus wore twice before three o'clock, might have displayed zeal and efficiency enough to run two miles, off the wind,[15] at five, to support a fight. Deliberate treachery is impossible. To this writer the Vice-Admiral's behaviour seems that of a man in a sulk, who will do only that which he can find no excuses for neglecting. In such cases of sailing close, men generally slip over the line into grievous wrong.

Keppel was cleared of all the charges preferred against him; the accuser had not thought best to embody among them the delay to recall the ships which his own example was detaining. Against Palliser no specific charge was preferred, but the Admiralty directed a general inquiry into his course on the 27th of July. The court found his conduct "in many instances highly exemplary and meritorious,"—he had fought well,—"but reprehensible in not having acquainted the Commander-in-Chief of his distress, which he might have done either by the *Fox*, or other means which he had in his power." Public opinion running strongly for Keppel, his acquittal was celebrated with bonfires and illuminations in London; the mob got drunk, smashed the windows of Palliser's friends, wrecked Palliser's own house, and came near to killing Palliser himself. The Admiralty, in 1780, made him Governor of Greenwich Hospital.

On the 28th of July, the British and French being no longer in sight of each other, Keppel, considering his fleet too injured aloft to cruise near the French coast, kept away for Plymouth, where he arrived on the 31st. Before putting to sea again, he provided against a recurrence of the misdemeanor of the 27th by a general order, that "in future the Line is always to be taken from the Centre." Had this been in force before, Palliser's captains would have taken station by the Commander-in-Chief, and the *Formidable* would have been left to windward by herself. At the same time Howe was closing his squadron upon the centre in America; and Rodney, two years later, experienced the ill-effects of distance taken from the next ahead, when the leading ship of a fleet disregarded an order.

Although privately censuring Palliser's conduct, the Commander-in-Chief made no official complaint, and it was not until the matter got into the papers, through the talk of the fleet, that the difficulty began which resulted in the trial of both officers, early in the following year. After this, Keppel, being dissatisfied with the Admiralty's treatment, intimated his wish to give up the command. The order to strike his flag was dated March 18th, 1779. He was not employed afloat again, but upon the change of administration in 1782 he became First Lord of the Admiralty, and so remained, with a brief intermission, until December, 1783.

It is perhaps necessary to mention that both British and French asserted, and assert to this day, that the other party abandoned the field.[16] The point is too trivial, in the author's opinion, to warrant further discussion of an episode the historical interest of which is very slight, though its professional lessons are valuable. The British case had the advantage—through the courts-martial—of the sworn testimony of twenty to thirty captains, who agreed that the British kept on the same tack under short sail throughout the night, and that in the morning only three French ships were visible. As far as known to the author, the French contention rests only on the usual reports.

1. *Ante*, p. 48.

2. Testimony of Captains Hood, Robinson, and Macbride, and of Rear-Admiral Campbell, captain of the fleet to Keppel.

3. See note 2.

4. A vessel is said to be on the port tack when she has the wind blowing on her port, or left side; on the starboard tack, when the wind is on the right side. Thus with an east wind, if she head north, she is on the starboard tack; if south, on the port.

5. See also note 5; *post*, p. 158.

6. Twenty-two degrees.

7. Column and line ahead are equivalent terms, each ship steering in the wake of its next ahead.

8. Forty-five degrees.

9. Chevalier says, p. 89, "The English passed out of range" of these ships. As these ships had the wind, they had the choice of range, barring signals from their own admiral. In truth, they were obeying his order.

10. This evidence of the captains of the *Ocean* and the *Elizabeth* contradicts Palliser's charge that his ship was not adequately supported.

11. It was actually quite equal, but this was due to an accidental explosion on board the *Formidable*.

12. Chevalier. Probably later by the other times used in this account.

13. The Order of Battle was constituted by the ships "of the line" ranging themselves one behind the other in a prescribed succession; the position of each and the intervals between being taken from the ship next ahead. This made the leading vessel the pivot of the order and of manœuvring, unless specially otherwise directed; which in an emergency could not always be easily done. Strictly, if circumstances favoured, the line on which the ships thus formed was one of the two close-hauled lines; "close-hauled" meaning to bring the vessel's head as "near" the direction of the wind as possible, usually to about 70 degrees. The advantage of the close-hauled line was that the vessels were more manageable than when "off" the wind.

14. Evidence of Captain John Laforey, of the *Ocean*.

15. "I do not recollect how many points I went from the wind; I must have bore down a pretty large course." Testimony of Captain J. Laforey, of the *Ocean*, on this point.

16. "During the night (of the 27th) Admiral Keppel kept away (*fit route*) for Portsmouth." Chevalier, "Marine Française," p. 90. Paris, 1877. Oddly enough, he adds that "on the evening of the 28th the French squadron, *carried eastward by the currents*, sighted Ushant."

VI

OPERATIONS IN THE WEST INDIES, GEORGIA AND SOUTH CAROLINA

C ONDITIONS OF SEASON EXERTED GREAT influence upon the time and place of hostilities during the maritime war of 1778; the opening scenes of which, in Europe and in North America, have just been narrated. In European seas it was realised that naval enterprises by fleets, requiring evolutions by masses of large vessels, were possible only in summer. Winter gales scattered ships, impeded manœuvres, and made gun-fire ineffective. The same consideration prevailed to limit activity in North American waters to the summer; and complementary to this was the fact that in the West Indies hurricanes of excessive violence occurred from July to October. The practice therefore was to transfer effort from one quarter to the other in the Western Hemisphere, according to the season.

In the recent treaty with the United States, the King of France had formally renounced all claim to acquire for himself any part of the American continent then in possession of Great Britain. On the other hand, he had reserved the express right to conquer any of her islands south of Bermuda. The West Indies were then the richest commercial region on the globe in the value of their products; and France wished not only to increase her already large possessions there, but also to establish more solidly her political and military tenure.

In September, 1778, the British Island of Dominica was seized by an expedition from the adjacent French colony of Martinique. The affair was a surprise, and possesses no special military interest; but it is instructive to observe that Great Britain was unprepared, in the West Indies as elsewhere, when the war began. A change had been made shortly before in the command of the Leeward Islands Station, as it was called, which extended from Antigua southward over the Lesser Antilles with headquarters at Barbados. Rear-Admiral the Hon. Samuel Barrington, the new-comer, leaving home before war had been declared, had orders not to quit Barbados till further instructions should arrive. These had not reached him when he learned of the loss of Dominica. The French had received their orders on the 17th of August. The blow was intrinsically somewhat serious, so far as the mere capture of a position can be, because the fortifications were strong, though they had been inadequately garrisoned. It is a mistake to build works and not man them, for their fall transfers to the enemy strength which he otherwise would need time to create. To the French the conquest was useful beyond its commercial value, because it closed a gap in their possessions. They now held four consecutive islands, from north to south, Guadeloupe, Dominica, Martinique, and Santa Lucia.

Barrington had two ships of the line: his flagship, the *Prince of Wales,* 74, and the *Boyne,* 70. If he had been cruising, these would probably have deterred the French. Upon receiving the news he put to sea, going as far as Antigua; but he did not venture to stay away because his expected instructions had not come yet, and, like Keppel, he feared an ungenerous construction of his actions. He therefore remained in Barbados, patiently watching for an opportunity to act.

The departure of Howe and the approach of winter determined the transference of British troops and ships from the continent to the Leeward Islands. Reinforcements had given the British fleet in America a numerical superiority, which for the time imposed a check upon d'Estaing; but Byron, proverbially unlucky in weather, was driven crippled to Newport, leaving the French free to quit Boston. The difficulty of provisioning so large a force as twelve ships of the line at first threatened to prevent the withdrawal, supplies being then extremely scarce in the port; but at the critical moment American privateers brought in large numbers of prizes, laden with provisions from Europe for the British army. Thus d'Estaing was enabled to sail for Martinique on the 4th of November. On the same day there left New York for Barbados a British squadron,—two 64s, three 50s, and three smaller craft,—under the command of Commodore William Hotham, convoying five thousand troops for service in the West Indies.

Being bound for nearly the same point, the two hostile bodies steered parallel courses, each ignorant of the other's nearness. In the latitude of Bermuda both suffered from a violent gale, but the French most; the flagship *Languedoc* losing her main and mizzen topmasts. On the 25th of November one[1] of Hotham's convoy fell into the hands of d'Estaing, who then first learned of the British sailing. Doubtful whether their destination was Barbados or Antigua,—their two chief stations,—he decided for the latter. Arriving off it on the 6th of December, he cruised for forty-eight hours, and then bore away for Fort Royal, Martinique, the principal French depôt in the West Indies, where he anchored on the 9th. On the 10th Hotham joined Barrington at Barbados.

Barrington knew already what he wanted to do, and therefore lost not a moment in deliberation. The troops were kept on board, Hotham's convoy arrangements being left as they were. On the morning of December 12th the entire force sailed again, the main changes in it being in the chief command, and in the addition of Barrington's two ships of the line. On the afternoon of the 13th the shipping anchored in the Grand Cul de Sac, an inlet on the west side of Santa Lucia, which is seventy miles east-north-east from Barbados. Part of the troops landed at once, and seized the batteries and heights on the north side of the bay. The remainder were put on shore the next morning. The French forces were inadequate to defend their works; but it is to be observed that they were driven with unremitting energy, and that to this promptness the British owed their ability to hold the position.

Three miles north of the Cul de Sac is a bay then called the Carénage; now Port Castries. At its northern extremity is a precipitous promontory, La Vigie, then fortified, upon the tenure of which depended not only control of that anchorage, but also access to the rear of the works which commanded the Cul de Sac. If those works fell, the British squadron must abandon its position and put to sea, where d'Estaing's much superior fleet would be in waiting. On the other hand, if the squadron were crushed at its anchors, the troops were isolated and must ultimately capitulate. Therefore La Vigie and the squadron were the two keys to the situation, and the loss of either would be decisive.

By the evening of the 14th the British held the shore line from La Vigie to the southern point of the Cul de Sac, as well as Morne Fortuné (Fort Charlotte), the capital of the island. The feeble French garrison retired to the interior, leaving its guns unspiked, and its ammunition and stores untouched,—another instance of the danger of works turning to one's own disadvantage. It was Barrington's purpose now to remove the transports to

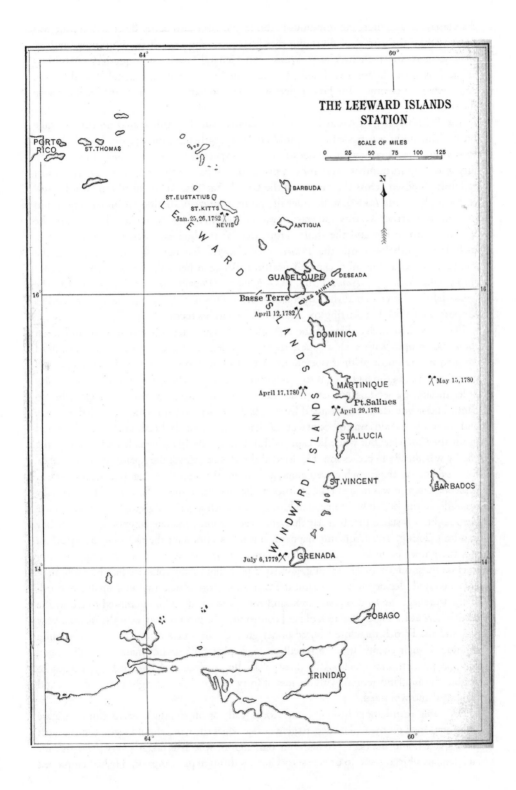

THE LEEWARD ISLANDS
STATION

SCALE OF MILES

0   25   50   75   100   125

N

PORTO
RICO

ST.THOMAS

BARBUDA

ST.EUSTATIUS
ST.KITTS
Jan.25,26,1782   NEVIS

ANTIGUA

L E E W A R D

GUADELOUPE   DESEADA

Basse Terre
April 12,1782
LES SAINTES

I S L A N D S

DOMINICA

MARTINIQUE
April 17,1780
May 15,1780

Pt.Salines
April 29,1781

STA.LUCIA

ST.VINCENT

BARBADOS

W I N D W A R D   I S L A N D S

July 6,1779   GRENADA

TOBAGO

TRINIDAD

the Carénage, as a more commodious harbour, probably also better defended; but he was prevented by the arrival of d'Estaing that afternoon. "Just as all the important stations were secured, the French colours struck, and General Grant's headquarters established at the Governor's house, the *Ariadne* frigate came in sight with the signal abroad for the approach of an enemy."[2] The French fleet was seen soon afterwards from the heights above the squadron.

The British had gained much so far by celerity, but they still spared no time to take breath. The night was passed by the soldiers in strengthening their positions, and by the Rear-Admiral in rectifying his order to meet the expected attack. The transports, between fifty and sixty in number, were moved inside the ships of war, and the latter were most carefully disposed across the mouth of the Cul de Sac bay. At the northern (windward)[3] end was placed the *Isis*, 50, well under the point to prevent anything from passing round her; but for further security she was supported by three frigates, anchored abreast of the interval between her and the shore. From the *Isis* the line extended to the southward, inclining slightly outward; the *Prince of Wales*, 74, Barrington's flagship, taking the southern flank, as the most exposed position. Between her and the *Isis* were five other ships,—the *Boyne*, 70, *Nonsuch*, 64, *St. Albans*, 64, *Preston*, 50, and *Centurion*, 50. The works left by the French at the north and south points of the bay may have been used to support the flanks, but Barrington does not say so in his report.

D'Estaing had twelve ships of the line, and two days after this was able to land seven thousand troops. With such a superiority it is evident that the British would have been stopped in the midst of their operations, if he had arrived twenty-four hours sooner. To gain time, Barrington had sought to prevent intelligence reaching Fort Royal, less than fifty miles distant, by sending cruisers in advance of his squadron, to cover the approaches to Santa Lucia; but, despite his care, d'Estaing had the news on the 14th. He sailed at once, and, as has been said, was off Santa Lucia that evening. At daybreak of the 15th he stood in for the Carénage; but when he came within range, a lively cannonade told him that the enemy was already in possession. He decided therefore to attack the squadron in the Cul de Sac, and at 11.30 the French passed along it from north to south, firing, but without effect. A second attempt was made in the afternoon, directed upon the lee flank, but it was equally unavailing. The British had three men killed; the French loss is not given, but is said to have been slight. It is stated that that day the sea breeze did not penetrate far enough into the bay to admit closing. This frequently happens, but it does not alter the fact that the squadron was the proper point of attack, and that, especially in the winter season, an opportunity to close must offer soon. D'Estaing, governed probably by the soldierly bias he more than once betrayed, decided now to assault the works on shore. Anchoring in a small bay north of the Carénage, he landed seven thousand men, and on the 18th attempted to storm the British lines at La Vigie. The neck of land connecting the promontory with the island is very flat, and the French therefore labored under great disadvantage through the commanding position of their enemy. It was a repetition of Bunker Hill, and of many other ill-judged and precipitate frontal attacks. After three gallant but ineffectual charges, led by d'Estaing in person, the assailants retired, with the loss of forty-one officers and eight hundred rank and file, killed and wounded.

D'Estaing reembarked his men, and stood ready again to attack Barrington; a frigate being stationed off the Cul de Sac, to give notice when the wind should serve. On the 24th she signalled, and the fleet weighed; but Barrington, who had taken a very great risk for an adequate object, took no unnecessary chances through presumption. He had employed

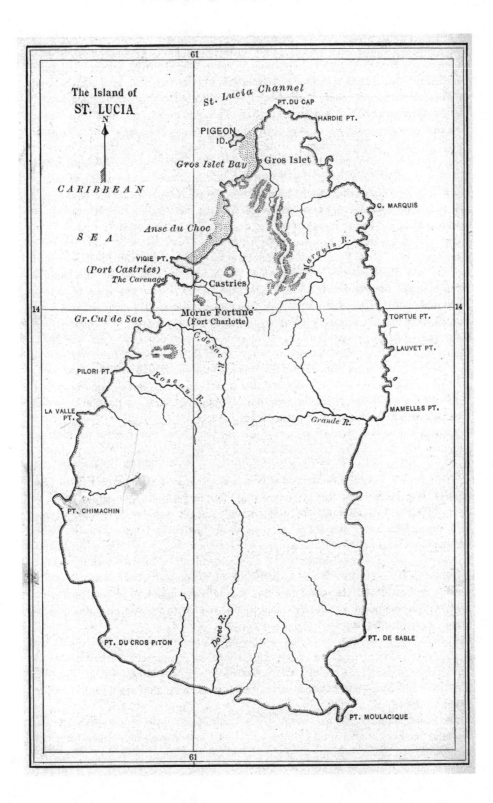

The Island of
ST. LUCIA

N

St. Lucia Channel

PT. DU CAP

HARDIE PT.

PIGEON
ID.

Gros Islet Bay   Gros Islet

CARIBBEAN

C. MARQUIS

Anse du Choc

SEA

VIGIE PT.

(Port Castries)
The Carenage   Castries

Marquis R.

Gr. Cul de Sac   Morne Fortuné
(Fort Charlotte)

TORTUE PT.

LAUVET PT.

C. de Sac R.

PILORI PT.

Roseau R.

LA VALLE
PT.

Grande R.

MAMELLES PT.

PT. CHIMACHIN

PT. DU CROS PITON

Doree R.

PT. DE SABLE

PT. MOULACIQUE

his respite to warp the ships of war farther in, where the breeze reached less certainly, and where narrower waters gave better support to the flanks. He had strengthened the latter also by new works, in which he had placed heavy guns from the ships, manned by seamen. For these or other reasons d'Estatng did not attack. On the 29th he quitted the island, and on the 30th the French governor, the Chevalier de Micoud, formally capitulated.

This achievement of Barrington and of Major-General James Grant, who was associated with him, was greeted at the time with an applause which will be echoed by the military judgment of a later age. There is a particular pleasure in finding the willingness to incur a great risk, conjoined with a care that chances nothing against which the utmost diligence and skill can provide. The celerity, forethought, wariness, and daring of Admiral Barrington have inscribed upon the records of the British Navy a success the distinction of which should be measured, not by the largeness of the scale, but by the perfection of the workmanship, and by the energy of the execution in face of great odds.

Santa Lucia remained in the hands of the British throughout the war. It was an important acquisition, because at its north-west extremity was a good and defensible anchorage, Gros Ilet Bay, only thirty miles from Fort Royal in Martinique. In it the British fleet could lie, when desirable to close-watch the enemy, yet not be worried for the safety of the port when away; for it was but an outpost, not a base of operations, as Fort Royal was. It was thus used continually, and from it Rodney issued for his great victory in April, 1782.

During the first six months of 1779 no important incident occurred in the West Indies. On the 6th of January, Vice-Admiral Byron, with ten ships of the line from Narragansett Bay, reached Santa Lucia, and relieved Barrington of the chief command. Both the British and the French fleets were reinforced in the course of the spring, but the relative strength remained nearly as before, until the 27th of June, when the arrival of a division from Brest made the French numbers somewhat superior.

Shortly before this, Byron had been constrained by one of the commercial exigencies which constantly embarrassed the military action of British admirals. A large convoy of trading ships, bound to England, was collecting at St. Kitts, and he thought necessary to accompany it part of the homeward way, until well clear of the French West India cruisers. For this purpose he left Santa Lucia early in June. As soon as the coast was clear, d'Estaing, informed of Byron's object, sent a small combined expedition against St. Vincent, which was surrendered on the 18th of the month. On the 30th the French admiral himself quitted Fort Royal with his whole fleet,—twenty-five ships of the line and several frigates,—directing his course for the British Island of Grenada, before which he anchored on the 2d of July. With commendable promptitude, he landed his troops that evening, and on the 4th the island capitulated. Except as represented by one small armed sloop, which was taken, the British Navy had no part in this transaction. Thirty richly laden merchant ships were captured in the port.

At daybreak of July 6th, Byron appeared with twenty-one sail of the line, one frigate, and a convoy of twenty-eight vessels, carrying troops and equipments. He had returned to Santa Lucia on the 1st, and there had heard of the loss of St. Vincent, with a rumor that the French had gone against Grenada. He consequently had put to sea on the 3d, with the force mentioned.

The British approach was reported to d'Estaing during the night of July 5th. Most of his fleet was then lying at anchor off Georgetown, at the south-west of the island; some vessels, which had been under way on look-out duty, had fallen to leeward.[4] At 4 A.M. the French began to lift their anchors, with orders to form line of battle on the starboard tack, in order of

ADMIRAL
THE HONOURABLE
SAMUEL BARRINGTON

speed; that is, as rapidly as possible without regard to usual stations. When daylight had fully made, the British fleet (A) was seen standing down from the northward, close inshore, on the port tack, with the wind free at north-east by east. It was not in order, as is evident from the fact that the ships nearest the enemy, and therefore first to close, ought to have been in the rear on the then tack. For this condition there is no evident excuse; for a fleet having a convoy necessarily proceeds so slowly that the warships can keep reasonable order for mutual support. Moreover, irregularities that are permissible in case of emergency, or when no enemy can be encountered suddenly, cease to be so when the imminent probability of a meeting exists. The worst results of the day are to be attributed to this fault. Being short of frigates, Byron had assigned three ships of the line (a), under Rear-Admiral Rowley, to the convoy, which of course was on the off hand from the enemy, and somewhat in the rear. It was understood, however, that these would be called into the line, if needed.

When the French (AA) were first perceived by Byron, their line was forming; the long thin column lengthening out gradually to the north-north-west, from the confused cluster[5] still to be seen at the anchorage. Hoping to profit by their disorder, he signalled "a general chase in that quarter,[6] as well as for Rear-Admiral Rowley to leave the convoy; and as not more than fourteen or fifteen of the enemy's ships appeared to be in line, the signal was made for the ships to engage, and form as they could get up."[7] It is clear from this not only that the ships were not in order, but also that they were to form under fire. Three ships, the *Sultan*, 74, the *Prince of Wales*, 74, and the *Boyne*, 70, in the order named,—the second carrying Barrington's flag,—were well ahead of the fleet (b). The direction prescribed for the attack, that of the clustered ships in the French rear, carried the British down on a south-south-west, or south by west, course; and as the enemy's van and centre were drawing out to the north-north-west, the two lines at that time resembled the legs of a "V," the point of which was the anchorage off Georgetown. Barrington's three ships therefore neared the French order gradually, and had to receive its fire for some time before they could reply, unless, by hauling to the wind, they diverged from the set course. This, and their isolation, made their loss very heavy. When they reached the rear of the French, the latter's column was tolerably formed, and Barrington's ships wore (w) in succession,—just as Harland's had done in Keppel's action,—to follow on the other tack. In doing this, the *Sultan* kept away under the stern of the enemy's rearmost ship, to rake her; to avoid which the latter bore up. The *Sultan* thus lost time and ground, and Barrington took the lead, standing along the French line, from rear to van, and to windward.

Meanwhile, the forming of the enemy had revealed to Byron for the first time, and to his dismay, that he had been deceived in thinking the French force inferior to his own. "However, the general chase was continued, and the signal made for close engagement."[8] The remainder of the ships stood down on the port tack, as the first three had done, and wore in the wake of the latter, whom they followed; but before reaching the point of wearing, three ships, "the *Grafton*, 74, the *Cornwall*, 74, and the *Lion*, 64 (c), *happening to be to leeward*,[9] sustained the fire of the enemy's whole line, as it passed on the starboard tack." It seems clear that, having had the wind, during the night and now, and being in search of an enemy, it should not have "happened" that any ships should have been so far to leeward as to be unsupported. Captain Thomas White, R.N., writing as an advocate of Byron, says,[10] "while the van was wearing . . . the sternmost ships were coming up under Rear-Admiral Hyde Parker. . . . Among these ships, the *Cornwall* and *Lion*, from being nearer the enemy than those about them (for the rear division had not then *formed into line*), drew upon themselves almost the whole of the enemy's fire." No words can show more clearly the disastrous, precipitate disorder in which this attack was conducted. The *Grafton*, White says, was similarly situated. In consequence, these three were so crippled, besides a heavy loss in men, that they dropped far to leeward and astern (c´, c″), when on the other tack.

When the British ships in general had got round, and were in line ahead on the starboard tack,—the same as the French,—ranging from rear to van of the enemy (Positions B, B, B), Byron signalled for the eight leading ships to close together, for mutual support, and to engage close. This, which should have been done—not with finikin precision, but with military adequacy—before engaging, was less easy now, in the din of battle and with crippled ships. A quick-eyed subordinate, however, did something to remedy the error of his chief. Rear-Admiral Rowley was still considerably astern, having to make up the distance between the convoy and the fleet. As he followed the latter, he saw Barrington's three ships unduly separated and doubtless visibly much mauled. Instead, therefore, of blindly following his leader, he cut straight across (aa) to the head of the column to support the van,—an act almost absolutely identical with that which won Nelson renown at Cape St. Vincent. In this he was followed by the *Monmouth*, 64, the brilliancy of whose bearing was so conspicuous to the two fleets that it is said the French officers after the battle toasted "the little black ship." She and the *Suffolk*, 74, Rowley's flagship, also suffered severely in this gallant feat.

It was imperative with Byron now to keep his van well up with the enemy, lest he should uncover the convoy, broad on the weather bow of the two fleets. "They seemed much inclined to cut off the convoy, and had it much in their power by means of their large frigates, independent of ships of the line."[11] On the other hand, the *Cornwall*, *Grafton*, and

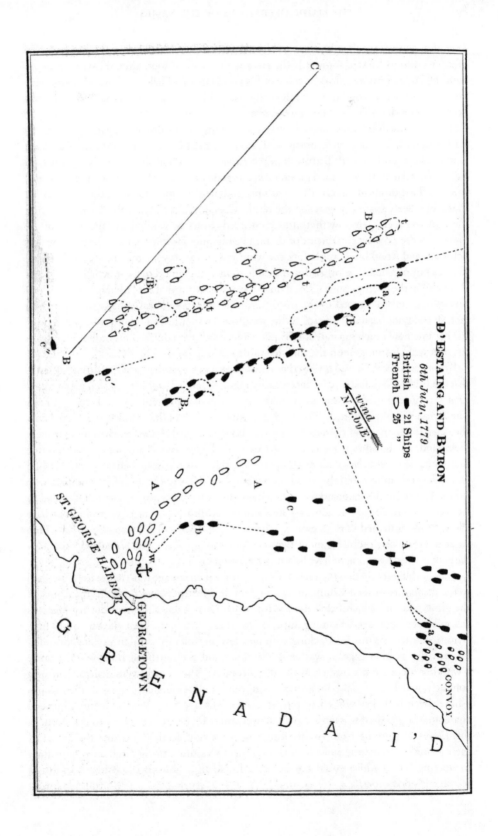

D'ESTAING AND BYRON

6th July, 1779

British ● 21 Ships
French ◁ 25 "

wind
N.E. ⅛ E.

C

B

t

B

E

t

t

t

a'

a

B

c"

B

c'

B'

wind N.E. ⅛ E.

A

A

c

A

D

w

A

ST. GEORGE HARBOR

GEORGETOWN

a
a
a

CONVOY

G R E N A D A   I ' D

Lion, though they got their heads round, could not keep up with the fleet (c´, c″), and were dropping also to leeward—towards the enemy. At noon, or soon after, d'Estaing bore up with the body of his force to join some of his vessels that had fallen to leeward. Byron very properly—under his conditions of inferiority—kept his wind; and the separation of the two fleets, thus produced, caused firing to cease at 1 P.M.

The enemies were now ranged on parallel lines, some distance apart; still on the starboard tack, heading north-north-west. Between the two, but far astern, the *Cornwall*, *Grafton*, *Lion*, and a fourth British ship, the *Fame*, were toiling along, greatly crippled. At 3 P.M., the French, now in good order, tacked together (t, t, t), which caused them to head towards these disabled vessels. Byron at once imitated the movement, and the eyes of all in the two fleets anxiously watched the result. Captain Cornwallis of the *Lion*, measuring the situation accurately, saw that, if he continued ahead, he would be in the midst of the French by the time he got abreast of them. Having only his foremast standing, he put his helm up, and stood broad off before the wind (c″), across the enemy's bows, for Jamaica. He was not pursued. The other three, unable to tack and afraid to wear, which would put them also in the enemy's power, stood on, passed to windward of the latter, receiving several broadsides, and so escaped to the northward. The *Monmouth* was equally maltreated; in fact, she had not been able to tack to the southward with the fleet. Continuing north (a´), she became now much separated. D'Estaing afterwards reestablished his order of battle on the port tack, forming upon the then leewardmost ship on the line BC.

Byron's action off Grenada, viewed as an isolated event, was the most disastrous in results that the British Navy had fought since Beachy Head, in 1690. That the *Cornwall*, *Grafton*, and *Lion* were not captured was due simply to the strained and inept caution of the French admiral. This Byron virtually admitted. "To my great surprise no ship of the enemy was detached after the *Lion*. The *Grafton* and *Cornwall* might have been weathered by the French, if they had kept their wind, . . . but they persevered so strictly in declining every chance of close action that they contented themselves with firing upon these ships when passing barely within gunshot, and suffered them to rejoin the squadron, without one effort to cut them off." Suffren,[12] who led the French on the starboard tack, and whose ship, the *Fantasque*, 64, lost 22 killed and 43 wounded, wrote: "Had our admiral's seamanship equalled his courage, we would not have allowed four dismasted ships to escape." That the *Monmouth* and *Fame* could also have been secured is extremely probable; and if Byron, in order to save them, had borne down to renew the action, the disaster might have become a catastrophe.

That nothing resulted to the French from their great advantage is therefore to be ascribed to the incapacity of their Commander-in-Chief. It is instructive to note also the causes of the grave calamity which befell the British, when twenty-one ships met twenty-four,[13]— a sensible but not overwhelming superiority. These facts have been shown sufficiently. Byron's disaster was due to attacking with needless precipitation, and in needless disorder. He had the weather-gage, it was early morning, and the northeast trade-wind, already a working breeze, must freshen as the day advanced. The French were tied to their new conquest, which they could not abandon without humiliation; not to speak of their troops ashore. Even had they wished to retreat, they could not have done so before a general chase, unless prepared to sacrifice their slower ships. If twenty-four ships could reconcile themselves to running from twenty-one, it was scarcely possible but that the fastest of these would overtake the slowest of those. There was time for fighting, an opportunity for forcing action which could not be evaded, and time also for the British to form in reasonably good order.

It is important to consider this, because, while Keppel must be approved for attacking in partial disorder, Byron must be blamed for attacking in utter disorder. Keppel had to snatch opportunity from an unwilling foe. Having himself the leegage, he could not pick and choose, nor yet manœuvre; yet he brought his fleet into action, giving mutual support throughout nearly, if not quite, the whole line. What Byron did has been set forth; the sting is that his bungling tactics can find no extenuation in any urgency of the case.

The loss of the two fleets, as given by the authorities of either nation, were: British, 183 killed, 346 wounded; French, 190 killed, 759 wounded. Of the British total, 126 killed and 235 wounded, or two thirds, fell to the two groups of three ships each, which by Byron's mismanagement were successively exposed to be cut up in detail by the concentrated fire of the enemy. The British loss in spars and sails—in motive-power—also exceeded greatly that of the French.

After the action d'Estaing returned quietly to Grenada. Byron went to St. Kitts to refit; but repairs were most difficult, owing to the dearth of stores in which the Admiralty had left the West Indies. With all the skill of the seamen of that day in making good damages, the ships remained long unserviceable, causing great apprehension for the other islands. This state of things d'Estaing left unimproved, as he had his advantage in the battle. He did, indeed, parade his superior force before Byron's fleet as it lay at anchor; but, beyond the humiliation naturally felt by a Navy which prided itself on ruling the sea, no further injury was done.

In August Byron sailed for England. Barrington had already gone home, wounded. The station therefore was left in command of Rear-Admiral Hyde Parker,[14] and, so remained until March, 1780, when the celebrated Rodney arrived as Commander-in-Chief on the Leeward Islands Station. The North American Station was given to Vice-Admiral Marriot Arbuthnot, who had under him a half-dozen ships of the line, with headquarters at New York. His command was ordinarily independent of Rodney's, but the latter had no hesitation in going to New York on emergency and taking charge there; in doing which he had the approval of the Admiralty.

The approach of winter in 1778 had determined the cessation of operations, both naval and military, in the northern part of the American continent, and had led to the transfer of five thousand troops to the West Indies, already noted. At the same time, an unjustifiable extension of British effort, having regard to the disposable means, was undertaken in the southern States of Georgia and South Carolina. On the 27th of November a small detachment of troops under Lieutenant-Colonel Archibald Campbell, sailed from Sandy Hook, convoyed by a division of frigates commanded by Captain Hyde Parker.[15] The expedition entered the Savannah River four weeks later, and soon afterwards occupied the city of the same name. Simultaneously with this, by Clinton's orders, General Prevost moved from Florida, then a British colony, with all the men he could spare from the defence of St. Augustine. Upon his arrival in Savannah he took command of the whole force thus assembled.

These operations, which during 1779 extended as far as the neighbourhood of Charleston, depended upon the control of the water, and are a conspicuous example of misapplication of power to the point of ultimate self-destruction. They were in 1778–79 essentially of a minor character, especially the maritime part, and will therefore be dismissed with the remark that the Navy, by small vessels, accompanied every movement in a country cut up in all directions by watercourses, big and little. "The defence of this province," wrote Parker, "must greatly depend on the naval force upon the different inland creeks.

I am therefore forming some galleys covered from musketry, which I believe will have a good effect." These were precursors of the "tin-clads" of the American War of Secession, a century later. Not even an armored ship is a new thing under the sun.

In the southern States, from Georgia to Virginia, the part of the Navy from first, to last was subsidiary, though important. It is therefore unnecessary to go into details, but most necessary to note that here, by misdirection of effort and abuse of means, was initiated the fatal movement which henceforth divided the small British army in North America into two sections, wholly out of mutual support. Here Sir William Howe's error of 1777 was reproduced on a larger scale and was therefore more fatal. This led directly, by the inevitable logic of a false position, to Cornwallis's march through North Carolina into Virginia, to Yorktown in 1781, and to the signal demonstration of sea power off Chesapeake Bay, which at a blow accomplished the independence of the United States. No hostile strategist could have severed the British army more hopelessly than did the British government; no fate could have been more inexorable than was its own perverse will. The personal alienation and official quarrel between Sir Henry Clinton and Lord Cornwallis, their divided counsels and divergent action, were but the natural result, and the reflection, of a situation essentially self-contradictory and exasperating.

As the hurricane season of 1779 advanced, d'Estaing, who had orders to bring back to France the ships of the line with which he had sailed from Toulon in 1778, resolved to go first upon the American coast, off South Carolina or Georgia. Arriving with his whole fleet at the mouth of the Savannah, August 31st, he decided to attempt to wrest the city of Savannah from the British. This would have been of real service to the latter, had it nipped in the bud their ex-centric undertaking; but, after three weeks of opening trenches, an assault upon the place failed. D'Estaing then sailed for Europe with the ships designated to accompany him, the others returning to the West Indies in two squadrons, under de Grasse and La Motte-Picquet. Though fruitless in its main object, this enterprise of d'Estaing had the important indirect effect of causing the British to abandon Narragansett Bay. Upon the news of his appearance, Sir Henry Clinton had felt that, with his greatly diminished army, he could not hold both Rhode Island and New York. He therefore ordered the evacuation of the former, thus surrendering, to use again Rodney's words, "the best and noblest harbour in America." The following summer it was occupied in force by the French.

D'Estaing was succeeded in the chief command, in the West Indies and North America, by Rear-Admiral de Guichen,[16] who arrived on the station in March, 1780, almost at the same moment as Rodney.

1. The French accounts say three.
2. Beatson, "Military and Naval Memoirs," iv. 390.
3. Santa Lucia being in the region of the north-east trade winds, north and east are always windwardly relatively to south and west.
4. To the westward. These islands lie in the trade-winds, which are constant in *general* direction from north-east.
5. Admiral Keppel, in his evidence before the Palliser Court, gave an interesting description of a similar scene, although the present writer is persuaded that he was narrating things as they seemed, rather than as they were—as at Grenada. "The French were forming their line exactly

in the manner M. Conflans did when attacked by Admiral Hawke." (Keppel had been in that action.) "It is a manner peculiar to themselves; and to those who do not understand it, it appears like confusion. They draw out ship by ship from a cluster."

6. That is, towards the ships at anchor,—the enemy's rear as matters then were.

7. Byron's Report. The italics are the author's.

8. Byron's Report.

9. *Ibid.* Author's italics.

10. "Naval Researches." London, 1830, p. 22.

11. Byron's Report.

12. Pierre A. de Suffren de Saint Tropez, a Bailli of the Order of Knights of Malta. Born, 1726. Present at two naval actions before he was twenty. Participated in 1756 in the attack on Port Mahon, and in 1759 in the action off Lagos. Chef d'escadre in 1779. Dispatched to the East Indies in 1781. Fought a British squadron in the Bay of Praya, and a succession of brilliant actions with Sir Edward Hughes, 1782–83. Vice-Admiral, 1783. Killed in a duel, 1788. One of the greatest of French naval officers.—W.L.C.

13. Troude says that one French seventy-four, having touched in leaving port, was not in the engagement.

14. First of the name. Born 1714. In 1780, he fell under Rodney's censure, and went home. In 1781, he commanded in the general action with the Dutch, known as the Dogger Bank. In 1782, he sailed for the East Indies in the *Cato*, 64; which ship was never again heard from.

15. Sir Hyde Parker, Kt. Second of the name, son of the first. Born, 1739. Captain, 1763. Rear-Admiral, 1793. Vice-Admiral, 1794. Admiral, 1799. Died, 1807. Nelson's chief at Copenhagen, in 1801.

16. Louis Urbain de Bouënic, Comte de Guichen. Born, 1712. Entered the navy, 1730. Commanded the *Illustre* with success in North America in 1756. Second in command in the action off Ushant in 1778. Thrice fought Rodney in the West Indies in 1780. Fought Kempenfelt off the Azores in 1781. Died, 1790.—W.L.C.

VII

THE NAVAL WAR IN EUROPEAN WATERS

I N JUNE, 1779, THE MARITIME situation of Great Britain had become much more serious by Spain's declaring war. At the same moment that d'Estaing with twenty-five ships of the line had confronted Byron's twenty-one, the Channel fleet of forty sail had seen gathering against it a host of sixty-six. Of this great number thirty-six were Spanish.

The open declaration of Spain had been preceded by a secret alliance with France, signed on the 12th of April. Fearing that the British government would take betimes the reasonable and proper step of blockading the Brest fleet of thirty with the Channel forty, thus assuming a central position with reference to its enemies and anticipating the policy of Lord St. Vincent, the French Ministry hurried its ships to sea on the 4th of June; Admiral d'Orvilliers, Keppel's opponent, still in command. His orders were to cruise near the island of Cizarga, off the north-west coast of Spain, where the Spaniards were to join him. On the 11th of June he was at the rendezvous, but not till the 23d of July did the bulk of the Spanish force appear. During this time, the French, insufficiently equipped from the first, owing to the haste of their departure, were consuming provisions and water, not to speak of wasting pleasant summer weather. Their ships also were ravaged by an epidemic fever. Upon the junction, d'Orvilliers found that the Spaniards had not been furnished with the French system of signals, although by the treaty the French admiral was to be in chief command. The rectification of this oversight caused further delay, but on the 11th of August the combined fleet sighted Ushant, and on the 14th was off the Lizard. On the 16th it appeared before Plymouth, and there on the 17th captured the British 64-gun ship *Ardent*.

Thirty-five ships of the Channel fleet had gone to sea on the 16th of June, and now were cruising outside, under the command of Admiral Sir Charles Hardy. His station was from ten to twenty leagues south-west of Scilly; consequently he had not been seen by the enemy, who from Ushant had stood up the Channel. The allies, now nearly double the numbers of the British, were between them and their ports,—a serious situation doubtless, but by no means desperate; not so dangerous for sailing ships as it probably will be for steamers to have an enemy between them and their coal.

The alarm in England was very great, especially in the south. On the 9th of July a royal proclamation had commanded all horses and cattle to be driven from the coasts, in case of invasion. Booms had been placed across the entrance to Plymouth Harbor, and orders were sent from the Admiralty to sink vessels across the harbour's mouth. Many who had the means withdrew into the interior, which increased the panic. Great merchant fleets were then on the sea, homeward bound. If d'Orvilliers were gone to cruise in the approaches to the Channel, instead of to the Spanish coast, these might be taken; and for some time his whereabouts were unknown. As it was, the Jamaica convoy, over two hundred sail, got in a few days before the allies appeared, and the Leeward Islands fleet had similar good fortune. Eight homeward bound East Indiamen were less lucky, but, being warned of their danger, took refuge in the Shannon, and there remained till the trouble blew over. On the other hand, the stock market stood firm. Nevertheless, it was justly felt that such a state of things as a vastly superior hostile fleet in the Channel should not have been. Sir John Jervis, afterward Earl St. Vincent, who commanded a ship in the fleet, wrote to his sister: "What a humiliating state is our country reduced to!" but he added that he laughed at the idea of invasion.

The French had placed a force of fifty thousand men at Le Havre and St. Malo, and collected four hundred vessels for their transport. Their plans were not certainly known, but enough had transpired to cause reasonable anxiety; and the crisis, on its face, was very serious. Not their own preparations, but the inefficiency of their enemies, in counsel and in preparation, saved the British Islands from invasion. What the results of this would have been is another question,—a question of land warfare. The original scheme of the French Ministry was to seize the Isle of Wight, securing Spithead as an anchorage for the fleet, and to prosecute their enterprise from this near and reasonably secure base. Referring to this first project, d'Orvilliers wrote: "We will seek the enemy at St. Helen's,[1] and then, if I find that roadstead unoccupied, or make myself master of it, I will send word to Marshal De Vaux, at Le Havre, and inform him of the measures I will take to insure his passage, which [measures] will depend upon the position of the English main fleet [dèpendront des forces supèrieures des Anglais]. That is to say, I myself will lead the combined fleet on that side [against their main body], to contain the enemy, and I will send, on the other side [to convoy], a light squadron, with a sufficient number of ships of the line and frigates; or I will propose to M. de Cordova to take this latter station, in order that the passage of the army may be free and sure. I assume that then, either by the engagement I shall have fought with the enemy, or *by their retreat into their ports*, I shall be certain of their situation and of the success of the operation."[2] It will be observed that d'Orvilliers, accounted then and now one of the best officers of his day in the French navy, takes here into full account the British "fleet in being." The main body of the allies, fifty ships, was to hold this in check, while a smaller force—Cordova had command of a special "squadron of observation," of sixteen ships of the line—was to convoy the crossing.

These projects all fell to pieces before a strong east wind, and a change of mind in the French government. On the 16th of August, before Plymouth, d'Orvilliers was notified that not the Isle of Wight, but the coast of Cornwall, near Falmouth, was to be the scene of landing. The effect of this was to deprive the huge fleet of any anchorage,—a resource necessary even to steamers, and far more to sailing vessels aiming to remain in a position. As a point to begin shore operations, too, as well as to sustain them, such a remote corner of the country to be invaded was absurd. D'Orvilliers duly represented all this, but could not stay where he was long enough to get a reply. An easterly gale came on, which blew hard for several days and drove the allies out of the Channel. On the 25th of August word was received that the British fleet was near Scilly. A council of war was then held, which decided that, in view of the terrible increase of disease in the shipping, and of the shortness of provisions, it was expedient not to re-enter the Channel, but to seek the enemy, and bring him to battle. This was done. On the 29th Hardy was sighted, being then on his return up Channel. With the disparity of force he could not but decline action, and the allies were unable to compel it. On the 3d of September he reached Spithead. D'Orvilliers soon afterwards received orders to return to Brest, and on the 14th the combined fleet anchored there.

The criticism to be passed on the conduct of this summer campaign by the British Ministry is twofold. In the first place, it was not ready according to the reasonable standard of the day, which recognised in the probable cooperation of the two Bourbon kingdoms, France and Spain, the measure of the minimum naval force permissible to Great Britain. Secondly, the entrance of Spain into the war had been foreseen months before. For the inferior force, therefore, it was essential to prevent a junction,—to take an interior position. The Channel fleet ought to have been off Brest before the French sailed. After they were gone, there was still fair ground for the contention of the Opposition, that they should have been followed, and attacked, off the coast of Spain. During the six weeks they waited there, they were inferior to Hardy's force. Allowance here must be made, however, for the inability of a representative government to disregard popular outcry, and to uncover the main approach to its own ports. This, indeed, does but magnify the error made in not watching Brest betimes; for in such case a fleet before Brest covered also the Channel.

With regard to the objects of the war in which they had become partners, the views of France and Spain accorded in but one point,—the desirability of injuring Great Britain. Each had its own special aim for its own advantage. This necessarily introduced divergence of effort; but, France having first embarked alone in the contest and then sought the aid of Spain, the particular objects of her ally naturally obtained from the beginning a certain precedence. Until near the close of the war, it may be said that the chief ambitions of France were in the West Indies; those of Spain, in Europe,—to regain Minorca and Gibraltar.

In this way Gibraltar became a leading factor in the contest, and affected, directly or indirectly, the major operations throughout the world, by the amount of force absorbed in attacking and preserving it. After the futile effort in the Channel, in 1779, Spain recalled her vessels from Brest. "The project of a descent upon England was abandoned provisionally. To blockade Gibraltar, to have in America and Asia force sufficient to hold the British in check, and to take the offensive in the West Indies,—such," wrote the French government to its ambassador in Madrid, "was the plan of campaign adopted for 1780." Immediately upon the declaration of war, intercourse between Gibraltar and the Spanish mainland was stopped. Soon afterwards a blockade by sea was instituted; fifteen cruisers being stationed at the entrance of the Bay, where they seized and sent into Spanish ports all vessels, neutral or British, bound to the Rock. This blockade was effectively supported from Cadiz, but a Spanish force of some ships of the line and many small vessels also maintained it more directly from Algeciras, on the Spanish side of the Bay of Gibraltar. The British Mediterranean squadron, then consisting only of one 60-gun ship, three frigates, and a sloop, was wholly unable to afford relief. At the close of the year 1779, flour in Gibraltar was fourteen guineas the barrel, and other provisions in proportion. It became therefore imminently necessary to throw in supplies of all kinds, as well as to reinforce the garrison. To this service Rodney was assigned; and with it he began the brilliant career, the chief scene of which was to be in the West Indies.

Rodney was appointed to command the Leeward Islands Station on the 1st of October, 1779. He was to be accompanied there immediately by only four or five ships of the line; but advantage was taken of his sailing, to place under the charge of an officer of his approved reputation a great force, composed of his small division and a large fraction of the Channel fleet, to convey supplies and reinforcements to Gibraltar and Minorca. On the 29th of December the whole body, after many delays in getting down Channel, put to sea from Plymouth: twenty-two ships of the line, fourteen frigates and smaller vessels, besides a huge collection of storeships, victuallers, ordnance vessels, troop-ships, and merchantmen, the last named being the "trade" for the West Indies and Portugal.

On the 7th of January, 1780, a hundred leagues west of Cape Finisterre, the West India ships parted for their destination, under convoy of a ship of the line and three frigates. At daylight on the 8th, twenty-two sail were seen to the north-east, the squadron apparently having passed them in the night. Chase was at once given, and the whole were taken in a few hours. Seven were ships of war, one 64 and six frigates; the remainder merchant vessels, laden with naval stores and provisions for the Spanish fleet at Cadiz. The provision ships, twelve in number, were diverted at once to the relief of Gibraltar, under charge of the Spanish sixty-four, which had been one of their convoy before capture, and was now manned by a British crew. Continuing on, intelligence was received from time to time by passing vessels that a Spanish squadron was cruising off Cape St. Vincent. Thus forewarned, orders were given to all captains to be prepared for battle as the Cape was neared. On the 16th it was passed, and at 1 P.M. sails in the south-east were signalled. These were a Spanish squadron of eleven ships of the line, and two 26-gun frigates. Rodney at once bore down for them under a press of canvas, making signal for the line abreast.[3] Seeing, however, that the enemy was trying to form line of battle ahead on the starboard tack, which with a westerly wind was with heads to the southward, towards Cadiz, a hundred miles to the south-east, he changed the orders to a "General Chase," the ships to engage as they came up; "to leeward," so as to get between the enemy and his port, and "in rotation," by which probably was meant that the leading British vessel should attack the sternmost of the Spaniards, and that her followers should pass her to leeward, successively engaging from the enemy's rear towards the van.

At 4 P.M. the signal for battle was made, and a few minutes later the four headmost of the pursuers got into action. At 4.40 one of the Spanish ships, the *Santo Domingo*, 80, blew up with all on board, and at 6 another struck. By this hour, it being January, darkness had set in. A night action therefore followed, which lasted until 2 A.M., when the headmost of the enemy surrendered, and all firing ceased. Of the eleven hostile ships of the line, only four escaped. Besides the one blown up, six were taken. These were the *Fénix*, 80, flag of the Spanish Admiral, Don Juan de Langara, the *Monarca*, 70, the *Princesa*, 70, the *Diligente*, 70, the *San Julian*, 70, and the *San Eugenio*, 70. The two latter drove ashore and were lost.[4] The remaining four were brought into Gibraltar, and were ultimately added to the Navy. All retained their old names, save the *Fénix*, which was renamed *Gibraltar*. "The weather during the night," by Rodney's report, "was at times very tempestuous, with a great sea. It continued very bad weather the next day, when the *Royal George*, 100, *Prince George*, 90, *Sandwich*, 90 (Rodney's flagship), and several other ships were in great danger, and under the necessity of making sail to avoid the shoals of San Lucar, nor did they get into deep water till the next morning."

It was in this danger from a lee shore, which was deliberately though promptly incurred, that the distinction of this action of Rodney's consists. The enemy's squadron, being only eleven ships of the line, was but half the force of the British, and it was taken by surprise; which, to be sure, is no excuse for a body of war-ships in war-time. Caught unawares, the Spaniards took to flight too late. It was Rodney's merit, and no slight one under the conditions of weather and navigation, that they were not permitted to retrieve their mistake. His action left nothing to be desired in resolution or readiness. It is true that Rodney discussed the matter with his flag-captain, Walter Young, and that rumor attributed the merit of the decision to the latter; but this sort of detraction is of too common occurrence to affect opinion. Sir Gilbert Blane, Physician to the Fleet, gives the following account: "When it was close upon sunset, it became a question whether the chase should be continued. After some discussion between the Admiral and Captain, at which I was present, the Admiral being confined with the gout, it was decided to persist in the same course, with the signal to engage to leeward." Rodney at that time was nearly sixty-two, and a constant martyr to gout in both feet and hands.

The two successes by the way imparted a slightly triumphal character to the welcome of the Admiral by the garrison, then sorely in need of some good news. The arrival of much-needed supplies from home was itself a matter of rejoicing; but it was more inspiriting still to see following in the train of the friendly fleet five hostile ships of the line, one of them bearing the flag of a Commander-in-Chief, and to hear that, besides these, three more had been sunk or destroyed. The exultation in England was even greater, and especially at the Admiralty, which was labouring under the just indignation of the people for the unpreparedness of the Navy. "You have taken more line-of-battle ships," wrote the First Lord to Rodney, "than had been captured in any one action in either of the two last preceding wars."

It should be remembered, too, as an element in the triumph, that this advantage over an exposed detachment had been snatched, as it were, in the teeth of a main fleet superior to Rodney's own; for twenty Spanish and four French ships of the line, under Admiral de Cordova, were lying then in Cadiz Bay. During the eighteen days when the British remained in and near the Straits, no attempt was made by Cordova to take revenge for the disaster, or to reap the benefit of superior force. The inaction was due, probably, to the poor condition of the Spanish ships in point of efficiency and equipment, and largely to their having uncoppered bottoms. This element of inferiority in the Spanish navy should be kept in mind as a factor in the general war, although Spanish fleets did not come much into battle. A French Commodore, then with the Spanish fleet in Ferrol, wrote as follows: "Their ships all sail so badly that they can neither overtake an enemy nor escape from one. The *Glorieux* is a bad sailer in the French navy, but better than the best among the Spaniards." He adds: "The vessels of Langara's squadron were surprised at immense distances one from the other. Thus they always sail, and their negligence and security on this point are incredible."

On approaching Gibraltar, the continuance of bad weather, and the strong easterly current of the Straits, set many of Rodney's ships and convoy to leeward, to the back of the Rock, and it was not till the 26th that the flagship herself anchored. The storeships for Minorca were sent on at once, under charge of three coppered ships of the line. The practice of coppering, though then fully adopted, had not yet been extended to all vessels. As an element of speed, it was an important factor on an occasion like this, when time pressed to get to the West Indies; as it also was in an engagement. The action on the 16th had been opened by the coppered ships of the line, which first overtook the retreating enemy and brought his rear to battle. In the French navy at the time, Suffren was urging the adoption upon an apparently reluctant Minister. It would seem to have been more general among the British, going far to compensate for the otherwise inferior qualities of their ships. "The Spanish men-of-war we have taken," wrote Rodney to his wife concerning these prizes, "are much superior to ours." It may be remembered that Nelson, thirteen years later, said the same of the Spanish vessels which came under his observation. "I never saw finer ships." "I perceive you cry out loudly for coppered ships," wrote the First Lord to Rodney after this action; "and I am therefore determined to stop your mouth. You shall have copper enough."

Upon the return of the Minorca ships, Rodney put to sea again on the 13th of February, for the West Indies. The detachment from the Channel fleet accompanied him three days sail on his way, and then parted for England with the prizes. On this return voyage it fell in with fifteen French supply vessels, convoyed by two 64s, bound for the Ile de France,[5] in the Indian Ocean. One of the ships of war, the *Protée*, and three of the storeships were taken. Though trivial, the incident illustrates the effect of operations in Europe upon war in India. It may be mentioned here as indicative of the government's dilemmas, that Rodney was censured for having left one ship of the line at the Rock. "It has given us the trouble *and risk* of sending a frigate on purpose to order her home immediately; and if you will look into your original instructions, you will find that there was no point more strongly guarded against than that of your leaving any line-of-battle ship behind you." These words clearly show the exigency and peril of the general situation, owing to the inadequate development of the naval force as compared with its foes. Such isolated ships ran the gauntlet of the fleets in Cadiz, Ferrol, and Brest flanking the routes.

1. An anchorage three miles to seaward of Spithead.
2. Chevalier, "Marine Française," 1778, p. 165. Author's italics.
3. In line "abreast," as the word indicates, the ships are not in each other's wake, as in line "ahead," but abreast; that is, ranged on a line perpendicular to the course steered.
4. Rodney's Report. Chevalier says that one of them was retaken by her crew and carried into Cadiz.
5. Now the British Mauritius.

VIII

RODNEY AND DE GUICHEN'S
NAVAL CAMPAIGN

WHEN RODNEY ARRIVED AT SANTA Lucia with his four ships of the line, on March 27, 1780, he found there a force of sixteen others, composed in about equal proportions of ships that had left England with Byron in the summer of 1778, and of a reinforcement brought by Rear-Admiral Rowley in the spring of 1779.

During the temporary command of Rear-Admiral Hyde Parker, between the departure of Byron and the arrival of Rodney, a smart affair had taken place between a detachment of the squadron and one from the French division, under La Motte-Picquet, then lying in Fort Royal, Martinique.

On the 18th of December, 1779, between 8 and 9 A.M., the British look-out ship, the *Preston*, 50, between Martinique and Santa Lucia made signal for a fleet to windward, which proved to be a body of French supply ships, twenty-six in number, under convoy of a frigate. Both the British and the French squadrons were in disarray, sails unbent, ships on the heel or partially disarmed, crews ashore for wood and water. In both, signals flew at once for certain ships to get under way, and in both the orders were executed with a rapidity gratifying to the two commanders, who also went out in person. The British, however, were outside first, with five sail of the line and a 50-gun ship. Nine of the supply vessels were captured by them, and four forced ashore. The French Rear-Admiral had by this time got out of Fort Royal with three ships of the line,—the *Annibal*, 74, *Vengeur*, 64, and *Réfléchi*, 64,—and, being to windward, covered the entrance of the remainder of the convoy. As the two hostile divisions were now near each other, with a fine working breeze, the British tried to beat up to the enemy; the *Conqueror*, 74, Captain Walter Griffith, being ahead and to windward of her consorts. Coming within range at 5, firing began between her and the French flagship, *Annibal*, 74, and subsequently between her and all the three vessels of the enemy. Towards sunset, the *Albion*, 74, had got close up with the *Conqueror*, and the other ships were within distant range; "but as they had worked not only well within the dangers of the shoals of the bay (Fort Royal), but within reach of the batteries, I called them off by night signal at a quarter before seven."[1] In this chivalrous skirmish,—for it was little more, although the injury to the French in the loss of the convoy was notable,—Parker was equally delighted with his own squadron and with his enemy. "The steadiness and coolness with which on every tack the *Conqueror* received the fire of these three ships, and returned her own, working his ship with as much exactness as if he had been turning into Spithead, and on every board gaining on the enemy, gave me infinite pleasure. It was with inexpressible concern," he added, "that I heard that Captain Walter Griffith, of the *Conqueror*, was killed by the last broadside."[2] Having occasion, a few days later, to exchange a flag of truce with the French Rear-Admiral, he wrote to him; "The conduct of your Excellency in the affair of the 18th of this month fully justifies the reputation which you enjoy among us, and I assure you that I could not witness without envy the skill you showed on that occasion. Our enmity is transient, depending upon our masters; but your merit has stamped upon my heart the greatest admiration for yourself." This was the officer who was commonly known in his time as "Vinegar" Parker; but these letters show that the epithet fitted the rind rather than the kernel.

Shortly after de Guichen[3] took command, in March, 1780, he arranged with the Marquis de Bouillé, Governor of Martinique, to make a combined attack upon some one of the British West India Islands. For this purpose three thousand troops were embarked in the fleet, which sailed on the night of the 13th of April, 1780, intending first to accompany a convoy for Santo Domingo, until it was safely out of reach of the British. Rodney, who was informed at once of the French departure, put to sea in chase with all his ships, twenty of the line, two of which were of 90 guns, and on the 16th came in sight of the enemy to leeward (westward) of Martinique, beating up against the north-east trade-winds, and intending to pass through the channel between that island and Dominica. "A general chase to the north-west followed, and at five in the evening we plainly discovered that they consisted of twenty-three sail of the line, and one 50 gun ship."[4]

As it fell dark Rodney formed his line of battle, standing still to the north-west, therefore on the starboard tack; and he was attentive to keep to windward of the enemy, whom his frigates watched diligently during the night. "Their manœuvres," he wrote, "indicated a wish to avoid battle," and he therefore was careful to counteract them. At daylight of April 17th, they were seen forming line of battle, on the port tack, four or five leagues to leeward,—that is, to the westward. The wind being east, or east by north, the French would be heading south-south-east (Fig. 1, aa). The British order now was rectified by signal from the irregularities of darkness, the ships being directed to keep two cables'[5] lengths apart, and steering as before to the northward and westward. At 7 A.M., considering this line too extended, the Admiral closed the intervals to one cable (aa). The two fleets thus were passing on nearly parallel lines, but in opposite directions, which tended to bring the whole force of Rodney, whose line was better and more compact than the enemy's, abreast the latter's rear, upon which he intended to concentrate. At 8 A.M. he made general signal that this was his purpose; and at 8.30, to execute it, he signalled for the ships to form line abreast, bearing from each other south by east and north by west, and stood down at once upon the enemy (Fig. 1, bb). The object of the British being evident, de Guichen made his fleet wear together to the starboard tack (bb). The French rear thus became the van, and their former van, which was stretched too far for prompt assistance to the threatened rear, now headed to support it.

Rodney, baulked in his first spring, hauled at once to the wind on the port tack (Fig. 1, cc) again contrary to the French, standing thus once more along their line, for their new rear. The intervals were opened out again to two cables. The fleets thus were passing once more on parallel lines, each having reversed its order; but the British still retained the advantage, on whatever course and interval, that they were much more compact than the French, whose line, by Rodney's estimate, extended four leagues in length.[6] The wariness of the two combatants, both trained in the school of the eighteenth century with its reverence for the line of battle, will appear to the careful reader. Rodney, although struggling through this chrysalis stage to the later vigor, and seriously bent on a deadly blow, still was constrained by the traditions of watchful fencing. Nor was his caution extravagant; conditions did not justify yet the apparent recklessness of Nelson's tactics.

"The different movements of the enemy," he wrote, "obliged me to be very attentive, and watch every opportunity that offered of attacking them to advantage."

The two fleets continued to stand on opposite parallel courses—the French north by west, the British south by east—until the flagship *Sandwich*, 90, (Fig. 2, S_I) was abreast the *Couronne*, 80, (C), the flagship of de Guichen. Then, at 10.10 A.M., the signal was made to wear together, forming on the same tack as the enemy. There being some delay in execution, this had to be repeated, and further enforced by the pennant of the *Stirling Castle*, which, as the rear ship, should begin the evolution. At half-past ten, apparently, the fleet was about (Fig. 2, aa), for an order was then given for rectifying the line, still at two cables. At 11 A.M. the Admiral made the signal to prepare for battle, "to convince the whole fleet I was determined to bring the enemy to an engagement,"[7] and to this succeeded shortly the order to alter the course to port (bb), towards the enemy.[8] Why he thought that any of the fleet should have required such assurance cannot certainly be said. Possibly, although he had so recently joined, he had already detected the ill-will, or the slackness, of which he afterwards complained; possibly he feared that the wariness of his tactics might lead men to believe that he did not mean to exceed the lukewarm and indecisive action of days scarce yet passed away, which had led Suffren to stigmatize tactics as a mere veil, behind which timidity thinks to hide its nakedness.

At 11.50 A.M. the decisive signal was made "for every ship to bear down, and steer for her *opposite in the enemy's line*, agreeable to the 21st article of the Additional Fighting Instructions." Five minutes later, when the ships, presumably, had altered their course for the enemy, the signal for battle was made, followed by the message that the Admiral's intention was to engage closely; he expecting, naturally, that every ship would follow the example he purposed to set. The captain of the ship which in the formation (aa) had been the leader, upon whose action depended that of those near her, unfortunately understood Rodney's signal to mean that he was to attack the enemy's leader, not the ship

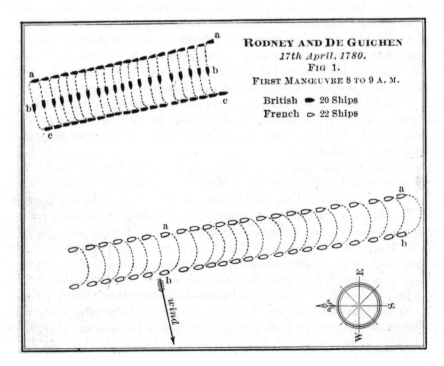

RODNEY AND DE GUICHEN
17th April, 1780.
FIG 1.
FIRST MANŒUVRE 8 TO 9 A. M.

British ➤ 20 Ships
French ▷ 22 Ships

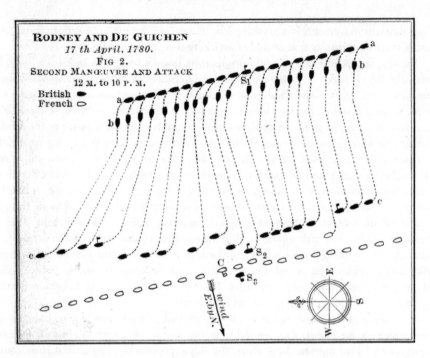

opposite to him at the moment of bearing away. This ship, therefore, diverged markedly from the Admiral's course, drawing after her many of the van. A few minutes before 1 P.M., one of the headmost ships began to engage at long range; but it was not till some time after 1 P.M. that the *Sandwich*, having received several broadsides, came into close action (S_2) with the second vessel astern from the French Admiral, the *Actionnaire*, 64. The latter was soon beat out of the line by the superiority of the *Sandwich's* battery, and the same lot befell the ship astern of her,—probably the *Intrépide*, 74,—which came up to close the gap. Towards 2.30 P.M., the *Sandwich*, either by her own efforts to close, or by her immediate opponents keeping away, was found to be to leeward (S_3) of the enemy's line; the *Couronne* (C) being on her weather bow. The fact was pointed out by Rodney to the captain of the ship, Walter Young, who was then in the lee gangway. Young, going over to look for himself, saw that it was so, and that the *Yarmouth*, 64, had hauled off to windward, where she lay with her main and mizzen topsails aback. Signals were then made to her, and to the *Cornwall*, 74, to come to closer engagement, they both being on the weather bow of the flagship.

De Guichen, recognising this state of affairs, then or a little later, attributed it to the deliberate purpose of the British Admiral to break his line. It does not appear that Rodney so intended. His tactical idea was to concentrate his whole fleet on the French rear and centre, but there is no indication that he now aimed at breaking the line. De Guichen so construing it, however, gave the signal to wear together, away from the British line. The effect of this, in any event, would have been to carry his fleet somewhat to leeward; but with ships more or less crippled, taking therefore greater room to manoeuvre, and with the exigency of reforming the line upon them, the tendency was exaggerated. The movement which the French called wearing together was therefore differently interpreted by Rodney. "The action in the centre continued till 4.15 P.M., when M. de Guichen, in the *Couronne*, the *Triomphant*, and the *Fendant*, after engaging the *Sandwich* for an hour and a half, bore away. The superiority of fire from the *Sandwich*, and the gallant behavior of the officers and men, enabled her to sustain so unequal a combat; though before attacked by them, she had beat three ships out of their line of battle, had entirely broke it, and was to leeward of the French Admiral." Possibly the French accounts, if they were not so very meagre, might dispute this prowess of the flagship; but there can be no doubt that Rodney had set an example, which, had it been followed by all, would have made this engagement memorable, if not decisive. He reported that the captains, with very few exceptions, had placed their ships improperly (cc). The *Sandwich* had eighty shot in her hull, had lost her foremast and mainyard, and had fired 3,288 rounds, an average of 73 to each gun of the broadside engaged. Three of her hits being below the water line, she was kept afloat with difficulty during the next twenty-four hours. With the wearing of the French the battle ceased.

In the advantage offered by the enemy, whose order was too greatly extended, and in his own plan of attack, Rodney always considered this action of April 17th, 1780, to have been the great opportunity of his life; and his wrath was bitter against those by whose misconduct he conceived it had been frustrated. "The French admiral, who appeared to me to be a brave and gallant officer, had the honour to be nobly supported during the whole action. It is with concern inexpressible, mixed with indignation, that the duty I owe my sovereign and my country obliges me to acquaint your Lordships that during the action between the French fleet, on the 17th inst, and his Majesty's, the British flag was not properly supported." Divided as the Navy was then into factions, with their hands at each other's throats or at the throat of the Admiralty, the latter thought it more discreet to suppress this paragraph, allowing to appear only the negative stigma of the encomium upon the French officers, unaccompanied by any upon his own. Rodney, however, in public and private letters did not conceal his feelings; and the censure found its way to the ears of those concerned. Subsequently, three months after the action, in a public letter, he bore testimony to the excellent conduct of five of the captains, Walter Young, of the flagship, George Bowyer of the *Albion*, John Douglas of the *Terrible*, John Houlton of the *Montagu*, and A.J.P. Molloy[9] of the *Trident*. "To them I have given certificates, under my hand," "free and unsolicited." Beyond these, "no consideration in life would induce" him to go; and the two junior flag-officers were implicitly condemned in the words, "to inattention to signals, both in the van and rear divisions, is to be attributed the loss of that glorious opportunity (perhaps never to be recovered) of terminating the naval contest in these seas." These junior admirals were Hyde Parker and Rowley; the latter the same who had behaved, not only so gallantly, but with such unusual initiative, in Byron's engagement. A singular incident in this case led him to a like independence of action, which displeased Rodney. The *Montagu*, of his division, when closing the French line, wore against the helm, and could only be brought into action on the wrong (port) tack. Immediately upon this, part of the French rear also wore, and Rowley followed them of his own motion. Being called to account by Rodney, he stated the facts, justifying the act by the order that "the greatest impression was to be made on the enemy's rear." Both parties soon wore back.

Hyde Parker went home in a rage a few weeks later. The certificates to Bowyer and Douglas, certainly, and probably to Molloy, all of Parker's division, bore the stinging words that these officers "meant well, and would have done their duty had they been permitted." It is stated that their ships, which were the rear of the van division, were going down to engage close, following Rodney's example, when Parker made them a signal to keep the line. If this be so, as Parker's courage was beyond all doubt, it was simply a recurrence of the old superstition of the line, aggravated by a misunderstanding of Rodney's later signals. These must be discussed, for the whole incident is part of the history of the British Navy, far more important than many an indecisive though bloody encounter.

One of the captains more expressly blamed, Carkett of the *Stirling Castle*, which had been the leading ship at the time the signal to alter the course toward the enemy was made, wrote to Rodney that he understood that his name had been mentioned, unfavourably of course, in the public letter. Rodney's reply makes perfectly apparent the point at issue, his own plan, the ideas running in his head as he made his successive signals, the misconceptions of the juniors, and the consequent fiasco. It must be said, however, that, granting the facts as they seem certainly to have occurred, no misunderstanding, no technical verbal allegation, can justify a military stupidity so great as that of which he complained. There are occasions in which not only is literal disobedience permissible, but literal obedience, flying in the face of the evident conditions, becomes a crime.

At 8 in the morning, Rodney had made a general signal of his purpose to attack the enemy's rear. This, having been understood and answered, was hauled down; all juniors had been acquainted with a general purpose, to which the subsequent manœuvres were to lead. How he meant to carry out his intention was evidenced by the consecutive course of action while on that tack,—the starboard; when the time came, the fleet bore up together, in line abreast, standing for the French rear. This attempt, being balked then by de Guichen's wearing, was renewed two hours later; only in place of the signal to form line abreast, was made one to alter the course to port,—towards the enemy. As this followed immediately upon that to prepare for battle, it indicated almost beyond question, that Rodney wished, for reasons of the moment, to run down at first in a slanting direction,—not in line abreast, as before,—ships taking course and interval from the flagship. Later again, at 11.50, the signal was made, "agreeable to the 21st Article of the Additional Fighting Instructions, for every ship to steer for her opposite in the enemy's line;" and here the trouble began. Rodney meant the ship opposite when the signal was hauled down. He had steered slanting, till he had gained as nearly as possible the position he wanted, probably till within long range; then it was desirable to cover the remaining ground as rapidly and orderly as possible, for which purpose the enemy's ship then abreast gave each of his fleet its convenient point of direction. He conceived that his signalled purpose to attack the enemy's rear, never having been altered, remained imperative; and further, that the signal for two cables' length interval should govern all ships, and would tie them to him, and to his movements, in the centre. Carkett construed "opposite" to mean opposite in numerical order, British van ship against French van ship, wherever the latter was. Rodney states—in his letter to Carkett—that the French van was then two leagues away. "You led to the van ship, notwithstanding you had answered my signals signifying that it was my intention to attack the enemy's rear; which signal I had never altered. . . . Your leading in the manner you did, induced others to follow so bad an example; and thereby, forgetting that the signal for the line was only at two cables' length distance from each other, the van division was led by you to more than two leagues' distance from the centre division, which was thereby not properly supported."[10]

Carkett was the oldest captain in the fleet, his post commission being dated March 12th, 1758. How far he may have been excusable in construing as he did Fighting Instructions, which originated in the inane conception that the supreme duty of a Commander-in-Chief was to oppose ship to ship, and that a fleet action was only an agglomeration of naval duels, is not very material, though historically interesting. There certainly was that in the past history of the British Navy which extenuated the offence of a man who must have been well on in middle life. But since the Fighting Instructions had been first issued there had been the courts-martial, also instructive, on Mathews, Lestock, Byng, Keppel, and Palliser, all of which turned more or less on the constraint of the line of battle, and the duty of supporting ships engaged,—above all, an engaged Commander-in-Chief. Rodney perhaps underestimated the weight of the Fighting Instructions upon a dull man; but he was justified in claiming that his previous signals, and the prescription of distance, created at the least a conflict of orders, a doubt, to which there should have been but one solution, namely: to support the ships engaged, and to close down upon the enemy, as near as possible to the Commander-in-Chief. And in moments of actual perplexity such will always be the truth. It is like marching towards the sound of guns, or, to use Nelson's words, "*In case* signals cannot be understood, no captain can do very wrong if he places his ship alongside that of an enemy." The "In Case," however, needs also to be kept in mind; and that it was Nelson who said it. Utterances of to-day, like utterances of all time, show how few are the men who can hold both sides of a truth firmly, without exaggeration or defect. Judicial impartiality can be had, and positive convictions too; but their combination is rare. A two-sided man is apt also to be double-minded.

The loss of men in this sharp encounter was: British, killed, 120, wounded, 354; French, killed, 222, wounded, 537.[11] This gives three French hit for every two British, from which, and from the much greater damage received aloft by the latter, it may be inferred that both followed their usual custom of aiming, the British at the hull, the French at the spars. To the latter conduced also the leegage, which the French had. The British, as the attacking party, suffered likewise a raking fire as they bore down.

Rodney repaired damages at sea, and pursued, taking care to keep between Martinique and the French. The latter going into Guadeloupe, he reconnoitred them there under the batteries, and then took his station off Fort Royal. "The only chance of bringing them to action," he wrote to the Admiralty on the 26th of April, "was to be off that port before them, where the fleet now is, in daily expectation of their arrival." The French represent that he avoided them, but as they assert that they came out best on the 17th, and yet admit that he appeared off Guadeloupe, the claim is not tenable. Rodney here showed thorough tenacity of purpose. De Guichen's orders were "to keep the sea, so far as the force maintained by England in the Windward Islands would permit, without too far compromising the fleet intrusted to him."[12] With such instructions, he naturally and consistently shrunk from decisive engagement. After landing his wounded and refitting in Guadeloupe, he again put to sea, with the intention of proceeding to Santa Lucia, resuming against that island the project which both he and De Bouillé continuously entertained. The latter and his troops remained with the fleet.

Rodney meantime had felt compelled to return momentarily to Santa Lucia. "The fleet continued before Fort Royal till the condition of many of the ships under my command, and the lee currents,[13] rendered it necessary to anchor in Choque Bay (Anse du Choc), St. Lucie, in order to put the wounded and sick men on shore, and to water and refit the fleet, frigates having been detached both to leeward and to windward of every island, in order to gain intelligence of the motions of the enemy, and timely notice of their approach towards Martinique, the only place they could refit at in these seas." In this last clause is seen the strategic idea of the British Admiral: the French must come back to Martinique.

From the vigilance of his frigates it resulted that when the look-outs of de Guichen, who passed to windward of Martinique on the 7th of May, came in sight of Gros Ilet on the 9th, it was simply to find the British getting under way to meet the enemy. During the five following days both fleets were engaged in constant movements, upon the character of which the writers of each nation put different constructions. Both are agreed, however, that the French were to windward throughout, except for a brief hour on the 15th, when a fleeting change of wind gave the British that advantage, only to lose it soon again. They at once used it to force action. As the windward position carries the power to attack, and as the French were twenty-three to the British twenty, it is probably not a strained inference to say that the latter were chasing to windward, and the former avoiding action, in favour, perhaps, of that ulterior motive, the conquest of Santa Lucia, for which they had sailed. Rodney states in his letter that, when the two fleets parted on the 20th of May, they were forty leagues to windward (eastward) of Martinique, in sight of which they had been on the 10th.

During these days de Guichen, whose fleet, according to Rodney, sailed the better, and certainly sufficiently well to preserve the advantage of the wind, bore down more than once, generally in the afternoon, when the breeze is steadiest, to within distant range of the British. Upon this movement, the French base the statement that the British Admiral was avoiding an encounter; it is equally open to the interpretation that he would not throw away ammunition until sure of effective distance. Both admirals showed much skill and mastery of their profession, great wariness also, and quickness of eye; but it is wholly untenable to claim that a fleet having the weather-gage for five days, in the tradewinds, was unable to bring its enemy to action, especially when it is admitted that the latter closed the instant the wind permitted him to do so.

On the afternoon of May 15th, about the usual hour, Rodney "made a great deal of sail upon the wind." The French, inferring that he was trying to get off, which he meant them to do, approached somewhat closer than on the previous days. Their van ship had come

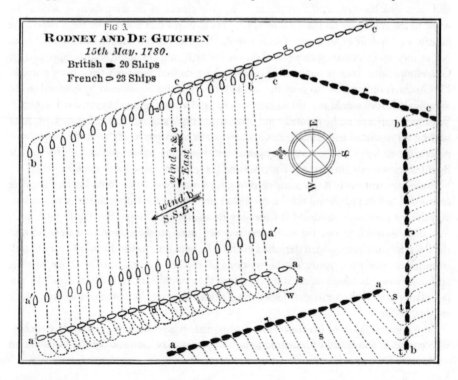

FIG 3.

RODNEY AND DE GUICHEN
15th May. 1780.
British ● 20 Ships
French ○ 23 Ships

within long range, abreast the centre of the British, who were on the port tack standing to
the south-south-east, with the wind at east (Fig. 3, aa, aa). Here the breeze suddenly hauled
to south-south-east (wind b). The heads of all the ships in both fleets were thus knocked
off to south-west (s, s), on the port tack, but the shift left the British rear, which on that
tack led the fleet, to windward of the French van. Rodney's signal flew at once, to tack in
succession and keep the wind of the enemy; the latter, unwilling to yield the advantage,
wore all together (w), hauling to the wind on the starboard tack, and to use Rodney's
words, "fled with a crowd of sail" (a', a').

The British fleet tacking in succession after their leaders (t, t), the immediate result was
that both were now standing on the starboard tack,—to the eastward,—the British having
a slight advantage of the wind, but well abaft the beam of the French (bb, bb). The result,
had the wind held, would have been a trial of speed and weatherliness. "His Majesty's
fleet," wrote Rodney, "by this manœuvre had gained the wind, and would have forced the
enemy to battle, had it not at once changed six points (back to east, its former direction,)
when near the enemy, and enabled them to recover that advantage." When the wind
thus shifted again, de Guichen tacked his ships together and stood across the bows of the
advancing enemy (cc, cc). The British leader struck the French line behind the centre, and
ran along to leeward, the British van exchanging a close cannonade with the enemy's rear.
Such an engagement, two lines passing on opposite tacks, is usually indecisive, even when
the entire fleets are engaged, as at Ushant; but where, as in this case, the engagement is
but partial, the result is naturally less. The French van and centre, having passed the head
of the enemy, diverged at that point farther and farther from the track of the on-coming
British ships, which from the centre rearwards did not fire. "As the enemy were under a
press of sail, none but the van of our fleet could come in for any part of the action without
wasting his Majesty's powder and shot, the enemy wantonly expending theirs at such a
distance as to have no effect." Here again the French were evidently taking the chance of
disabling the distant enemy in his spars. The British loss in the action of May 15th was 21
killed and 100 wounded.

The fleets continued their respective movements, each acting as before, until the 19th,
when another encounter took place, of exactly the same character as the last, although
without the same preliminary manœuvring. On that occasion the British, who in the
interim had been reinforced by one 74 and one 50-gun ship, lost 47 killed and 113
wounded. The result was equally indecisive, tactically considered; but both by this time
had exhausted their staying powers. The French, having been absent from Martinique
since the 13th of April, had now but six days' provisions.[14] Rodney found the *Conqueror*,
Cornwall, and *Boyne* so shattered that he sent them before the wind to Santa Lucia, while
he himself with the rest of the fleet stood for Barbados, where he arrived on the 22d. The
French anchored on the same day at Fort Royal. "The English," says Chevalier, "stood on
upon the starboard tack, to the southward, after the action of the 19th, and the next day
were not to be seen." "The enemy," reported Rodney, "stood to the northward with all
the sail they could possibly press, and were out of sight the 21st inst. The condition of his
Majesty's ships was such as not to allow a longer pursuit."

By their dexterity and vigilance each admiral had thwarted the other's aims. Rodney, by a
pronounced, if cautious, offensive effort, had absolutely prevented the "ulterior object" of the
French, which he clearly understood to be Santa Lucia. De Guichen had been successful in
avoiding decisive action, and he had momentarily so crippled a few of the British ships that
the fleet must await their repairs before again taking the sea. The tactical gain was his, the

GEORGE BRYDGES,
LORD RODNEY

strategic victory rested with his opponent; but that his ships also had been much maltreated is shown by the fact that half a dozen could not put to sea three weeks later. The French admiral broke down under the strain, to which was added the grief of losing a son, killed in the recent engagements. He asked for his recall. "The command of so large a fleet," he wrote, "is infinitely beyond my capacity in all respects. My health cannot endure such continual fatigue and anxiety." Certainly this seems a tacit testimony to Rodney's skill, persistence, and offensive purpose. The latter wrote to his wife: "For fourteen days and nights the fleets were so near each other that neither officers nor men could be said to sleep. Nothing but the goodness of the weather and climate would have enabled us to endure so continual a fatigue. Had it been in Europe, half the people must have sunk under it. For my part, it did me good."

Rodney stated also in his home letters that the action of his subordinates in the last affairs had been efficient; but he gave them little credit for it. "As I had given public notice to all my captains, etc., that I expected implicit obedience to every signal made, under the certain penalty of being instantly superseded, it had an admirable effect; as they were all convinced, after their late gross behaviour, that they had nothing to expect at my hands but instant punishment to those who neglected their duty. My eye on them had more dread than the enemy's fire, and they knew it would be fatal. No regard was paid to rank: admirals as well as captains, if out of their station, were instantly reprimanded by signals, or messages sent by frigates; and, in spite of themselves, I taught them to be, what they had never been before,—*officers*." Rodney told his officers also that he would shift his flag into a frigate, if necessary, to watch them better. It is by

COMTE DE GUICHEN

no means obligatory to accept these gross aspersions as significant of anything worse than the suspiciousness prevalent throughout the Navy, traceable ultimately to a corrupt administration of the Admiralty. The latter, like the government of 1756, was open to censure through political maladministration; every one feared that blame would be shifted on to him, as it had been on to Byng,—who deserved it; and not only so, but that blame would be pushed on to ruin, as in his case. The Navy was honeycombed with distrust, falling little short of panic. In this state of apprehension and doubt, the tradition of the line of battle, resting upon men who did not stop to study facts or analyse impressions, and who had seen officers censured, cashiered, and shot, for errors of judgment or of action, naturally produced hesitations and misunderstandings. An order of battle is a good thing, necessary to insure mutual support and to develop a plan. The error of the century, not then exploded, was to observe it in the letter rather than in the spirit; to regard the order as an end rather than a means; and to seek in it not merely efficiency, which admits broad construction in positions, but preciseness, which is as narrowing as a brace of handcuffs. Rodney himself, Tory though he was, found fault with the administration. With all his severity and hauteur, he did not lose sight of justice, as is shown by a sentence in his letter to Carkett. "Could I have imagined your conduct and inattention to signals had proceeded from anything but error in judgment, I had certainly superseded you, but God forbid I should do so for error in judgment only,"—again an illusion, not obscure, to Byng's fate.

In Barbados, Rodney received certain information that a Spanish squadron of twelve ships of the line, with a large convoy of ten thousand troops, had sailed from Cadiz on

April 28th for the West Indies. The vessel bringing the news had fallen in with them on the way. Rodney spread a line of frigates "to windward, from Barbados to Barbuda," to obtain timely warning, and with the fleet put to sea on the 7th of June, to cruise to the eastward of Martinique to intercept the enemy. The latter had been discovered on the 5th by a frigate, fifty leagues east of the island, steering for it; but the Spanish admiral, seeing that he would be reported, changed his course, and passed north of Gaudeloupe. On the 9th he was joined in that neighbourhood by de Guichen, who was able to bring with him only fifteen sail,—a fact which shows that he had suffered in the late brushes quite as severely as Rodney, who had with him seventeen of his twenty.

Having evaded the British, the allies anchored at Fort Royal; but the Spanish admiral absolutely refused to join in any undertaking against the enemy's fleet or possessions. Not only so, but he insisted on being accompanied to leeward. The Spanish squadron was ravaged by an epidemic, due to unsanitary conditions of the ships and the uncleanliness of the crews, and the disease was communicated to their allies. De Guichen had already orders to leave the Windward Islands when winter approached. He decided now to anticipate that time, and on the 5th of July sailed from Fort Royal with the Spaniards. Having accompanied the latter to the east end of Cuba, he went to Cap François, in Haïti, then a principal French station. The Spaniards continued on to Havana.

At Cap François, de Guichen found urgent entreaties from the French Minister to the United States, and from Lafayette, to carry his fleet to the continent, where the clear-sighted genius of Washington had recognised already that the issue of the contest depended upon the navies. The French admiral declined to comply, as contrary to his instructions, and on the 16th of August sailed for Europe, with nineteen sail of the line, leaving ten at Cap François. Sealed orders, opened at sea, directed him to proceed to Cadiz, where he anchored on the 24th of October. His arrival raised the allied force there assembled to fifty-one sail of the line, besides the ninety-five sugar and coffee ships which he had convoyed from Haïti. It is significant of the weakness of Great Britain in the Mediterranean at that time, that these extremely valuable merchant ships were sent on to Toulon, instead of to the more convenient Atlantic ports, only five ships of the line accompanying them past Gibraltar. The French government had feared to trust them to Brest, even with de Guichen's nineteen sail.

The allied operations in the Windward Islands for the season of 1780 had thus ended in nothing, notwithstanding an incontestable inferiority of the British to the French alone, of which Rodney strongly complained. It was, however, contrary to the intentions of the Admiralty that things so happened. Orders had been sent to Vice-Admiral Marriot Arbuthnot, at New York, to detach ships to Rodney; but the vessel carrying them was driven by weather to the Bahamas, and her captain neglected to notify Arbuthnot of his whereabouts, or of his dispatches. A detachment of five ships of the line under Commodore the Hon. Robert Boyle Walsingham was detained three months in England, windbound. They consequently did not join till July 12th. The dispositions at once made by Rodney afford a very good illustration of the kind of duties that a British Admiral had then to discharge. He detailed five ships of the line to remain with Hotham at Santa Lucia, for the protection of the Windward Islands. On the 17th, taking with him a large merchant convoy, he put to sea with the fleet for St. Kitts, where the Leeward Islands "trade" was collecting for England. On the way he received precise information as to the route and force of the Franco-Spanish fleet under de Guichen, of the sickness on board it, and of the dissension between the allies. From St. Kitts the July "trade" was sent home with two ships of the line. Three others, he wrote to the Admiralty, would accompany the September fleet, "and the remainder of the ships on this station, which are in want of great repair and are not copper-bottomed, shall proceed with them or with the convoy which their Lordships have been pleased to order shall sail from hence in October next." If these arrived before winter, he argued, they would be available by spring as a reinforcement for the Channel fleet, and would enable the Admiralty to send him an equivalent number for the winter work on his station.

As de Guichen had taken the whole French homeward merchant fleet from Martinique to Cap François and as the height of the hurricane season was near, Rodney reasoned that but a small French force would remain in Haïti, and consequently that Jamaica would not require all the British fleet to save it from any possible attack. He therefore sent thither ten sail of the line, notifying Vice-Admiral Sir Peter Parker that they were not merely to defend the island, but to enable him to send home its great trade in reasonable security.

These things being done by July 31st, Rodney, reasoning that the allies had practically abandoned all enterprises in the West Indies for that year, and that a hurricane might at any moment overtake the fleet at its anchors, possibly making for it a lee shore, went to sea, to cruise with the fleet off Barbuda. His mind, however, was inclined already to go to the continent, whither he inferred, correctly but mistakenly, that the greater part of de Guichen's fleet would go, because it should. His purpose was confirmed by information from an American vessel that a French squadron of seven ships of the line, convoying six thousand troops, had anchored in Narragansett Bay on the 12th of July. He started at once for the coast of South Carolina, where he communicated with the army in Charleston, and thence, "sweeping the southern coast of America," anchored with fourteen ships of the line at Sandy Hook, on the 14th of September, unexpected and unwelcome to friends and foes alike.

Vice-Admiral Arbuthnot, being junior to Rodney, showed plainly and with insubordination his wrath at this intrusion into his command, which superseded his authority and divided the prize-money of a lucrative station. This, however, was a detail. To Washington, Rodney's coming was a deathblow to the hopes raised by the arrival of the French division at Newport, which he had expected to see reinforced by de Guichen. Actually, the departure of the latter made immaterial Rodney's appearance on the scene; but this Washington did not know then. As it was, Rodney's force joined to Arbuthnot's constituted a fleet of over twenty sail of the line, before which, vigorously used, there can be little doubt that the French squadron in Newport must have fallen. But Rodney, though he had shown great energy in the West Indies, and unusual resolution in quitting his own station for a more remote service, was sixty-two, and suffered from gout. "The sudden change of climate makes it necessary for me to go on shore for some short time," he wrote; and although he added that his illness was "not of such a nature as shall cause one moment's delay in his Majesty's service," he probably lost a chance at Rhode Island. He did not overlook the matter, it is true; but he decided upon the information of Arbuthnot and Sir Henry Clinton, and did not inspect the ground himself. Nothing of consequence came of his visit; and on the 16th of November he sailed again for the West Indies, taking with him only nine sail of the line.

The arrival of de Ternay's seven ships at Newport was more than offset by a British reinforcement of six ships of the line under Rear-Admiral Thomas Graves which entered New York on July 13th,—only one day later. Arbuthnot's force was thus raised to ten of the line, one of which was of 98 guns. After Rodney had come and gone, the French division was watched by cruisers, resting upon Gardiner's Bay,—a commodious anchorage at the east end of Long Island, between thirty and forty miles from Rhode Island. When a movement of the enemy was apprehended, the squadron assembled there, but nothing of consequence occurred during the remainder of the year.

The year 1780 had been one of great discouragement to the Americans, but the injury, except as the lapse of time taxed their staying power, was more superficial than real. The successes of the British in the southern States, though undeniable, and seemingly substantial, were involving them ever more deeply in a ruinously ex-centric movement. They need here only to be summarised, as steps in the process leading to the catastrophe of Yorktown,—a disaster which, as Washington said, exemplified naval rather than military power.

The failure of d'Estaing's attack upon Savannah in the autumn of 1779[15] had left that place in the possession of the British as a base for further advances in South Carolina and Georgia; lasting success in which was expected from the numbers of royalists in those States. When the departure of the French fleet was ascertained, Sir Henry Clinton put to sea from New York in December, 1779, for the Savannah River, escorted by Vice-Admiral Arbuthnot. The details of the operations, which were leisurely and methodical, will not be given here; for, although the Navy took an active part in them, they scarcely can be considered of major importance. On the 12th of May, 1780, the city of Charleston capitulated, between six and seven thousand prisoners being taken. Clinton then returned to New York, leaving Lord Cornwallis in command in the south. The latter proposed to remain quiet during the hot months; but the activity of the American partisan troops prevented this, and in July the approach of a small, but relatively formidable force, under General Gates, compelled him to take the field. On the 16th of August the two little armies met at Camden, and the Americans, who were much the more numerous, but largely irregulars, were routed decisively. This news reached General Washington in the north nearly at the same moment that the treason of Benedict Arnold became known. Although the objects of his treachery were frustrated, the sorrowful words, "Whom now can we trust?" show the deep gloom which for the moment shadowed the constant mind of the American Commander-in-Chief. It was just at this period, too, that Rodney arrived at New York.

Cornwallis, not content with his late success, decided to push on into North Carolina. Thus doing, he separated himself from his naval base in Charleston, communication with which by land he had not force to maintain, and could recover effective touch with the sea only in Chesapeake Bay. This conclusion was not apparent from the first. In North Carolina, the British general did not receive from the inhabitants the substantial support which he had expected, and found himself instead in a very difficult and wild country, confronted by General Greene, the second in ability of all the American leaders. Harassed and baffled, he was compelled to order supplies to be sent by sea to Wilmington, North Carolina, an out-of-the-way and inferior port, to which he turned aside, arriving exhausted on the 7th of April, 1781. The question as to his future course remained to be settled. To return to Charleston by sea was in his power, but to do so would be an open confession of failure,—that he could not return by land, through the country by which he had come—much the same dilemma as that of Howe and Clinton in Philadelphia. To support him in his distress by a diversion, Sir Henry Clinton had sent two successive detachments to ravage the valley of the James River in Virginia. These were still there, under the command of General Phillips; and Cornwallis, in the circumstances, could see many reasons that thither was the very scene to carry the British operations. On the 25th of April, 1781, he left Wilmington, and a month later joined the division at Petersburg, Virginia, then commanded by Benedict Arnold; Phillips having died. There, in touch now with his fate, we must leave him for the moment.

To complete the naval transactions of 1780, it is necessary to mention briefly two incidents, trivial in themselves, but significant, not only as associated with the greater movements of the campaign, but as indicative of the naval policy of the States which were at war. The two, though not otherwise connected, have a certain unity of interest, in that the same British officer commanded on both occasions.

It will be remembered that in Byron's action off Grenada, in July, 1779, the 64-gun ship *Lion* received such injuries that her commander, Captain Cornwallis, had been compelled to run down before the trade-winds to Jamaica, in order to save her from capture. Since that time she had remained there, as one of the squadron of Vice-Admiral Sir Peter Parker. In March, 1780, still commanded by Cornwallis, she was making an ordinary service cruise off the north side of Haïti, having in company the *Bristol*, 50, and the *Janus*, 44. On the 20th of March, off Monte Christi, a number of sail were sighted to the eastward, which proved to be a French convoy, on its way from Martinique to Cap François, protected by La Motte-Picquet's squadron of two 74s, one 64, one 50, and a frigate. The French merchant ships were ordered to crowd sail for their port, while the men-of-war chased to the north-west. La Motte-Picquet's flagship, the *Annibal*, 74, got within range at 5 P.M., when a distant cannonade began, which lasted till past midnight, and was resumed on the following morning. From it the *Janus* was the chief sufferer, losing her mizzen topmast and foretopgallant mast. It falling nearly calm, the *Bristol* and *Lion* got out their boats and were towed by them to her support. The two other French ships of the line got up during the forenoon of the 21st, so that the action that afternoon, though desultory, might be called general.

The two opposing commodores differ in their expressed opinions as to the power of the French to make the affair more decisive. Some of La Motte-Picquet's language seems to show that he felt the responsibility of his position. "The *Janus*, being smaller and more easily worked, lay upon our quarter and under our stern, where she did considerable damage. A little breeze springing up enabled us (the *Annibal*) to stand towards our own ships, which did everything possible to come up and cover us, without which we should have been *surrounded*." It is easy to see in such an expression the reflection of the commands of the French Cabinet, to economise the ships. This was still more evident in La Motte-Picquet's conduct next day. On the morning of the 22d, "at daylight we were within one and a half cannon-shot, breeze fresh at the east-north-east, and I expected to overtake the British squadron in an hour, when we perceived four ships in chase of us. At 6.30 A.M. three were seen to be men-of-war. This superiority of force compelled me to desist, and to make signal to haul our wind for Cap François." These three new-comers were the *Ruby*, 64, and two frigates, the *Pomona*, 28, and *Niger*, 32. The comparison of forces, therefore, would be: French, two 74s, one 64, one 50, and one frigate, opposed to, British, two 64s, one 50, and three frigates. La Motte-Picquet evidently did not wait to ascertain the size of the approaching ships. His courage was beyond all dispute, and, as Hyde Parker had said, he was among the most distinguished of French officers; but, like his comrades, he was dominated by the faulty theory of his government.

The captain of the *Janus* died a natural death during the encounter. It may be interesting to note that the ship was given to Nelson, who was recalled for that purpose from the expedition to San Juan, Nicaragua, one of the minor operations of the war. His health, however, prevented this command from being more than nominal, and not long afterward he returned to England with Cornwallis, in the *Lion*.

Three months later, Cornwallis was sent by Parker to accompany a body of merchant ships for England as far as the neighborhood of Bermuda. This duty being fulfilled, he was returning toward his station, having with him two 74s, two 64s, and one 50, when, on the morning of June 20, a number of sail were seen from north-east to east (Fig. 4, a); the British squadron (aa) then steering east, with the wind at south-south-east. The strangers were a body of French transports, carrying the six thousand troops destined for Rhode Island, and convoyed by a division of seven ships of the line—one 80, two 74s, and four 64s—under the command of Commodore de Ternay. Two of the ships of war were with the convoy, the other five very properly to windward of it. The latter therefore stood on, across the bows of the British, to rejoin their consorts, and then all hauled their wind to the south-west, standing in column (bb) towards the enemy. Cornwallis on his part had kept on (b) to reconnoitre the force opposed to him; but one of his ships, the *Ruby*, 64, was so far to leeward (b′) that the French, by keeping near the wind, could pass between her and her squadron (b, b, b′). She therefore went about (t) and steered southwest, on the port tack (c′), close to the wind. The French, who were already heading the same way, were thus brought on her weather quarter in chase. Cornwallis then wore his division (w), formed line of battle on the same tack as the others (c), and edged down towards the *Ruby*. If the French now kept their wind, either the *Ruby* (c′) must be cut off, or Cornwallis, to save her, must fight the large odds against him. De Ternay, however, did not keep his wind but bore up,—yielded ground (cc). "The enemy," wrote Cornwallis, "kept edging off and forming line, though within gunshot. At 5.30 P.M., seeing we had pushed the French ships to leeward sufficiently to enable the *Ruby*, on our lee bow, to join us, I made the signal to tack." As the British squadron went about to stand east again (d), the French, heading now west-south-west (cc), hoisted their colours and opened fire in passing. The *Ruby* kept on till she fetched the wake of the British column (d′), when she too tacked. The French then tacked also, in succession (d), and the two columns stood on for awhile in parallel lines, exchanging shots at long range, the British to windward. Cornwallis very properly declined further engagement with so superior a force. He had already done much in saving a ship so greatly exposed.

The account above followed is that of the British commander, but it does not differ in essentials from the French, whose captains were greatly incensed at the cautious action of their chief. A French *commissaire* in the squadron, who afterwards published his journal, tells that de Ternay a few days later asked the captain of one of the ships what English admiral he thought they had engaged, and received the reply, "We have lost our opportunity of finding out." He gives also many details of the talk that went on in the ships, which need not be repeated. Chevalier points out correctly, however, that de Ternay had to consider that an equal or even a superior force might be encountered as Narragansett Bay was approached, and that he should not risk crippling his squadron for such a contingency. The charge of six thousand troops, under the then conditions, was no light responsibility, and at the least must silence off-hand criticism now. Comment upon his action does not belong to British naval history, to which the firmness and seamanship of Captain Cornwallis added a lasting glory. It may be noted that fifteen years later, in the French Revolution, the same officer, then a Vice-Admiral, again

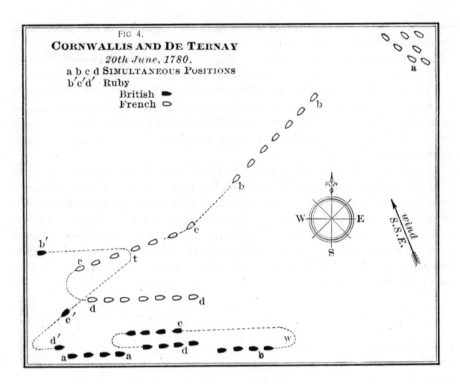

FIG 4.

CORNWALLIS AND DE TERNAY

20th June, 1780.

a b c d SIMULTANEOUS POSITIONS

b'c'd' Ruby

British ➤

French ○

distinguished himself by his bearing in face of great odds, bringing five ships safe off, out of the jaws of a dozen. It illustrates how luck seems in many cases to characterise a man's personality, much as temperament does. Cornwallis, familiarly known as "Billy Blue" to the seamen of his day, never won a victory, nor had a chance of winning one; but in command both of ships and of divisions, he repeatedly distinguished himself by successfully facing odds which he could not overcome.

The year 1780 was uneventful also in European waters, after Rodney's relief of Gibraltar in January. The detachment of the Channel Fleet which accompanied him on that mission returned safely to England. The "Grand Fleet," as it still was styled occasionally, cruised at sea from June 8th to August 18th, an imposing force of thirty-one ships of the line, eleven of them three-deckers of 90 guns and upwards. Admiral Francis Geary was then Commander-in-Chief, but, his health failing, and Barrington refusing to take the position, through professed distrust of himself and actual distrust of the Admiralty, Vice-Admiral George Darby succeeded to it, and held it during the year 1781.

The most notable maritime event in 1780 in Europe was the capture on August 9th of a large British convoy, two or three hundred miles west of Cape St. Vincent, by the allied fleets from Cadiz. As out of sixty-three sail only eight escaped, and as of those taken sixteen were carrying troops and supplies necessary for the West India garrisons, such a disaster claims mention among the greater operations of war, the success of which it could not fail to influence. Captain John Moutray, the officer commanding the convoy, was brought to trial and dismissed his ship; but there were not wanting those who charged the misadventure to the Admiralty, and saw in the captain a victim. It was the greatest single blow that British commerce had received in war during the memory of men then living, and "a general inclination prevailed to lay the blame upon some individual, who might be punished according to the magnitude of the object, rather than in proportion to his demerit."[16]

During the year 1780 was formed the League of the Baltic Powers, known historically as the Armed Neutrality, to exact from Great Britain the concession of certain points thought essential to neutral interests. The accession of Holland to this combination, together with other motives of dissatisfaction, caused Great Britain to declare war against the United Provinces on the 20th of December. Orders were at once sent to the East and West Indies to seize Dutch possessions and ships, but these did not issue in action until the following year.

Towards the end of 1780 the French Government, dissatisfied with the lack of results from the immense combined force assembled in Cadiz during the summer months, decided to recall its ships, and to refit them during the winter for the more extensive and aggressive movements planned for the campaign of 1781. D'Estaing was sent from France for the purpose; and under his command thirty-eight ships of the line, in which were included those brought by de Guichen from the West Indies, sailed on the 7th of November for Brest. Extraordinary as it may seem, this fleet did not reach its port until the 3d of January, 1781.

1. Parker's Report.

2. *Ibid.*

3. *Ante*, p. 82.

4 Rodney's Report. The French authorities give their line of battle as twenty-two ships of the line. There was no 90-gun ship among them—no three-decker; but there were two of 80 guns, of which also the British had none.

5. A cable was then assumed to have a length of 120 fathoms,—720 feet.

6. A properly formed line of twenty ships, at two cables' interval, would be about five miles long. Rodney seems to have been satisfied that this was about the condition of his fleet at this moment.

7. Rodney's Report.

8. Testimony of the signal officer at the court-martial on Captain Bateman.

9. Singularly enough, this officer was afterwards court-martialled for misbehaviour, on the 1st of June, 1794, of precisely the same character as that from all share in which Rodney now cleared him.

10. The words in Rodney's public letter, suppressed at the time by the Admiralty, agree with these, but are even more explicit. "I cannot conclude this letter without acquainting their Lordships that had Captain Carkett, who led the van, properly obeyed my signal for attacking the enemy, and agreeable to the 21st Article of the Additional Fighting Instructions, bore down instantly to the ship at that time abreast of him, instead of leading as he did to the van ship, the action had commenced much sooner, and the fleet engaged in a more compact manner. . . ." This clearly implies that the *Additional* Fighting Instructions prescribed the direction which Rodney expected Carkett to take. If these Additional Instructions are to be found, their testimony would be interesting.

Since this account was written, the Navy Records Society has published (1905) a volume, "Fighting Instructions, 1530–1816," by Mr. Julian Corbett, whose diligent researches in matters of naval history and warfare are appreciated by those interested in such subjects. The specific "Additional Instructions" quoted by Rodney appear not to have been found. Among those given prior to 1780 there is none that extends to twenty-one articles. In a set issued by Rodney in 1782 an article (No. 17, p. 227) is apparently designed to prevent the recurrence of Carkett's mistake. This, like one by Hawke, in 1756 (p. 217), prescribes the intended action rather by directing that the line of battle shall not prevent each ship engaging its opponent, irrespective of the conduct of other ships, than by making clear which that opponent was. Lucidity on this point cannot be claimed for either.

11. Lapeyrouse Bonfils, "Histoire de la Marine Francaise," iii, 132. Chevalier gives much smaller numbers, but the former has particularised the ships.

12. Chevalier, "Marine Française," 1778, p. 185.

13. A lee current is one that sets to leeward, with the wind, in this case the trade-wind.

14. Chevalier, p. 91.

15. *Ante*, p. 82.

16. Beatson, "Military and Naval Memoirs."

IX

NAVAL CAMPAIGN
IN THE WEST INDIES, 1781

Rodney, returning to the West Indies from New York, reached Barbados on December 6th, 1780. There he seems first to have learned of the disastrous effects of the great October hurricanes of that year. Not only had several ships—among them two of the line—been wrecked, with the loss of almost all on board, but the greater part of those which survived had been dismasted, wholly or in part, as well as injured in the hull. There were in the West Indies no docking facilities; under-water damage could be repaired only by careening or heaving-down. Furthermore, as Barbados, Santa Lucia, and Jamaica, all had been swept, their supplies were mainly destroyed. Antigua, it is true, had escaped, the hurricane passing south of St. Kitts; but Rodney wrote home that no stores for refitting were obtainable in the Caribbee Islands. He was hoping then that Sir Peter Parker might supply his needs in part; for when writing from Santa Lucia on December 10th, two months after the storm, he was still ignorant that the Jamaica Station had suffered to the full as severely as the eastern islands. The fact shows not merely the ordinary slowness of communications in those days, but also the paralysis that fell upon all movements in consequence of that great disaster. "The most beautiful island in the world," he said of Barbados, "has the appearance of a country laid waste by fire and sword."

Hearing that the fortifications at St. Vincent had been almost destroyed by the hurricane, Rodney, in combination with General Vaughan, commanding the troops on the station, made an attempt to reconquer the island, landing there on December 15th; but the intelligence proved erroneous, and the fleet returned to Santa Lucia. "I have only nine sail of the line now with me capable of going to sea," wrote the Admiral on the 22d, "and not one of them has spare rigging or sails." In the course of January, 1781, he was joined by a division of eight ships of the line from England, under the command of Rear-Admiral Sir Samuel Hood,—Nelson's Lord Hood. These, with four others refitted during that month, not improbably from stores brought in Hood's convoy of over a hundred sail, raised the disposable force to twenty-one ships of the line: two 90s, one 80, fifteen 74s, and three 64s.

On the 27th of January, an express arrived from England, directing the seizure of the Dutch possessions in the Caribbean, and specifying, as first to be attacked, St. Eustatius and St. Martin, two small islands lying within fifty miles north of the British St. Kitts. St. Eustatius, a rocky patch six miles in length by three in breadth, had been conspicuous, since the war began, as a great trade centre, where supplies of all kinds were gathered under the protection of its neutral flag, to be distributed afterwards in the belligerent islands and the North American continent. The British, owing to their extensive commerce and maritime aptitudes, derived from such an intermediary much less benefit than their enemies; and the island had been jealously regarded by Rodney for some time. He asserted that when de Guichen's fleet could not regain Fort Royal, because of its injuries received in the action of April 17th, it was refitted to meet him by mechanics and materials sent from St. Eustatius. On the other hand, when cordage was to be bought for the British vessels after the hurricanes of 1780, the merchants of the island, he said, alleged that there was none there; although, when he took the island soon afterwards, many hundred tons were found that had been long in stock.

Rodney and Vaughan moved promptly. Three days after their orders arrived, they sailed for St. Eustatius. There being in Fort Royal four French ships of the line, six British were left to check them, and on the 3d of February the fleet reached its destination. A peremptory summons from the commander of a dozen ships of the line secured immediate submission. Over a hundred and fifty merchant ships were taken; and a convoy of thirty sail, which had left the island two days before, was pursued and brought back. The merchandise found was valued at over £3,000,000. The neighbouring islands of St. Martin and Saba were seized also at this time.

Rodney's imagination, as is shown in his letters, was greatly impressed by the magnitude of the prize and by the defenceless condition of his capture. He alleged these as the motives for staying in person at St. Eustatius, to settle the complicated tangle of neutral and belligerent rights in the property involved, and to provide against the enemy's again possessing himself of a place now so equipped for transactions harmful to Great Britain. The storehouses and conveniences provided for the particular traffic, if not properly guarded, were like fortifications insufficiently garrisoned. If they passed into the hands of the enemy, they became sources of injury. The illicit trade could start again at once in full force, with means which elsewhere would have first to be created. There were a mile and a half of storehouses in the lower town, he said, and these he must leave at the least roofless, if not wholly demolished.

For such reasons he remained at St. Eustatius throughout February, March, and April. The amount of money involved, and the arbitrary methods pursued by him and by Vaughan, gave rise to much scandal, which was not diminished by the King's relinquishing all the booty to the captors, nor by the latters' professed disinterestedness. Men thought they did protest too much. Meanwhile, other matters arose to claim attention. A week after the capture, a vessel arrived from the Bay of Biscay announcing that eight or ten French sail of the line, with a large convoy, had been seen on the 31st of December steering for the West Indies. Rodney at once detached Sir Samuel Hood with eleven ships of the line, directing him to take also under his command the six left before Fort Royal, and to cruise with them to windward of Martinique, to intercept the force reported. Hood sailed February 12th. The particular intelligence proved afterwards to be false, but Hood was continued on his duty. A month later he was ordered to move from the windward to the leeward side of the island, and to blockade Fort Royal closely. Against this change he remonstrated, and the event showed him to be right; but Rodney insisted, saying that from his experience he knew that a fleet could remain off Fort Royal for months without dropping to leeward, and that there ships detached to Santa Lucia, for water and refreshments, could rejoin before an enemy's fleet, discovered to windward, could come up. Hood thought the Admiral's object was merely to shelter his own doings at St. Eustatius; and he considered the blockade of Fort Royal to be futile, if no descent upon the island were intended. "It would doubtless have been fortunate for the public," he remarked afterwards, "had Sir George been with his fleet, as I am confident he would have been to windward instead of to leeward, when de Grasse made his approach."

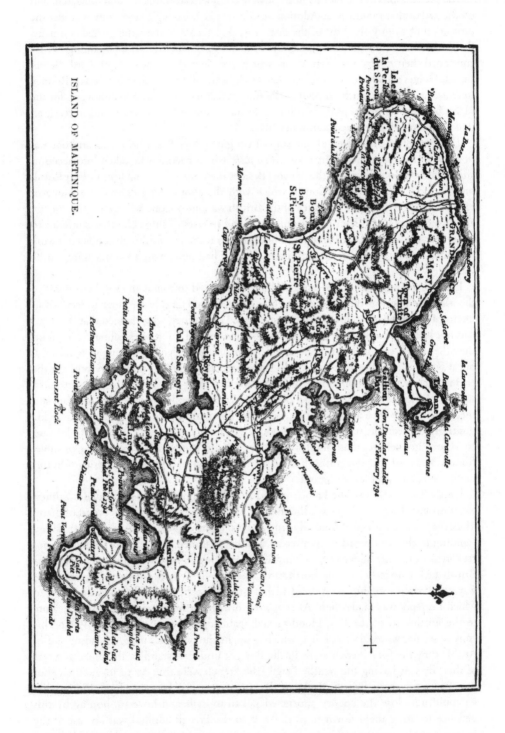

ISLAND OF MARTINIQUE.

The preparations of the French in Brest were completed towards the end of March, and on the 22d of that month Rear-Admiral de Grasse sailed, having a large convoy under the protection of twenty-six ships of the line. A week, later six of the latter parted company, five under Suffren for the East Indies and one for North America. The remaining twenty continued their course for Martinique, which was sighted on the 28th of April. Before sunset, Hood's squadron also was discovered to leeward of the island, as ordered by Rodney to cruise, and off the southern point,—Pointe des Salines. De Grasse then hove-to for the night, but sent an officer ashore both to give and to obtain intelligence, and to reach an understanding for concerted action next day.

The French fleet consisted of one ship of 110 guns, three 80s, fifteen 74s, and one 64, in all 20 of the line, besides three armed *en flûte*[1] which need not be taken into account, although they served to cover the convoy. Besides these there were the four in Fort Royal, one 74 and three 64s, a junction of which with the approaching enemy it was one of Hood's objects to prevent. The force of the British was one 90, one 80, twelve 74s, one 70, and two 64s: total, 17. Thus both in numbers and in rates of ships Hood was inferior to the main body alone of the French; but he had the advantage of ships all coppered, owing to Rodney's insistence with the Admiralty. He also had no convoy to worry him; but he was to leeward.

Early in the morning of the 29th, de Grasse advanced to round the southern point of the island, which was the usual course for sailing ships. Hood was too far to leeward to intercept this movement, for which he was blamed by Rodney, who claimed that the night had not been properly utilised by beating to windward of Pointe des Salines.[2] Hood, on the other hand, said in a private letter: "I never once lost sight of getting to windward, but it was totally impossible. . . . Had I fortunately been there, I must have brought the enemy to close action upon more equal terms, or they must have given up their transports, trade, etc." Hood's subsequent career places it beyond doubt that had he been to windward there would have been a severe action, whatever the result; but it is not possible to decide positively between his statement and Rodney's, as to where the fault of being to leeward lay. The writer believes that Hood would have been to windward, if in any way possible. It must be added that the British had no word that so great a force was coming. On this point Hood and Rodney are agreed.

Under the conditions, the French passed without difficulty round Pointe des Salines, the transports hugging the coast, the ships of war being outside and to leeward of them. Thus they headed up to the northward for Fort Royal Bay (Cul de Sac Royal), Hood standing to the southward until after 10, and being joined at 9.20 by a sixty-four (not reckoned in the list above) from Santa Lucia, making his force eighteen. At 10.35 the British tacked together to the northward. The two fleets were now steering the same way, the French van abreast of the British centre. At 11 the French opened their fire, to which no reply was made then. At 11.20, the British van being close in with the shore to the northward of the Bay, Hood tacked again together, and the enemy, seeing his convoy secure, wore, also together, which brought the two lines nearer, heading south. At this time the four French ships in the Bay got under way and easily joined the rear of their fleet, it having the weather-gage. The French were thus 24 to 18. As their shot were passing over the British, the latter now began to reply. At noon Hood, finding that he could not close the enemy, shortened sail to topsails and hove-to, hoping by this defiance to bring them down to him. At 12.30 the French admiral was abreast of the British flagship, and the action became general, but at too long range. "Never, I believe," wrote Hood, "was more powder and shot thrown away in one day before." The French continuing to stand on, Hood filled his sails again at 1 P.M., as their van had stretched beyond his.

As the leading ships, heading south, opened the channel between Santa Lucia and Martinique, they got the breeze fresher, which caused them to draw away from the centre. Hood, therefore, at 1.34 made the signal for a close order, and immediately afterwards ceased firing, finding not one in ten of the enemy's shot to reach. The engagement, however, continued somewhat longer between the southern—van—ships, where, by the account of Captain Sutherland, who was in that part of the line, four of the British were attacked very smartly by eight of the French. The *Centaur, Russell, Intrepid*, and *Shrewsbury* appear to have been the ships that suffered most heavily, either in hull, spars, or crews. They were all in the van on the southern tack. The *Russell*, having several shot between wind and water, was with difficulty kept afloat, the water rising over the platform of the magazine. Hood sent her off at nightfall to St. Eustatius, where she arrived on the 4th of May, bringing Rodney the first news of the action, and of the numbers of the French reinforcement. During the 30th Hood held his ground, still endeavouring to get to windward of the enemy; but failing in that attempt, and finding two of his squadron much disabled, he decided at sunset to bear away to the northward, because to the southward the westerly currents set so strong that the crippled ships could not regain Santa Lucia. On the 11th of May, between St. Kitts and Antigua, he joined Rodney, who, after hurried repairs to the *Russell*, had left St. Eustatius on the 5th, with that ship, the *Sandwich*, and the *Triumph*.

It is somewhat difficult to criticise positively the conduct of Hood and of de Grasse in this affair. It is clear that Hood on the first day seriously sought action, though his force was but three-fourths that of his foe. He tried first to take the offensive, and, failing that, to induce his enemy to attack frankly and decisively. Troude is doubtless correct in saying that it was optional with de Grasse to bring on a general engagement; and the writer finds himself in agreement also with another French authority, Captain Chevalier, that "Count de Grasse seems to have been too much preoccupied with the safety of his convoy on the 29th, Admiral Hood having shown himself much less circumspect on that day than he was on the next. Notwithstanding our numerical superiority, Count de Grasse kept near the land until all the convoy were safe." He represents Hood as fencing cautiously on the following day, keeping on the field, but avoiding a decisive encounter. This differs somewhat from the version of Hood himself, who mentions signalling a general chase to windward at 12.30 P.M. of the 30th. The two statements are not irreconcilable. Hood having coppered ships, had the speed of the French, whose vessels, being partly coppered and partly not, sailed unevenly. The British commander consequently could afford to take risks, and he therefore played with the enemy, watching for a chance. Hood was an officer of exceptional capacity, much in advance of his time. He thoroughly understood a watching game, and that an opportunity might offer to seize an advantage over part of the enemy, if the eagerness of pursuit, or any mishap, caused the French to separate. From any dilemma that ensued, the reserve of speed gave him a power of withdrawal, in relying upon which he was right. The present writer adopts here also Chevalier's conclusion: "Admiral Hood evidently had the very great advantage over his enemy of commanding a squadron of coppered ships. Nevertheless, homage is due to his skill and to the confidence shown by him in his captains. If some of his ships had dropped behind through injuries received, he would have had to sacrifice them, or to fight a superior force." This means that Hood for an adequate gain ran a great risk; that he thoroughly understood both the advantages and the disadvantages of his situation; and that he acted not only with great skill, but warily and boldly,—a rare combination. The British loss in this affair was 39 killed, including Captain Nott, of the *Centaur*, and 162 wounded. The French loss is given by Chevalier as 18 killed and 56 wounded; by Beatson, as 119 killed and 150 wounded.

Rodney, having collected his fleet, proceeded south, and on the 18th of May put into Barbados for water. Much anxiety had been felt at first for Santa Lucia, which Hood's retreat had uncovered. As was feared, the French had attacked it at once, their fleet, with the exception of one or two ships, going there, and twelve hundred troops landing at Gros Ilet Bay; but the batteries on Pigeon Island, which Rodney had erected and manned, kept them at arms' length. The works elsewhere being found too strong, the attempt was abandoned.

At the same time, two French ships of the line and thirteen hundred troops had sailed from Martinique against Tobago. When de Grasse returned from the failure at Santa Lucia, he learned that the British were at sea, apparently bound for Barbados. Alarmed for his detachment before Tobago, he again sailed with the fleet for that island on the 25th of May, accompanied by three thousand more troops. Rodney learned at Barbados of the attempt on Tobago, and on the 29th dispatched a squadron of six sail of the line, under Rear-Admiral Francis Samuel Drake, to support the defence. On the 30th he heard that the French main fleet had been seen to windward of Santa Lucia, steering south, evidently for Tobago. On the same day Drake and de Grasse encountered one another off the latter island, the French being to leeward, nearest the land. Drake necessarily retired, and on the morning of June 3d was again off Barbados, whereupon Rodney at once sailed for Tobago with the whole fleet. On the 4th the island was sighted, and next morning information was received that it had capitulated on the 2d.

The two fleets returning north were in presence of one another on the 9th; but no engagement took place. Rodney, who was to windward, having twenty sail to twenty-three,[3] was unwilling to attack unless he could get a clear sea. The strength of the currents, he said, would throw his fleet too far to leeward, in case of reverse, into the foul ground between St. Vincent and Grenada, thus exposing Barbados, which had not recovered sufficiently from the hurricane to stand alone. He therefore put into Barbados. De Grasse went to Martinique to prepare the expedition to the American continent, which resulted in the surrender of Cornwallis at Yorktown. On the 5th of July he sailed from Fort Royal taking with him the "trade" for France, and on the 26th anchored with it at Cap François in Haïti, where he found a division of four ships of the line which had been left the year before by de Guichen. There also was a frigate, which had left Boston on the 20th of June, and by which De Grasse received dispatches from Washington, and from Rochambeau, the general commanding the French troops in America. These acquainted him with the state of affairs on the continent, and requested that the fleet should come to either the Chesapeake or New York, to strike a decisive blow at the British power in one quarter or the other.

1. This latter is applied to vessels, usually ships of war, which are used as transports or supply ships, and therefore carry only a part of their normal battery.

2. Rodney said that Hood "lay-to" for the night. This is antecedently incredible of an officer of Hood's character, and is expressly contradicted by Captain Sutherland of the *Russell*. "At 6 P.M. (of the 28th) our fleet tacked to the north, and *kept moving* across the bay (Fort Royal) for the right (*sic*), in line of battle." Ekins, "Naval Battles," p. 136. The word "right" is evidently a misprint for "night." Rodney's criticisms seem to the author captious throughout.

3. One French ship had left the fleet, disabled.

X

NAVAL OPERATIONS PRECEDING AND DETERMINING THE FALL OF YORKTOWN

Having now brought the major naval transactions in the West Indies to the eve of the great events which determined the independence of the American States, it is expedient here to resume the thread of operations, both sea and land, on the American continent, so as to bring these also up to the same decisive moment, when the military and naval blended and in mutual support forced the surrender of the British army at Yorktown under Lord Cornwallis.

It has been said that, to support the operations of Cornwallis in the Carolinas, Clinton had begun a series of diversions in the valley of the James River.[1] The first detachment so sent, under General Leslie, had been transferred speedily to South Carolina, to meet the exigencies of Cornwallis's campaign. The second, of sixteen hundred troops under Benedict Arnold, left New York at the end of December, and began its work on the banks of the James at the end of January, 1781. It advanced to Richmond, nearly a hundred miles from the sea, wasting the country round about, and finding no opposition adequate to check its freedom of movement. Returning down stream, on the 20th it occupied Portsmouth, south of the James River; near the sea, and valuable as a naval station.

Washington urged Commodore des Touches, who by de Ternay's death had been left in command of the French squadron at Newport, to interrupt these proceedings, by dispatching a strong detachment to Chesapeake Bay; and he asked Rochambeau also to let some troops accompany the naval division, to support the scanty force which he himself could spare to Virginia. It happened, however, that a gale of wind just then had inflicted severe injury upon Arbuthnot's squadron, three of which had gone to sea from Gardiner's Bay upon a report that three French ships of the line had left Newport to meet an expected convoy. One seventy-four, the *Bedford*, was wholly dismasted; another, the *Culloden*, drove ashore on Long Island and was wrecked. The French ships had returned to port the day before the gale, but the incident indisposed des Touches to risk his vessels at sea at that time. He sent only a sixty-four, with two frigates. These left Newport on February 9th, and entered the Chesapeake, but were unable to reach the British vessels, which, being smaller, withdrew up the Elizabeth River. Arbuthnot, hearing of this expedition, sent orders to some frigates off Charleston to go to the scene. The French division, when leaving the Bay, met one of these, the *Romulus*, 44, off the Capes, captured her, and returned to Newport on February 25th. On the 8th of March, Arnold reported to Clinton that the Chesapeake was clear of French vessels.

On the same day Arbuthnot also was writing to Clinton, from Gardiner's Bay, that the French were evidently preparing to quit Newport. His utmost diligence had failed as yet to repair entirely the damage done his squadron by the storm, but on the 9th it was ready for sea. On the evening of the 8th the French had sailed. On the 10th Arbuthnot knew it, and, having taken the precaution to move down to the entrance of the bay, he was able to follow at once. On the 13th he spoke a vessel which had seen the enemy and gave him their course. Favoured by a strong north-west wind, and his ships being coppered, he outstripped the French, only three of which had coppered bottoms. At 6 A.M. of March 16th a British frigate reported that the enemy were astern—to the north-east—about a league distant, a thick haze preventing the squadron from seeing them even at that distance (Fig. 1, A, A). Cape Henry, the southern point of the entrance to the Chesapeake, then bore southwest by west, distant forty miles. The wind as stated by Arbuthnot was west; by the French, south-west.

The British admiral at once went about, steering in the direction reported, and the opposing squadrons soon sighted one another. The French finding the British between them and their port, hauled to the wind, which between 8 and 9 shifted to north by west, putting them to windward. Some preliminary manœuvres then followed, both parties seeking the weather-gage. The weather remained thick and squally, often intercepting the view; and the wind continued to shift until towards noon, when it settled at north-east. The better sailing, or the better seamanship, of the British had enabled them to gain so far upon their opponents that at 1 P.M. they were lying nearly up in their wake, on the port tack, overhauling them; both squadrons in line of battle, heading east-south-east, the French bearing from their pursuers east by south,—one point on the weather bow (B,B). The wind was rising with squalls, so that the ships lay over well to their canvas, and the sea was getting big.

As the enemy now was threatening his rear, and had the speed to overtake, des Touches felt it necessary to resort to the usual parry to such a thrust, by wearing his squadron and passing on the other tack. This could be done either together, reversing the order of the ships, or in succession, preserving the natural order; depending much upon the distance of the enemy. Having room enough, des Touches chose the latter, but, as fighting was inevitable, he decided also to utilise the manœuvre by surrendering the weather-gage, and passing to leeward. The advantage of this course was that, with the existing sea and wind, and the inclination of the ships, the party that had the opponent on his weather side could open the lower-deck ports and use those guns. There was thus a great increase of battery power, for the lower guns were the heaviest. Des Touches accordingly put his helm up, his line passing in succession to the southward (c) across the head of the advancing British column, and then hauling up so as to run parallel to the latter, to leeward, with the wind four points free.

Arbuthnot accepted the position offered, stood on as he was until nearly abreast of the French, and at 2 P.M. made the signal to wear. It does not appear certainly how this was executed; but from the expression in the official report, "the van of the squadron wore in the line," and from the fact that the ships which led in the attack were those which were leading on the port tack,—the tack before the signal was made,—it seems likely that the movement was made in succession (a). The whole squadron then stood down into action, but with the customary result. The ships in the van and centre were all engaged by 2.30, so Arbuthnot states; but the brunt of the engagement had already fallen upon the three leading vessels, which got the first raking fire, and, as is also usual, came to closer action than those which followed them (C). They therefore not only lost most heavily in men, but also were so damaged aloft as to be crippled. The British Vice-Admiral, keeping the signal for the line flying, and not hoisting that for close action, appears to have caused a movement of indecision in the squadron,—an evidence again of the hold which the line

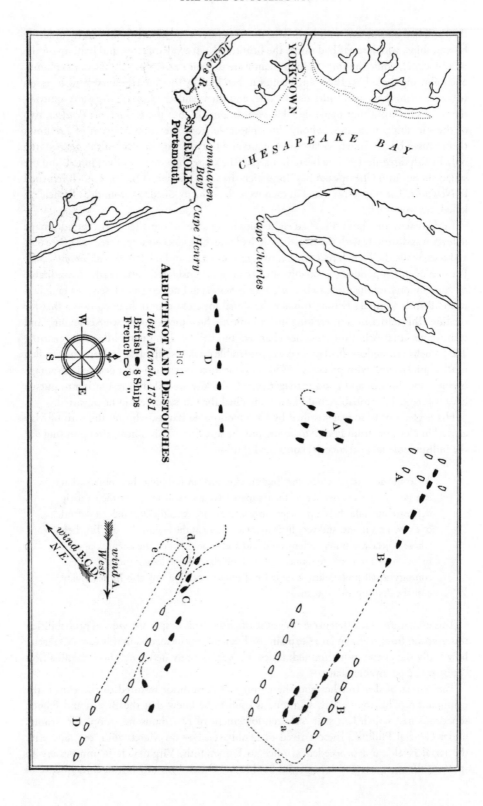

YORKTOWN

James R.

Lynnhaven Bay

NORFOLK

Portsmouth

Cape Henry

CHESAPEAKE BAY

Cape Charles

FIG 1.

ARBUTHNOT AND DESTOUCHES

16th March, 1781

British ● 8 Ships
French ◯ 8 "

W

S   E

wind B.C.D.
N.E.

wind A.
West

then still had upon men's minds. Of this des Touches cleverly availed himself, by ordering his van ships, which so far had borne the brunt, to keep away together and haul up on the other tack (e), while the ships behind them were to wear in succession; that is, in column, one following the other. The French column then filed by the three disabled British vessels (d), gave them their broadsides one by one, and then hauled off to the eastward, quitting the field (D). Arbuthnot made signal to wear in pursuit, but the *Robust* and *Prudent*, two of the van ships, were now wholly unmanageable from the concentration of fire upon them caused by des Touches's last movement; and the maintopsail yard of the *London*, the only British three-decker, had been shot away. The chase therefore was abandoned, and the squadron put into Chesapeake Bay, for which the wind was fair (D). The French returned to Newport. The respective losses in men were: British, 30 killed, 73 wounded; French, 72 killed, 112 wounded.

In this encounter, both sides had eight ships in line, besides smaller craft. The advantage in force was distinctly with the British, who had one three-decked ship, three 74s, three 64s, and a 50; while the French had one 84, two 74s, four 64s, and the late British *Romulus*, 44. Because of this superiority, probably, the action was considered particularly discreditable by contemporaries; the more so because several vessels did not engage closely,—a fault laid to the British admiral's failure to make the signal for close action, hauling down that for the line. This criticism is interesting, for it indicates how men's minds were changing; and it shows also that Arbuthnot had not changed, but still lived in the middle of the century. The French commodore displayed very considerable tactical skill; his squadron was handled neatly, quickly, and with precision. With inferior force he carried off a decided advantage by sheer intelligence and good management. Unluckily, he failed in resolution to pursue his advantage. He probably could have controlled the Chesapeake had he persisted.

His neglect to do so was justified by Commodore de Barras, who on the 10th of May arrived in Newport from France to command the squadron. This officer, after pointing out the indisputable tactical success, continued thus:—

> As to the advantage which the English obtained, in fulfilling their object, that is a necessary consequence of their superiority, and, still more, of their purely defensive attitude. It is a principle in war that one should risk much to defend one's own positions, and very little to attack those of the enemy. M. des Touches, whose object was purely offensive, could and should, when the enemy opposed to him superior forces, renounce a project which could no longer succeed, unless, contrary to all probability, it ended not only in beating but also in destroying entirely, that superior squadron.

This exaltation of the defensive above the offensive, this despairing view of probabilities, this aversion from risks, go far to explain the French want of success in this war. No matter how badly the enemy was thrashed, unless he were entirely destroyed, he was still a fleet "in being," a paralysing factor.

The retreat of des Touches and the coming of Arbuthnot restored to the British the command of Chesapeake Bay. Clinton, as soon as he knew that the British and French squadrons had sailed, had sent off a reinforcement of two thousand troops for Arnold, under General Phillips. These arrived in Lynnhaven Bay on March 26th, ten days after the naval battle, and proceeded at once to Portsmouth, Virginia. It is unnecessary to speak of the various operations of this land force. On the 9th of May, in consequence of letters received from Cornwallis, it moved to Petersburg. There on the 13th Phillips died, the command reverting momentarily to Arnold. On the 20th Cornwallis joined from Wilmington, North Carolina,[2] and Arnold soon after returned to New York.

Cornwallis now had with him about seven thousand troops, including the garrison at Portsmouth; but a serious difference of opinion existed between him and Clinton, the Commander-in-Chief. The latter had begun the conquest of South Carolina, and did not welcome the conclusion of his lieutenant that the conquest could not be maintained away from the seaboard, unless Virginia also were subdued; for from there, a rich and populous region, men and supplies supported the American cause in the south. Cornwallis had tested the asserted strength of the Royalists in the Carolinas, and had found it wanting. Offensive operations in Virginia were what he wished; but Clinton did not approve this project, nor feel that he could spare troops enough for the purpose. Between October, 1780, and June, 1781, he said, seven thousand seven hundred and twenty-four effectives had been sent from New York to the Chesapeake; and he could not understand the failure to cut off the greatly inferior force of the enemy in Virginia. This at least did not indicate probable success for a renewed offensive. The garrison of New York was now short of eleven thousand and could not be diminished further, as he was threatened with a siege. In short, the British situation in America had become essentially false, by the concurring effect of insufficient force and ex-centric—double—operations. Sent to conquer, their numbers now were so divided that they could barely maintain the defensive. Cornwallis therefore was ordered to occupy a defensive position which should control an anchorage for ships of the line, and to strengthen himself in it. After some discussion, which revealed further disagreement, he placed himself at Yorktown, on the peninsula formed by the James and York rivers. Portsmouth was evacuated, the garrison reaching Yorktown on the 22d of August. Cornwallis's force was then seven thousand troops; and there were with him besides about a thousand seamen, belonging to some half-dozen small vessels, which were shut up in the York by the arrival from Haïti of the French fleet under de Grasse, which on August 30th, 1781, had anchored in Lynnhaven Bay, inside of Cape Henry.

On July 2d Arbuthnot had sailed for England, leaving the command at New York to Rear-Admiral Thomas Graves. Graves on the same day wrote to Rodney by the brig *Active*, that intercepted dispatches of the enemy had revealed that a large division from the West Indies was to arrive on the American coast during the summer, to cooperate with the force already in Newport. Rodney, on the other hand, dispatched to New York on July 7th the *Swallow* sloop, 16, with word that, if he sent reinforcements from the West Indies, they would be ordered to make the Capes of the Chesapeake, and to coast thence to New York. He asked, therefore, that cruisers with information might be stationed along that route. Two days later, having then certain news that de Grasse had sailed for Cap François, he sent this intelligence to Sir Peter Parker at Jamaica, and gave Sir Samuel Hood preparatory orders to command a reinforcement of ships destined for the continent. This, however, was limited in numbers to fifteen sail of the line, Rodney being misled by his intelligence, which gave fourteen ships as the size of the French division having the same destination, and reported that de Grasse himself would convoy the trade from Cap François to France. On the 24th instructions were issued for Hood to proceed on this duty. He was first to convoy the trade from Jamaica as far as the passage between Cuba and Haïti, and thence to make the utmost speed to the Chesapeake. A false rumour, of French ships reaching Martinique from Europe, slightly delayed this movement. The convoy was dispatched to Jamaica with two ships of the line, which Sir Peter Parker was directed to send at once to America, and requested to reinforce with others from his own squadron. Hood was detained until the rumour could be verified. On the 1st of August Rodney sailed for England on leave of absence. On the 10th Hood left Antigua with fourteen ships of the line, direct for the Capes. He had already received, on August 3d, Graves's letter by the *Active*, which he sent back on the 8th with his answers and with a notification of his speedy departure.

The *Swallow* and the *Active* should have reached Graves before Hood; but neither got to him at all. The *Swallow* arrived safely in New York on the 27th of July; but Graves had sailed with all his squadron on the 21st, for Boston Bay, hoping there to intercept an expected convoy from France, concerning which a special caution had been sent him by the Admiralty. The *Swallow* was at once sent on by the senior naval officer at New York, but was attacked by hostile vessels, forced ashore on Long Island, and lost. The *Active* was captured before she reached New York. Graves, thus uninformed of the momentous crisis at hand, continued cruising until the 16th of August, when he returned to Sandy Hook. There he found the duplicates of the *Swallow's* letters, but they only notified him of the course a reinforcement would take, not that Hood had started. On August 25th the latter, being then off the Chesapeake, sent duplicates of the *Active's* dispatches, but these preceded by little his own arrival on the 28th. That evening news was received in New York that de Barras had sailed from Newport on the 25th, with his whole division. Hood anchored outside the Hook, where Graves, who was senior to him, undertook to join at once. On the 31st five sail of the line and a 50-gun ship, all that could be got ready in time, crossed the bar, and the entire body of nineteen ships of the line started at once for the Chesapeake, whither it was understood now that both the French fleet and the united armies of Washington and Rochambeau were hurrying.

Count de Grasse upon his arrival at Cap François had found that many things must be done before he could sail for the continent. Measures needed to be taken for the security of Haïti; and a large sum of money, with a considerable reinforcement of troops, was required to insure the success of the projected operation, for which but a short time was allowed, as it was now August and he must be again in the West Indies in October. It was not the least among the fortunate concurrences for the American cause at that moment, that de Grasse, whose military capacity was not conspicuous, showed then a remarkable energy, politic tact, and breadth of view. He decided to take with him every ship he could command, postponing the sailing of the convoys; and by dexterous arrangement with the Spaniards he contrived to secure both the funds required and an efficient corps of thirty-three hundred French troops, without stripping Haïti too closely. On the 5th of August he left Cap François, with twenty-eight ships of the line, taking the route through the Old Bahama Channel,[3] and anchored in Lynnhaven Bay, just within the entrance of the Chesapeake, on the 30th, the day before Graves sailed from New York for the same place. The troops were landed instantly on the south side of the James River, and soon reached La Fayette, who commanded the forces so far opposed to Cornwallis, which were thus raised to eight thousand men. At the same time Washington, having thrown Clinton off his guard, was crossing the Delaware on his way south, with six thousand regular troops, two thousand American and four thousand French, to join La Fayette. French cruisers took position in the James River, to prevent Cornwallis from crossing, and escaping to the southward into Carolina. Others were sent to close the mouth of the York. By these detachments the main fleet was reduced to twenty-four sail of the line.

On the 5th of September, at 8 A.M., the French look-out frigate, cruising outside Cape Henry, made the signal for a fleet steering for the Bay. It was hoped at first that this was de Barras's squadron from Newport, known to be on its way, but it was soon evident from the numbers that it must be an enemy. The forces now about to be opposed, nineteen British sail of the line to twenty-four French, were constituted as follows: British, two 98s (three-deckers); twelve 74s, one 70, four 64s, besides frigates; French, one 104 (three-decker),[4] three 80s, seventeen 74s, three 64s.

The mouth of the Chesapeake is about ten miles wide, from Cape Charles on the north to Cape Henry on the south. The main channel is between the latter and a shoal, three miles to the northward, called the Middle Ground. The British fleet, when the French were first seen from it, was steering south-west for the entrance, under foresails and topgallant sails, and it so continued, forming line as it approached. The wind was north-north-east. At noon the ebb-tide made, and the French began to get under way, but many of their ships had to make several tacks to clear Cape Henry. Their line was consequently late in forming, and was by no means regular or closed as they got outside.

At 1 P.M. Graves made the signal to form column on an east and west line, which with the wind as it was would be the close-hauled line heading out to sea, on the other tack from that on which his fleet still was. In this order he continued to head in for the entrance. At 2 P.M. the French van, standing out, three miles distant by estimate, bore south from the *London*, Graves's flagship, and was therefore abreast of the centre of the British line. As the British van came near the Middle Ground, at 2.13 P.M., the ships wore together. This put them on the same tack as the French, Hood's division, which had been leading, being now the rear in the reversed order. The fleet then brought-to,—stopped,—in order to allow the centre of the enemy to come abreast of the centre of the British (Fig. 2, aa, aa). The two lines now were nearly parallel, but the British, being five ships fewer, naturally did not extend so far as the rear of the French, which in fact was not yet clear of the Cape. At 2.30 Graves made the signal for the van ship (the *Shrewsbury*), to lead more to starboard (l)—towards the enemy. As each ship in succession would take her course to follow the leader, the effect of this was to put the British on a line inclined to that of the enemy, the van nearest, and as the signal was renewed three quarters of an hour later,—at 3.17,—this angle became still more marked (bb).[5] This was the original and enduring cause of a lamentable failure by which seven of the rear ships, in an inferior force undertaking to attack, never came into battle at all. At 3.34 the van was ordered again to keep still more toward the enemy.

At 3.46 the signal was made for ships to close to one cable, followed almost immediately by that to bear down and engage the enemy,—the signal for the line still flying. Graves's flagship, the *London*, 98 (f), which was hove-to, filled and bore down. Under the conditions, the van ships of course got first under fire, and the action gradually extended from them to the twelfth in the order, two ships astern of the *London*. According to the log of the latter, at 4.11 the signal for the line ahead was hauled down, that it might not interfere with that for close action, but at 4.22 it was rehoisted, "the ships not being sufficiently extended." The meaning of this expression may be inferred from Beatson's account:—

> The *London*, by taking the lead, had advanced farther towards the enemy than some of the ships stationed immediately ahead of her in the line of battle; and upon luffing up (f') to bring her broadside to bear, they having done the same thing, her second ahead (m) was brought nearly upon her weather beam. The other ships ahead of her were likewise too much crowded together.

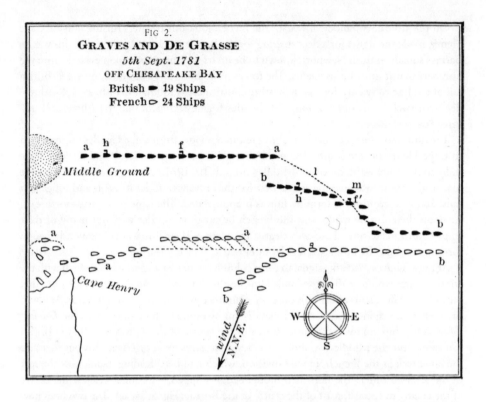

FIG 2.

GRAVES AND DE GRASSE
5th Sept. 1781
OFF CHESAPEAKE BAY
British ► 19 Ships
French ▻ 24 Ships

As the ship on the *London's* weather beam could not fire upon the enemy unless she drew ahead, this condition probably accounts for the flagship being again hove-to, while firing, as Hood says that she was. The signal for the line was hauled down again at 4.27, by the *London's* log, that for close action being up, and repeated at 5.20, when Hood (h) at last bore down with his division (h′), but the French ships bearing up also, he did not near them. Firing ceased shortly after sunset. The loss of the British was 90 killed, 246 wounded; that of the French is given only in round numbers, as about 200 killed and wounded.

Hood's statement introduces certain important qualifications into the above account:—

> Our centre began to engage at the same time as the van, at four, but at a most *improper* distance, and our rear, being barely within random shot, did not fire while the signal for the line was flying. The *London* had the signal for close action flying, as well as the signal for the line ahead at *half a cable* was under her topsails, with the main topsail to the mast,[6] though the enemy's ships were pushing on.

As showing the improper distance at which the *London* brought-to to fire, he says:

> The second ship astern of her (of the *London*) received but trifling damage, and the third astern of her received no damage at all, which most clearly proves [at] how much too great a distance was the centre division engaged.

The day after the action Hood made a memorandum of his criticisms upon it, which has been published. The gist of this is as follows. As the French stood out, their line was not regular or connected. The van was much separated from the centre and rear, and it appears also, from the French narratives, that it was to windward of the rest of the fleet. From these causes it was much exposed to be attacked unsupported. There was, by Hood's estimate, "a full hour and a half to have engaged it before any of the rear could have come up." The line of battle on the port tack with the then wind, was east and west, and Graves had first ranged his fleet on it, as the French were doing; but afterwards, owing to his method of approach, by the van bearing down and the other ships following in its wake, the two lines, instead of being parallel, formed an angle, the British centre and rear being much more distant from the enemy than the van was. This alone would cause the ships to come into battle successively instead of together, a fault of itself; but the Commander-in-Chief, according to Hood, committed the further mistake that he kept the signal for the line of battle flying until 5.30 P.M., near to sunset. In Hood's understanding, while that signal flew the position of each ship was determined by that of Graves's flagship. None could go closer than the line through her parallel to the enemy. Hence Hood's criticism, which is marked by much acerbity towards his superior, but does not betray any consciousness that he himself needed any justification for his division not having taken part.

> Had the centre gone to the support of the van, and *the signal for the line been hauled down*, or the Commander-in-Chief had set the example of close action, *even with the signal for the line flying*, the van of the enemy must have been cut to pieces, and the rear division of the British fleet would have been opposed to those ships the centre division fired at, and at the proper distance for engaging, or the Rear-Admiral who commanded it[7] would have a great deal to answer for.[8]

So much for the tactical failure of that day. The question remained what next was to be done. Graves contemplated renewing the action, but early in the night was informed that several of the van ships were too crippled to permit this. He held his ground, however, in sight of the French, until dark on the 9th, when they were seen for the last time. They were then under a cloud of sail, and on the morning of the 10th had disappeared. From their actions during this interval, Hood had inferred that de Grasse meant to get back into the Chesapeake without further fighting; and he implies that he advised Graves to anticipate the enemy in so doing. Though some ships were crippled aloft, the British batteries were practically intact, nor had men enough been disabled to prevent any gun in the fleet from being fought. Could but a single working day be gained in taking up an anchorage, a defensive order could be assumed, practically impregnable to the enemy, covering Cornwallis, and not impossibly intercepting the French ships left in the Bay. In the case of many men such comment might be dismissed as the idle talk of the captious fault-finder, always to the fore in life; but in the case of Hood it must be received with deference, for, but a few months later, when confronted with greater odds, he himself did the very thing he here recommended, for an object less vital than the relief of Cornwallis. Having regard to the character of de Grasse, it is reasonable to believe that, if he had found the British fleet thus drawn up at anchor in Chesapeake Bay, as he found Hood at St. Kitts in the following January, he would have waited off the entrance for de Barras, and then have gone to sea, leaving Washington and Rochambeau to look at Cornwallis slipping out of their grasp.

On the 10th of September Graves decided to burn the *Terrible,* 74, which had been kept afloat with difficulty since the action. This done, the fleet stood towards the Chesapeake, a frigate going ahead to reconnoitre. On the 13th, at 6 A.M., Graves wrote to Hood that the look-outs reported the French at anchor above the Horse Shoe (shoal) in the Chesapeake, and desired his opinion what to do with the fleet. To this Hood sent the comforting reply that it was no more than what he had expected, as the press of sail the (French) fleet carried on the 9th, and on the night of the 8th, made it very clear to him what de Grasse's intentions were. He "would be very glad to send an opinion, but he really knows not what to say in the truly lamentable state [to which] we have brought ourselves."[9] On the 10th de Barras had reached the Bay, where he was joined by de Grasse on the 11th, so that there were then present thirty-six French ships of the line. Graves, therefore, returned to New York, reaching Sandy Hook September 19th. On the 14th Washington had arrived before Yorktown, where he took the chief command; and the armies closed in upon Cornwallis by land as the French fleets had done already by water. On the 19th of October the British force was compelled to surrender, seven thousand two hundred and forty-seven troops and eight hundred and forty seamen laying down their arms. During the siege the latter had served in the works, the batteries of which were largely composed of ships' guns.

After Graves's return to New York, Rear-Admiral the Hon. Robert Digby arrived from England on the 24th of September, to take command of the station in Arbuthnot's place. He brought with him three ships of the line; and the two which Sir Peter Parker had been ordered by Rodney to send on at once had also reached the port. It was decided by the land and sea officers concerned to attempt the relief of Cornwallis, and that it was expedient for Graves to remain in command until after this expedition. He could not start, however, until the 18th of October, by which time Cornwallis's fate was decided. Graves then departed for Jamaica to supersede Sir Peter Parker. On the 11th of November Hood sailed from Sandy Hook with eighteen ships of the line, and on the 5th of December anchored at Barbados. On the 5th of November de Grasse also quitted the continent with his whole fleet, and returned to the West Indies.

1. *Ante,* p. 105.

2. *Ante,* p. 104.

3. Along the north coast of Cuba, between it and the Bahama Banks.

4. The *Ville de Paris,* to which Troude attributes 104 guns. She was considered the biggest and finest ship of her day.

5. This reproduced the blunder of Byng, between whose action and the one now under discussion there is a marked resemblance.

6. *i.e.* she had stopped.

7. Hood himself.

8. Letters of Lord Hood, p. 32. Navy Records Society. My italics. Concerning the crucial fact of the signal for the line of battle being kept flying continuously until 5.30 P.M., upon which there is a direct contradiction between Hood and the log of the *London,* it is necessary to give the statement of Captain Thomas White, who was present in the action in one of the rear ships. "If the *London's* log, or the log of any other individual ship in the fleet, confirm this

statement," (that Hood was dilatory in obeying the order for close action), "I shall be induced to fancy that what I that day saw and heard was a mere chimera of the brain, and that what I believed to be the signal for the line was not a union jack, but an *ignis fatuus* conjured up to mock me." White and Hood also agree that the signal for the line was rehoisted at 6.30. (White: "Naval Researches," London, 1830, p. 45.)

9. "Letters of Lord Hood." Navy Records Society, p. 35.

XI

NAVAL EVENTS OF 1781 IN EUROPE

IN EUROPE, DURING THE YEAR 1781, the two leading questions which dominated the action of the belligerents were the protection, or destruction, of commerce, and the attack and defence of Gibraltar. The British Channel Fleet was much inferior to the aggregate sea forces of France and Spain in the waters of Europe; and the Dutch navy also was now hostile. The French government represented to its allies that by concentrating their squadrons near the entrance of the Channel they would control the situation in every point of view; but the Spaniards, intent upon Gibraltar, declined to withdraw their fleet from Cadiz until late in the summer, while the French persisted in keeping their own at Brest. The Channel Fleet was decisively superior to the latter, and inferior to the Spaniards in numbers only.

No relief having been given Gibraltar since Rodney had left it in February, 1780, the question of supplying the fortress became pressing. For this purpose, twenty-eight ships of the line, under Vice-Admiral George Darby, sailed from St. Helen's on the 13th of March, 1781, with a large convoy. Off Cork a number of victuallers joined, and the whole body then proceeded for Gibraltar, accompanied by five ships of the line which were destined for the East Indies, as well as by the West India and American "trade." These several attachments parted from time to time on the way, and on the 11th of April the main expedition sighted Cape Spartel, on the African coast. No attempt to intercept it was made by the great Spanish fleet in Cadiz; and on the 12th of April, at noon, the convoy anchored in the Bay of Gibraltar. That night thirteen sail of the transports, under charge of two frigates, slipped out and made their way to Minorca, then a British possession. The British ships of war continued under way, cruising in the Bay and Gut of Gibraltar.

As the convoy entered, the besiegers opened a tremendous cannonade, which was ineffectual, however, to stop the landing of the stores. More annoyance was caused by a flotilla of gunboats, specially built for this siege, the peculiar fighting power of which lay in one 26-pounder, whose great length gave a range superior to the batteries of ships of the line. Being moved by oars as well as by sails, these little vessels could choose their distance in light airs and calms, and were used so actively to harass the transports at anchor that Darby was obliged to cover them with three ships of the line. These proved powerless effectually to injure the gunboats; but, while the latter caused great annoyance and petty injury, they did not hinder the unlading nor even greatly delay it. The experience illustrates again the unlikelihood that great results can be obtained by petty means, or that massed force, force concentrated, can be effectually counteracted either by cheap and ingenious expedients, or by the cooperative exertions of many small independent units. "They were only capable of producing trouble and vexation. So far were they from preventing the succours from being thrown into the garrison, or from burning the convoy, that the only damage of any consequence that they did to the shipping was the wounding of the mizzen-mast of the *Nonsuch* so much that it required to be shifted."[1] On the 19th of April—in one week—the revictualling was completed, and the expedition started back for England. The fleet anchored again at Spithead on the 22d of May.

While Darby was returning, La Motte Picquet had gone to sea from Brest with six ships of the line and some frigates to cruise in the approaches to the Channel. There, on the 2d of May, he fell in with the convoy returning from the West Indies with the spoils of St. Eustatius. The ships of war for the most part escaped, but La Motte Picquet carried twenty-two out of thirty merchant ships into Brest before he could be intercepted, although a detachment of eight sail sent by Darby got close upon his heels.

After a long refit, Darby put to sea again, about the 1st of August, to cover the approach of the large convoys then expected to arrive. Being greatly delayed by head winds, he had got no further than the Lizard, when news was brought him that the Franco-Spanish grand fleet, of forty-nine ships of the line, was cruising near the Scilly Isles. Having himself but thirty of the line, he put into Tor Bay on the 24th of August, and moored his squadron across the entrance to the Bay.

This appearance of the allies was a surprise to the British authorities, who saw thus unexpectedly renewed the invasion of the Channel made in 1779. Spain, mortified justly by her failure even to molest the intrusion of succours into Gibraltar, had thought to retrieve her honour by an attack upon Minorca, for which she asked the cooperation of France. De Guichen was sent in July with nineteen ships of the line; and the combined fleets, under the chief command of the Spanish admiral, Don Luis de Cordova, convoyed the troops into the Mediterranean beyond the reach of Gibraltar cruisers. Returning thence into the Atlantic, de Cordova directed his course for the Channel, keeping far out to sea to conceal his movements. But though thus successful in reaching his ground unheralded, he made no attempt to profit by the advantage gained. The question of attacking Darby at his anchors was discussed in a council of war, at which de Guichen strongly advocated the measure; but a majority of votes decided that Great Britain would be less hurt by ruining her fleet than by intercepting the expected convoys. Even for the latter purpose, however, de Cordova could not wait. On the 5th of September he informed de Guichen that he was at liberty to return to Brest; and he himself went back to Cadiz with thirty-nine ships, nine of which were French. "This cruise of the combined fleet," says Chevalier, "diminished the consideration of France and Spain. These two powers had made a great display of force, without producing the slightest result." It may be mentioned here that Minorca, after a six months' siege, capitulated in February, 1782.

While Darby was beating down Channel in the early days of August, 1781, Vice-Admiral Hyde Parker, lately Rodney's second in command in the West Indies, was returning to England convoying a large merchant fleet from the Baltic. On the 5th of August, at daylight, a Dutch squadron, also with a convoy, but outward bound, from the Texel to the Baltic, was discovered in the south-west, near the Doggers-bank. Heading as the two enemies then were, their courses must shortly intersect. Parker, therefore, ordered his convoy to steer to the westward for England, while he himself bore down for the enemy. The Dutch Rear-Admiral, Johan Arnold Zoutman, on the contrary, kept the merchant vessels with him, under his lee, but drew out the ships of war from among them, to form his order on the side towards the enemy. Each opponent put seven sail into the line. The British vessels, besides being of different rates, were chiefly very old ships, dragged out from Rotten Row to meet the pressing emergency caused by the greatly superior forces which were in coalition against Great Britain. Owing to the decayed condition of some of them, their batteries had been lightened, to the detriment of their fighting power. Two of them, however, were good and new seventy-fours. It is probable that the Dutch vessels, after a long peace, were not much better than their antagonists. In fact, each squadron was a scratch lot, in the worst sense of the phrase. The conduct of the affair by the two admirals, even to the very intensity of their pugnaciousness, contributes a tinge of the comic to the history of a desperately fought action.

The breeze was fresh at north-east, and the sea smooth. The Dutch, being to leeward, awaited attack, forming line on the port tack, heading south-east by east, a point off the wind, under topsails and foresails, a cable's length apart. There is little room to doubt that an adversary who thus holds his ground means to make a stand-up fight, but Parker, although the sun of a midsummer day had scarcely risen, thought advisable to order a general chase. Of course, no ship spared her canvas to this, while the worse sailers had to set their studdingsails to keep up; and the handling of the sails took the men off from the preparations for battle. Parker, who doubtless was still sore over Rodney's censure of the year before, and who moreover had incurred the Admiralty's rebuke, for apparent hesitation to attack the enemy's islands while temporarily in command in the West Indies, was determined now to show the fight that was in him. "It is related that, upon being informed of the force of the Dutch squadron in the morning, he replied (pulling up his breeches), 'It matters little what their force is; we must fight them if they are double the number.'" At 6.10 A.M. the signal was made for line abreast, the ships running down nearly before the wind. This of course introduced more regularity, the leading ships taking in their lighter sails to permit the others to reach their places; but the pace still was rapid. At 6.45 the order was closed to one cable, and at 7.56 the signal for battle was hoisted. It is said that at that moment the 80-gun ship was still securing a studdingsail-boom, which indicates how closely action trod on the heels of preparation.

The Dutch admiral was as deliberate as Parker was headlong. An English witness writes:—

> They appeared to be in great order; and their hammocks, quarter-cloths, etc., were spread in as nice order as if for show in harbour. Their marines also were well drawn up, and stood with their muskets shouldered, with all the regularity and exactness of a review. Their politeness ought to be remembered by every man in our line; for, as if certain of what happened, we came down almost end-on upon their broadsides; yet did not the Dutch admiral fire a gun, or make the signal to engage, till the red flag was at the *Fortitude's* masthead, and her shot finding their way into his ship. This was a manœuvre which Admiral Zutman should not be warmly thanked for by their High Mightinesses; as he had it in his power to have done infinite mischief to our fleet, coming down in that unofficer-like manner. Having suffered Admiral Parker to place himself as he pleased, he calmly waited till the signal was hoisted on board the *Fortitude*, and at the same time we saw the signal going up on board Admiral Zutman's ship.

The British, thus unmolested, rounded-to just to windward of the enemy. A pilot who was on board their leading ship was for some reason told to assist in laying her close to her opponent. "By close," he asked, "do you mean about a ship's breadth?" "Not a gun was fired on either side," says the official British report, "until within the distance of half musket-shot." Parker, whom an on-looker describes as full of life and spirits, here made a mistake, of a routine character, which somewhat dislocated his order. It was a matter of tradition for flagship to seek flagship, just as it was to signal a general chase, and to bear down together, each ship for its opposite, well extended with the enemy. Now Parker, as was usual, was in the centre of his line, the fourth ship; but Zoutman was for some reason in the fifth. Parker therefore placed his fourth by the enemy's fifth. In consequence, the rear British ship overlapped the enemy, and for a time had no opponent; while the second and third found themselves engaged with three of the Dutch. At 8 A.M. the signal for the line was hauled down, and that for close action hoisted,—thus avoiding a mistake often made.

All the vessels were soon satisfactorily and hotly at work, and the action continued with varying phases till 11.35 A.M. The leading two ships in both orders got well to leeward of the lines, the British two having to tack to regain their places to windward. Towards the middle of the engagement the Dutch convoy bore away, back to the Texel, as the British had steered for England before it began; the difference being that the voyage was abandoned by the Dutch and completed by the British. At eleven o'clock Parker made sail, and passed with the flagship between the enemy and the *Buffalo*, his next ahead and third in the British order; the three rear ships following close in his wake, in obedience to the signal for line ahead, which had been rehoisted at 10.43.[2] A heavy cannonade attended this evolution, the Dutch fighting gloriously to the last. When it was completed, the British fleet wore and the action ceased. "I made an effort to form the line, in order to renew the action," wrote Parker in his report, "but found it impracticable. The enemy appeared to be in as bad a condition. Both squadrons lay-to a considerable time near each other, when the Dutch, with their convoy, bore away for the Texel. We were not in a condition to follow them."

This was a most satisfactory exhibition of valour, and a most unsatisfactory battle; magnificent, but not war. The completion of their voyage by the British merchant ships, while the Dutch were obliged to return to the port which they had just left, may be considered to award success, and therefore the essentials of victory, to Parker's fleet. With this exception the *status quo* remained much as before, although one of the Dutch ships sank next day; yet the British loss 104 killed and 339 wounded, was nearly as great as in Keppel's action, where thirty ships fought on each side, or in Rodney's of April 17th, 1780, where the British had twenty sail; greater than with Graves off the Chesapeake, and, in proportion, fully equal to the sanguinary conflicts between Suffren and Hughes in the East Indies. The Dutch loss is reported as 142 killed, 403 wounded. Both sides aimed at the hull, as is shown by the injuries; for though much harm was done aloft, few spars were wholly shot away. The *Buffalo*, a small ship, had 39 shot through and through her, and a very great number pierced between wind and water; in the British van ship as many as 14, another proof that the Dutch fired low.

With the rudimentary notions of manœuvring evinced, it is not surprising that Parker was found an unsatisfactory second by an enlightened tactician like Rodney. The Vice-Admiral, however, laid his unsuccess to the indifferent quality of his ships. George III visited the squadron after the action, but Parker was not open to compliments. "I wish your Majesty better ships and younger officers," he said. "For myself, I am now too old for service." No rewards were given, and it is asserted that Parker made no secret that none would be accepted, if offered, at the hands of the then Admiralty. He voiced the protest of the Navy and of the nation against the mal-administration of the peace days, which had left the country unprepared for war. The gallant veteran was ordered soon afterwards to command in the East Indies. He sailed for his station in the *Cato*, which was never heard of again.

Though unfruitful in substantial results, Parker's action merits commemoration; for, after all, even where skill does its utmost, staunchness such as his shows the sound constitution of a military body.

1. Beatson, "Military and Naval Memoirs," v. 347.

2. Sir John Ross, in his "Life of Saumarez," who was lieutenant in the flagship, says that the flagship only passed ahead of the *Buffalo*, and that the rear ships closed upon the latter. The version in the text rests upon the detailed and circumstantial statements of another lieutenant of the squadron, in Ekins's "Naval Battles." As Ekins also was present as a midshipman, this gives, as it were, the confirmation of two witnesses.

XII

THE FINAL NAVAL CAMPAIGN
IN THE WEST INDIES

T HE YEAR 1781 CLOSED WITH an incident more decisive in character than most of the
events that occurred in European waters during its course; one also which transfers
the interest, by natural transition, again to the West Indies. The French government had
felt throughout the summer the necessity of sending de Grasse reinforcements both of
ships and of supplies, but the transports and material of war needed could not be collected
before December. As the British probably would attempt to intercept a convoy upon
which the next campaign so much depended, Rear-Admiral de Guichen was ordered to
accompany it clear of the Bay of Biscay, with twelve ships of the line, and then to go to
Cadiz. Five ships of the line destined to de Grasse, and two going to the East Indies, raised
to nineteen the total force with which de Guichen left Brest on the 10th of December.
On the afternoon of the 12th, the French being then one hundred and fifty miles to
the southward and westward of Ushant, with a south-east wind, the weather, which had
been thick and squally, suddenly cleared and showed sails to windward. These were twelve
ships of the line, one 50, and some frigates, under Rear-Admiral Richard Kempenfelt,
who had left England on the 2d of the month, to cruise in wait for this expedition. The
French numbers were amply sufficient to frustrate any attack, but de Guichen, ordinarily
a careful officer, had allowed his ships of war to be to leeward and ahead of the convoy.
The latter scattered in every direction, as the British swooped down upon them, but all
could not escape; and the French ships of war remained helpless spectators, while the
victims were hauling down their flags right and left. Night coming on, some prizes could
not be secured, but Kempenfelt carried off fifteen, laden with military and naval stores
of great money value and greater military importance. A few days later a violent storm
dispersed and shattered the remainder of the French body. Two ships of the line only, the
Triomphant, 84, and *Brave*, 74, and five transports, could pursue their way to the West
Indies. The rest went back to Brest. This event may be considered as opening the naval
campaign of 1782 in the West Indies.

Kempenfelt, before returning to England, sent off express to Hood in the West Indies
the fireship *Tisiphone*, 8, Commander James Saumarez,[1]—afterwards the distinguished
admiral,—with news of the French approach. Saumarez, having been first to Barbados,
joined Hood on the 31st of January, 1782, in Basse Terre Roads, on the lee side of St.
Kitts; a position from which Hood had dislodged de Grasse six days before by a brilliant
manœuvre, resembling that which he had contemplated[2] as open to Graves the previous
September at Chesapeake Bay for the relief of Cornwallis. The campaign for the year
1782 had opened already with an attack upon St. Kitts by the French army and navy; and
the French fleet was even then cruising close at hand to leeward, between St. Kitts and
Nevis.

The original intention of de Grasse and de Bouillé had been to capture Barbados, the most important of the Eastern Antilles still remaining to the British; but the heavy trade-winds, which in those days made a winter passage to windward so long and dreary a beat, twice drove them back to port. "The whole French fleet," wrote Hood, "appeared off Santa Lucia on the 17th of last month, endeavouring to get to windward, and having carried away many topmasts and yards in struggling against very squally weather, returned to Fort Royal Bay on the 23d, and on the 28th came out again with forty transports, manœuvring as before." On the 2d of January it disappeared from Santa Lucia, and, after a short stay again at Martinique, proceeded on the 5th to St. Kitts, anchoring in Basse Terre Roads on the 11th. The British garrison retired to Brimstone Hill, a fortified position at the north-west of the island, while the inhabitants surrendered the government to the French, pledging themselves to neutrality. The adjacent island of Nevis capitulated on the same terms on the 20th.

On the 14th of January, an express sent by General Shirley, governor of St. Kitts, had informed Hood at Barbados that a great fleet approaching had been seen from the heights of Nevis on the 10th. Hood at once put to sea, though short of bread and flour, which could not be had, and with the material of his ships in wretched condition. "When the *President*[3] joins," he wrote the Admiralty, "I shall be twenty-two strong, with which I beg you will assure their Lordships I will seek and give battle to the Count de Grasse, be his numbers as they may." On the way a ship reached him with word that the French fleet had invested St. Kitts. On the 21st he anchored at Antigua for repairs and supplies, indispensable for keeping the sea in the operations which he contemplated, the duration of which could not be foreseen. About a thousand troops also were embarked, which, with the marines that could be spared from the squadron, would give a landing force of twenty-four hundred men.

St. Kitts being less than fifty miles from Antigua, Hood doubtless now got accurate information of the enemy's dispositions, and could form a definite, well-matured plan. This seems to have been carefully imparted to all his captains, as was the practice of Nelson, who was the pupil of Hood, if of any one. "At 9.15 A.M. the Admiral made the signal for all flag-officers," says the log of the *Canada*; "and at 4 P.M. the Admirals and Commodore made the signals for all captains of their divisions." At 5 P.M. of the same day, January 23d, the fleet weighed and stood over for Nevis, round the southern point of which Basse Terre must be approached; for, the channel between Nevis and St. Kitts being impracticable for ships of the line, the two islands were virtually one, and, their common axis lying north-west and south-east, the trade-wind is fair only when coming from the south.

Basse Terre, where de Grasse then was, is about fifteen miles from the south point of Nevis. The roadstead lies east and west, and the French fleet, then twenty-four of the line and two fifties, were anchored without attention to order, three or four deep; the eastern ships so placed that an enemy coming from the southward could reach them with the prevailing trade-wind, against which the western ships could not beat up quickly to their support. This being so, we are told that Hood, starting shortly before sunset with a fair, and probably fresh wind, from a point only sixty miles distant, hoped to come upon the French by surprise at early daybreak, to attack the weather ships, and from them to sail along the hostile order so far as might seem expedient. His column, thus passing in its entirety close to a certain exposed fraction of the enemy, the latter would be cut up in detail by the concentration upon it. The British then, wearing to the southward, would haul their wind, tack, and again stand up to the assault, if the enemy continued to await it.

This reasonable expectation, and skilful conception, was thwarted by a collision, during the night, between a frigate, the *Nymphe*, 36, and the leading ship of the line, the *Alfred*, 74. The repairs to the latter delayed the fleet, the approach of which was discovered by daylight. De Grasse therefore put to sea. He imagined Hood's purpose was to throw succours into Brimstone Hill; and moreover the position of the enemy now was between him and four ships of the line momentarily expected from Martinique, one of which joined him on the same day. The French were all under way by sunset, standing to the southward under easy sail, towards the British, who had rounded the south point of Nevis at 1 P.M. Towards dark, Hood went about and stood also to the southward, seemingly in retreat.

During the following night the British tacked several times, to keep their position to windward. At daylight of January 25th, the two fleets were to the westward of Nevis; the British near the island, the French abreast, but several miles to leeward. Foiled in his first spring by an unexpected accident, Hood had not relinquished his enterprise, and now proposed to seize the anchorage quitted by the French, so establishing himself there,—as he had proposed to Graves to do in the Chesapeake,—that he could not be dislodged. For such a defensive position St. Kitts offered special advantages. The anchorage was a narrow ledge, dropping precipitately to very deep water; and it was possible so to place the ships that the enemy could not easily anchor near them.

At 5.30 A.M. of the 25th Hood made the signal to form line of battle on the starboard tack, at one cable interval.[4] It is mentioned in the log of the *Canada*, 74, Captain Cornwallis, that that ship brought-to in her station, fourth from the rear, at 7 o'clock. By 10 o'clock the line was formed, and the ships hove-to in it. At 10.45 the signal was made to fill [to go ahead], the van ships to carry the same sail as the Admiral,—topsails and foresails,—followed, just before noon, by the order to prepare to anchor, with springs on the cables. The French, who were steering south, on the port tack, while the British

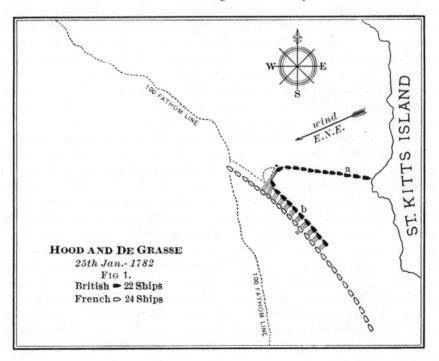

HOOD AND DE GRASSE
25th Jan.- 1782
Fig 1.
British ➤ 22 Ships
French ➲ 24 Ships

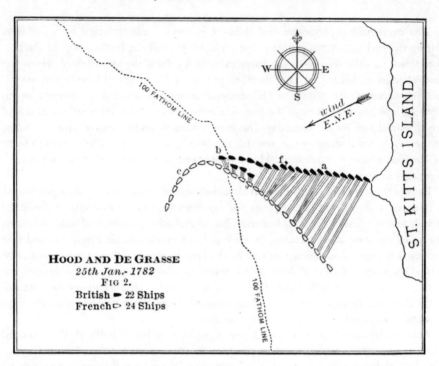

HOOD AND DE GRASSE
25th Jan.- 1782
FIG 2.
British ➤ 22 Ships
French ⊃ 24 Ships

were hove-to, went about as soon as the latter filled, and stood towards them in bow and quarter line.[5]

At noon the British fleet was running along close under the high land of Nevis; so close that the *Solebay*, 28, one of the frigates inshore of the line, grounded and was wrecked. No signals were needed, except to correct irregularities in the order, for the captains knew what they were to do. The French were approaching steadily, but inevitably dropping astern with reference to the point of the enemy's line for which they were heading. At 2 P.M. de Grasse's flagship, the *Ville de Paris*, fired several shot at the British rear, which alone she could reach, while his left wing was nearing the *Barfleur*, Hood's flagship, and the vessels astern of her, the centre of the column, which opened their fire at 2.30. Hood, trusting to his captains, disregarded this threat to the rear half of his force. Signals flew for the van to crowd sail and take its anchorage, and at 3.30 P.M. the leading ships began to anchor in line ahead (Fig. 1, a), covered as they did so by the broadsides of the rear and the rear centre (b). Upon the latter the French were now keeping up a smart fire. Between the *Canada* and her next astern, the *Prudent*, 64,—which was a dull sailer,—there was a considerable interval. Towards it the French admiral pressed, aiming to cut off the three rear vessels; but Cornwallis threw everything aback and closed down upon his consort,—a stirring deed in which he was imitated by the *Resolution* and *Bedford*, 74s, immediately ahead of him. De Grasse was thus foiled, but so narrowly, that an officer, looking from one of the ships which had anchored, asserted that for a moment he could perceive the *Ville de Paris's* jib inside the British line. As the rear of the latter pushed on to its place, it cleared the broadsides of the now anchored van and centre (Fig. 2, a), and these opened upon the enemy, a great part of whom were strung out behind the British column, without opponents as yet, but hastening up to get their share of the action. Hood's flagship (f), which anchored at 4.03, opened fire again at 4.40 P.M. Thus, as the *Canada* and her few companions, who bore the brunt of the day, were shortening sail and rounding-to (b), still under a hot cannonade, the batteries of their predecessors were ringing out their welcome, and at the same time covering their movements by giving the enemy much else to think about. The *Canada*, fetching up near the tail of the column and letting go in a hurry, ran out two cables on end, and found upon sounding that she had dropped her anchor in a hundred and fifty fathoms of water. The French column stood on, off soundings, though close to, firing as it passed, and then, wearing to the southward in succession, stood out of action on the port tack, (c), its ineffectual broadsides adding to the grandeur and excitement of the scene, and swelling the glory of Hood's successful daring, of which it is difficult to speak too highly. Lord Robert Manners, the captain of the *Resolution*, which was fifth ship from the British rear, writing a week later, passed upon this achievement a verdict, which posterity will confirm. "The taking possession of this road was well judged, well conducted, and well executed, though indeed the French had an opportunity—which they missed—of bringing our rear to a very severe account. The van and centre divisions brought to an anchor under the fire of the rear, which was engaged with the enemy's centre (Fig. 1); and then the centre, being at an anchor and properly placed, covered us while we anchored (Fig. 2), making, I think, the most masterly manœuvre I ever saw." Whether regard be had to the thoughtful preparation, the crafty management of the fleet antecedent to the final push, the calculated audacity of the latter, or the firm and sagacious tactical handling from the first moment to the last, Nelson himself never did a more brilliant deed than this of Hood's.[6] All firing ceased at 5.30.

Naturally, an order taken up under such conditions needed some rectifying before further battle. As the proper stationing of the fleet depended in great measure upon the position of the van ship, Hood had put a local pilot on board her; but when the action ceased, he found that she was not as close to the shore as he had intended. The rear, on the other hand, was naturally in the most disorder, owing to the circumstances attending its anchorage. Three ships from the rear were consequently directed to place themselves

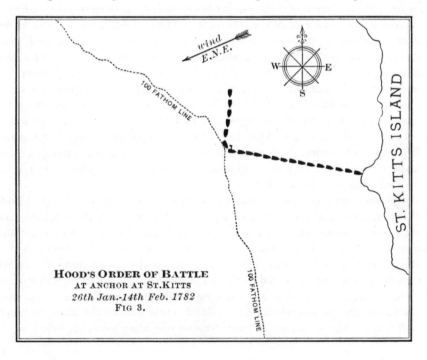

HOOD'S ORDER OF BATTLE
AT ANCHOR AT ST.KITTS
26th Jan.-14th Feb. 1782
FIG 3.

ahead of the van, closing the interval, while others shifted their berths, according to specific directions. The order as finally assumed (Fig. 3) was as follows. The van ship was anchored so close to the shore that it was impossible to pass within her, or, with the prevailing wind, even to reach her, because of a point and shoal just outside, covering her position. From her the line extended in a west-north-west direction to the fifteenth ship,—the *Barfleur*, 98, Hood's flagship,—when it turned to north, the last six ships being on a north and south line. These six, with their broadsides turned to the westward, prevented a column passing from south to north, the only way one could pass, from enfilading the main line with impunity. The latter covered with its guns the approach from the south. All the ships had springs on their cables, enabling them to turn their sides so as to cover a large arc of a circle with their batteries.

At daylight on the following morning, January 26th, the ships began changing their places, the French being then seven or eight miles distant in the south-south-east. At 7 A.M. they were seen to be approaching in line of battle, under a press of sail, heading for the British van. The *Canada*, which had begun at 5 A.M. to tackle her 200-odd fathoms of cable, was obliged to cut, whereby "we lost the small bower anchor and two cables with one 8-inch and one 9-inch hawsers, which were bent for springs." The ship had to work to windward to close with the fleet, and was therefore ordered by the Rear-Admiral to keep engaging under way, until 10.50, when a message was sent her to anchor in support of the rear. The action began between 8.30 and 9 A.M., the leading French ship heading for the British van, seemingly with the view of passing round and inside it. Against this attempt Hood's precautions probably were sufficient; but as the enemy's vessel approached, the wind headed her, so that she could only fetch the third ship. The latter, with the vessels ahead and astern, sprung their batteries upon her. "The crash occasioned by their destructive broadsides was so tremendous on board her that whole pieces of plank were seen flying from her off side, ere she could escape the cool concentrated fire of her determined adversaries."[7] She put her helm up, and ran along outside the British line, receiving the first fire of each successive ship. Her movement was imitated by her followers, some keeping off sooner, some later; but de Grasse in his flagship not only came close, but pointed his after yards to the wind,[8] to move the slower. As he ported his helm when leaving the *Barfleur*, this brought these sails aback, keeping him a still longer time before the British ships thrown to the rear. "In this he was supported by those ships which were astern, or immediately ahead of him. During this short but tremendous conflict in that part of the field of battle, nothing whatever could be seen of them for upwards of twenty minutes, save de Grasse's white flag at the main-topgallant masthead of the *Ville de Paris*, gracefully floating above the immense volumes of smoke that enveloped them, or the pennants of those ships which were occasionally perceptible, when an increase of breeze would waft away the smoke."[9]

Though most gallantly done, no such routine manœuvre as this could shake Hood's solidly assumed position. The attempt was repeated in the afternoon, but more feebly, and upon the centre and rear only. This also was ineffectual; and Hood was left in triumphant possession of the field. The losses in the several affairs of the two days had been: British, 72 killed, 244 wounded; French, 107 killed, 207 wounded. Thenceforth the French fleet continued cruising to leeward of the island, approaching almost daily, frequently threatening attack, and occasionally exchanging distant shots; but no serious encounter took place. Interest was centred on Brimstone Hill, where alone on the island the British flag still flew. De Grasse awaited its surrender, flattering himself that the British would be forced then to put to sea, and that his fleet, increased by successive arrivals to thirty-two of the line, would then find an opportunity to crush the man who had outwitted and out-manœuvred him on January 25th and 26th. In this hope he was deceived by his own inaptness and his adversary's readiness. Hood was unable to succour Brimstone Hill, for want of troops; the French having landed six thousand men, against which the British twenty-four hundred could effect nothing, either alone or in cooperation with the garrison, which was but twelve hundred strong. The work capitulated on the 13th of February. De Grasse, who had neglected to keep his ships provisioned, went next day to Nevis and anchored there to empty the storeships. That evening Hood called his captains on board, explained his intentions, had them set their watches by his, and at 11 p.m. the cables were cut one by one, lights being left on the buoys, and the fleet silently decamped, passing round the north end of St. Kitts, and so towards Antigua. When de Grasse opened his eyes next morning, the British were no longer to be seen. "Nothing could have been more fortunately executed," wrote Lord Robert Manners, "as not one accident happened from it. Taking the whole in one light, though not successful in the point we aimed at, nevertheless it was well conducted, and has given the enemy a pretty severe check; and if you give him half the credit the enemy does, Sir Samuel Hood will stand very high in the public estimation."

Hood's intention had been to return to Barbados; but on the 25th of February he was joined, to windward of Antigua, by Rodney, who had arrived from England a week earlier, bringing with him twelve ships of the line. The new Commander-in-Chief endeavoured to cut off de Grasse from Martinique, but the French fleet got in there on the 26th. Rodney consequently went to Santa Lucia, to refit Hood's ships, and to prepare for the coming campaign, in which it was understood that the conquest of Jamaica was to be the first object of the allies. An important condition to their success was the arrival of a great convoy, known to be on its way from Brest to repair the losses which Kempenfelt's raid and subsequent bad weather had inflicted in December. Hood suggested to Rodney to halve the fleet, which then numbered thirty-six of the line, letting one part cruise north of Dominica, between that island and Deseada, while the other guarded the southern approach, between Martinique and Santa Lucia. Rodney, however, was unwilling to do this, and adopted a half-measure,—Hood's division being stationed to windward of the north end of Martinique, reaching only as far north as the latitude of Dominica, while the center and rear were abreast of the centre and south of Martinique; all in mutual touch by intermediate vessels. It would seem—reading between the lines—that Hood tried to stretch his cruising ground northwards, in pursuance of his own ideas, but Rodney recalled him. The French convoy consequently passed north of Deseada, convoyed by two ships of the line, and on the 20th of March reached Martinique safely. De Grasse's force was thus raised to thirty-five of the line, including two 50-gun ships, as against the British thirty-six. At the end of the month Rodney returned to Santa Lucia, and there remained at anchor, vigilantly watching the French fleet in Fort Royal by means of a chain of frigates.

The problem now immediately confronting de Grasse—the first step towards the conquest of Jamaica—was extremely difficult. It was to convoy to Cap François the supply vessels essential to his enterprise, besides the merchant fleet bound for France; making in all one hundred and fifty unarmed ships to be protected by his thirty-five sail of the line, in face of the British thirty-six. The trade-wind being fair, he purposed to skirt the inner northern edge of the Caribbean Sea; by which means he would keep close to a succession of friendly ports, wherein the convoy might find refuge in case of need.

With this plan the French armament put to sea on the 8th of April, 1782. The fact being reported promptly to Rodney, by noon his whole fleet was clear of its anchorage and in pursuit. Then was evident the vital importance of Barrington's conquest of Santa Lucia; for, had the British been at Barbados, the most probable alternative, the French movement not only would have been longer unknown, but pursuit would have started from a hundred miles distant, instead of thirty. If the British had met this disadvantage by cruising before Martinique, they would have encountered the difficulty of keeping their ships supplied with water and other necessaries, which Santa Lucia afforded. In truth, without in any degree minimizing the faults of the loser, or the merits of the winner, in the exciting week that followed, the opening situation may be said to have represented on either side an accumulation of neglects or of successes, which at the moment of their occurrence may have seemed individually trivial; a conspicuous warning against the risk incurred by losing single points in the game of war. De Grasse was tremendously handicapped from the outset by the errors of his predecessors and of himself. That the British had Santa Lucia as their outpost was due not only to Barrington's diligence, but also to d'Estaing's slackness and professional timidity; and it may be questioned whether de Grasse himself had shown a proper understanding of strategic conditions, when he neglected that island in favour of Tobago and St. Kitts. Certainly Hood had feared for it greatly the year before. That the convoy was there to embarrass his movements, may not have been the fault of the French admiral; but it was greatly and entirely his fault that, of the thirty-six ships pursuing him, twenty-one represented a force that he might have crushed in detail a few weeks before,— not to mention the similar failure of April, 1781.[10]

Large bodies of ships commonly will move less rapidly than small. By 2.30 P.M. of the day of starting, Rodney's lookouts had sighted the French fleet; and before sundown it could be seen from the mastheads of the main body. At 6 next morning, April 9th, the

FRANCOIS-JOSEPH-PAUL,
COMTE DE GRASSE,
MARQUIS DE TILLY

enemy, both fleet and convoy, was visible from the deck of the *Barfleur*, the flagship of Hood's division, then in the British van. The French bore north-east, distant four to twelve miles, extending from abreast of the centre of Dominica northwards towards Guadeloupe. The British had gained much during the night, and their centre was now off Dominica to leeward of the enemy's rear, which was becalmed under the island. Some fourteen or fifteen of the French van, having opened out the channel between Dominica and Guadeloupe, felt a fresh trade-wind, from east by north, with which they steered north; and their number was gradually increased as individual ships, utilising the catspaws, stole clear of the high land of Dominica. Hood's division in like manner, first among the British, got the breeze, and, with eight ships, the commander of the van stood north in order of battle. To the north-west of him were two French vessels, separated from their consorts and threatened to be cut off. These stood boldly down and crossed the head of Hood's column; one passing so close to the leading ship, the *Alfred*, that the latter had to bear up to let her pass. Rodney had hoisted a signal to engage at 6.38 A.M., but had hauled it down almost immediately, and Hood would not fire without orders. These ships therefore rejoined their main body unharmed. At 8.30 the French hoisted their colours, and shortly afterwards the vessels which had cleared Dominica tacked and stood south, opposite to Hood.

De Grasse now had recognised that he could not escape action, if the convoy kept company. He therefore directed the two 50-gun ships, *Experiment* and *Sagittaire*, to accompany it into Guadeloupe, where it arrived safely that day (Fig. 4, dd) and he decided that the fleet should ply to windward through the channel between Dominica and Guadeloupe, nearly midway in which lies a group of small islands called Les Saintes,—a name at times given to the battle of April 12th. By this course he hoped not only to lead the enemy away from the convoy, but also to throw off pursuit through his superior speed, and so to accomplish his mission unharmed. The French ships, larger,

ADMIRAL LORD HOOD

deeper, and with better lines than their opponents, were naturally better sailers, and it may be inferred that even coppering had not entirely overcome this original disadvantage of the British.

At the very moment of beginning his new policy, however, a subtle temptation assailed de Grasse irresistibly, in the exposed position of Hood's column (h); and he met it, not by a frank and hearty acceptance of a great opportunity, but by a half-measure. Hood thoroughly crushed, the British fleet became hopelessly inferior to the French; Hood damaged, and it became somewhat inferior: possibly it would be deterred from further pursuit. De Grasse decided for this second course, and ordered part of his fleet to attack. This operation was carried out under the orders of the Marquis de Vaudreuil, the second in command. The ships engaged in it bore down from the windward, attacked Hood's rear ships, stood along northward (f) on the weather side of his column at long range, and, having passed ahead, tacked (t) in succession and formed again in the rear (f₂), whence they repeated the same manœuvre (Figs. 4 & 5). Thus a procession of fifteen ships kept passing by eight, describing a continuous curve of elliptical form. They were able to do this because Hood was condemned to a low speed, lest he should draw too far away from the British centre (a) and rear (c), still becalmed under Dominica (Fig. 5). The French, having choice of distance, kept at long gunshot, because they were deficient in carronades, of which the British had many. These guns, of short range but large calibre, were thus rendered useless. Could they have come into play, the French rigging and sails would have suffered severely. This first engagement (Fig. 4) lasted, by Hood's log, from 9.48 to 10.25 A.M. It was resumed in stronger force (Fig. 5) at 14 minutes past noon, and continued till 1.45 P.M., when firing ceased for that day; Rodney hauling down the signal for battle at 2. Between the two affairs, which were identical in general character. Hood's column was reinforced, and great part of the British centre also got into action with some of the French main body, though at long range only. "Except the two rear ships," wrote Rodney to Hood that night, "the others fired at such a distance that I returned none."

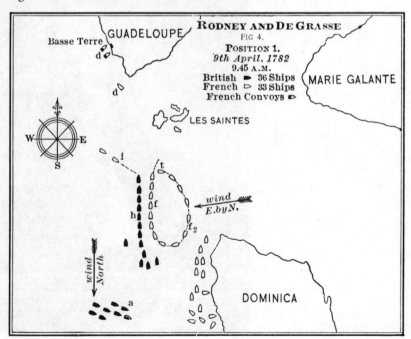

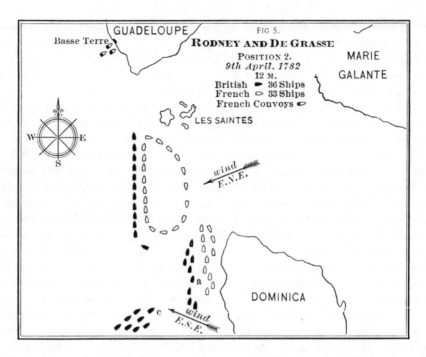

The injuries to the British ships engaged were not such as to compel them to leave the fleet. The *Royal Oak* lost her main topmast, and that of the *Warrior* fell two days later, not improbably from wounds; but in these was nothing that the ready hands of seamen could not repair so as to continue the chase. Rodney, therefore, contented himself with reversing the order of sailing, putting Hood in the rear, whereby he was able to refit, and yet follow fast enough not to be out of supporting distance. This circumstance caused Hood's division to be in the rear in the battle of the 12th. One of the French ships, the *Caton*, 64, had been so injured that de Grasse detached her into Guadeloupe. It must be remembered that a crippled ship in a chased fleet not only embarrasses movement, but may compromise the whole body, if the latter delay to protect it; whereas the chaser keeps between his lame birds and the enemy.

During the night of the 9th the British lay-to for repairs. The next morning they resumed the pursuit, turning to windward after the enemy, but upon the whole losing throughout the 10th and the 11th. At daylight of the 10th the French, by the logs of Hood and Cornwallis, were "from four to five leagues distant," "just in sight from the deck." During that night, however, the *Zélé*, 74, had collided with the *Jason*, 64; and the latter was injured so far as to be compelled to follow the *Caton* into Guadeloupe. At sunset of that day Rodney signalled a general chase to windward, the effect of which was to enable each ship to do her best according to her captain's judgment during the dark hours. Nevertheless, on the morning of the 11th the French seem again to have gained, for Hood, who, it will be remembered, was now in the rear, notes that at 10 A.M. twenty-two French sail (not all the fleet) could be counted *from the masthead*; Cornwallis, further to windward, could count thirty-three. Troude, a French authority, says that at that time nearly all the French had doubled The Saintes, that is, had got to windward of them, and it looked as though de Grasse might succeed in throwing off his pursuer. Unluckily, two ships, the *Magnanime*, 74, and the *Zélé*, 74, the latter of which had lost her main topmast, were several miles to leeward of the French main body. It was necessary to delay, or to drop those vessels. Again, trivial circumstances conspired to further a great disaster, and de Grasse bore down to cover the crippled ships; so losing much of his hard-won ground, and entailing a further misfortune that night. Rodney hung doggedly on, relying on the chapter of accidents, as one who knows that all things come to him who endures. To be sure, there was not much else he could do; yet he deserves credit for unremitting industry and pluck. During the afternoon, the signals noted in the British logs—to call in all cruisers and for the fleet to close—attest mutely the movement of de Grasse in bearing down,—coming nearer.

During the night, at 2 A.M. of April 12th, the *Zélé* and de Grasse's flagship, the *Ville de Paris*, 110, crossing on opposite tacks, came into collision. The former lost both foremast and bowsprit. It has been stated by John Paul Jones, who by permission of Congress embarked a few months later on board the French fleet as a volunteer, and doubtless thus heard many personal narratives, that this accident was due to the deficiency of watch-officers in the French navy; the deck of the *Zélé* being in charge of a young ensign, instead of an experienced lieutenant. It was necessary to rid the fleet of the *Zélé* at once, or an action could not be avoided; so a frigate was summoned to tow her, and the two were left to make their way to Guadeloupe, while the others resumed the beat to windward. At 5 A.M. she and the frigate were again under way, steering for Guadeloupe, to the north-west, making from five to six miles (Fig. 6, a); but in the interval they had been nearly motionless, and consequently when day broke at 5.30 they were only two leagues from the *Barfleur*, Hood's flagship, which, still in the British rear, was then standing south on the port tack. The body of the French (Fig. 6), was at about the same distance as on the previous evening,—ten to fifteen miles,—but the *Ville de Paris* (c) not more than eight. Just before 6 A.M. Rodney signalled Hood, who was nearest, to chase the *Zélé*; and four of the rearmost ships of the line were detached for that purpose (b). De Grasse, seeing this, signalled his vessels at 6 A.M. to close the flagship, making all sail; and he himself bore down to the westward (cc′), on the port tack, but running free, to frighten away Rodney's chasers. The British Admiral kept them out until 7 o'clock, by which time de Grasse was fairly committed to his false step. All cruisers were then called in, and the line was closed to one cable.[11] Within an hour were heard the opening guns of the great battle, since known by the names of the 12th of April, or of The Saintes, and, in the French navy, of Dominica. The successive losses of the *Caton, Jason*, and *Zélé*, with the previous detachment of the two 50-gun ships with the convoy, had reduced the French numbers from thirty-five to thirty effective vessels. The thirty-six British remained undiminished.

The British appear to have been standing to the south on the port tack at daylight; but, soon after sending out the chasers, Rodney had ordered the line of bearing (from ship to ship) to be north-north-east to south-south-west, evidently in preparation for a close-hauled line of battle on the starboard tack, heading northerly to an east wind. Somewhat unusually, the wind that morning held at south-east for some time, enabling the British to lie up as high as east-north-east on the starboard tack (Fig. 6, d), on which they were when the battle joined; and this circumstance, being very favourable for gaining to windward,—to the eastward,—doubtless led to the annulling of the signal for the line of bearing, half an hour after it was made, and the substitution for it of the line of battle ahead at one cable. It is to be inferred that Rodney's first purpose was to tack together, thus restoring Hood to the van, his natural station; but the accident of the wind holding to the southward placed the actual van—regularly the rear—most to windward, and rendered it expedient to tack in succession, instead of all together, preserving to the full the opportunity which chance

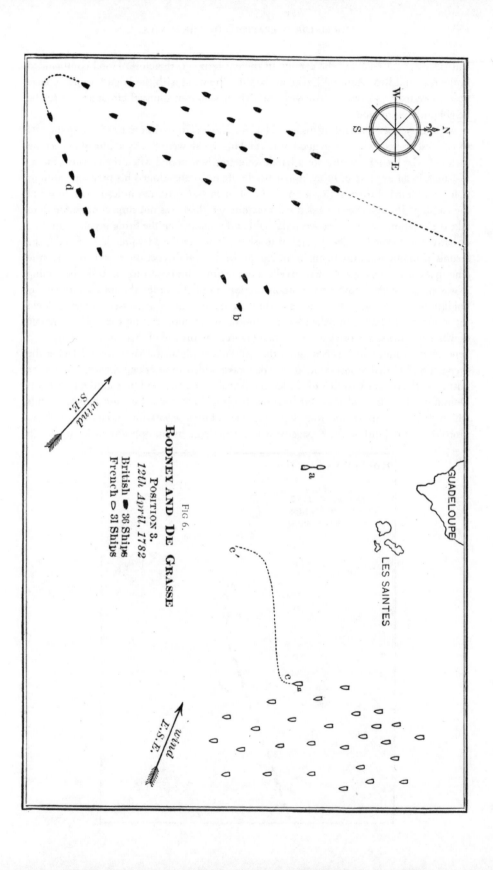

Fig 6.

RODNEY AND DE GRASSE

POSITION 3.

12th April, 1782

British ● 36 Ships
French ○ 31 Ships

GUADELOUPE

LES SAINTES

wind S.E.

wind E.S.E.

had extended for reaching the enemy. In the engagement, therefore, Hood commanded in the rear, and Rear-Admiral Drake in the van. The wind with the French seems to have been more to the eastward than with the British,—not an unusual circumstance in the neighbourhood of land.

As Rodney, notwithstanding his haste, had formed line from time to time during the past three days, his fleet was now in good order, and his signals were chiefly confined to keeping it closed. The French, on the other hand, were greatly scattered when their Commander-in-Chief, in an impulse of hasty, unbalanced judgment, abandoned his previous cautious policy and hurried them into action. Some of them were over ten miles to windward of the flagship. Though they crowded sail to rejoin her, there was not time enough for all to take their stations properly, between daylight and 8 A.M., when the firing began. "Our line of battle was formed under the fire of musketry,"[12] wrote the Marquis de Vaudreuil, the second in command, who, being in the rear of the fleet on this occasion, and consequently among the last to be engaged, had excellent opportunity for observation. At the beginning it was in de Grasse's power to postpone action, until the order should be formed, by holding his wind under short canvas; while the mere sight of his vessels hurrying down for action would have compelled Rodney to call in the ships chasing the *Zélé*, the rescue of which was the sole motive of the French manœuvre. Instead of this, the French flagship kept off the wind; which precipitated the collision, while at the same time delaying the preparations needed to sustain it. To this de Grasse added another fault by forming on the port tack, the contrary to that on which the British were, and standing southerly towards Dominica. The effect of this was to bring his ships into the calms and baffling winds which cling to the shore-line, thus depriving them of their power of manœuvre. His object probably was to confine the engagement to a mere pass-by on opposite tacks, by which

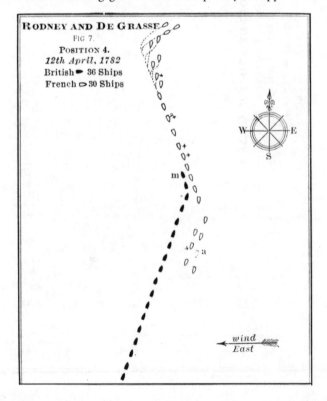

RODNEY AND DE GRASSE
FIG 7.
POSITION 4.
12th April, 1782
British ➤ 36 Ships
French ➲ 30 Ships

W———E

S

wind
East

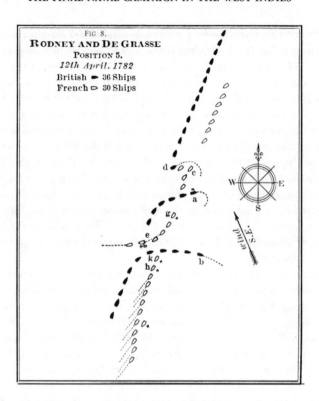

FIG 8.
RODNEY AND DE GRASSE
POSITION 5.
12th April, 1782
British — 36 Ships
French ⊃ 30 Ships

in all previous instances the French had thwarted the decisive action that Rodney sought. Nevertheless, the blunder was evident at once to French eyes. "What evil genius has inspired the admiral?" exclaimed du Pavillon, Vaudreuil's flag-captain, who was esteemed one of the best tacticians in France, and who fell in the battle.

As the two lines drew near to one another, standing, the French south, the British east-north-east, the wind shifted back to the eastward, allowing the French to head higher, to south-south-east, and knocking the British off to north-north-east (Fig. 7). The head of the French column thus passed out of gunshot, across the bows of Rodney's leading vessel, the *Marlborough* (m), which came within range when abreast the eighth ship. The first shots were fired by the *Brave*, 74, ninth in the French line, at 8 A.M. The British captain then put his helm up and ran slowly along, north-north-west, under the lee of the French, towards their rear. The rest of the British fleet followed in his wake. The battle thus assumed the form of passing in opposite directions on parallel lines; except that the French ships, as they successively cleared the point where the British column struck their line, would draw out of fire, their course diverging thenceforth from that of the British approach. The effect of this would be that the British rear, when it reached that point, would be fresh, having undergone no fire, and with that advantage would encounter the French rear, which had received already the fire of the British van and centre. To obviate this, by bringing his own van into action, de Grasse signalled the van ships to lead south-south-west, parallel with the British north-north-east (a). The engagement thus became general all along the lines; but it is probable that the French van was never well formed. Its commander, at all events, reached his post later than the commander of the rear did his.[13]

At five minutes past eight, Rodney made a general signal for close action, followed immediately by another for the leading ships to head one point to starboard—towards the enemy—which indicates that he was not satisfied with the distance first taken by the *Marlborough.* The *Formidable,* his flagship, eighteenth in the column, began to fire at 8.23;[14] but the *Barfleur,* Hood's flagship, which was thirty-first, not till 9.25. This difference in time is to be accounted for chiefly by the light airs near Dominica, contrasted with the fresh trades in the open channel to the northward, which the leading British vessels felt before their rear. De Grasse now, too late, had realised the disastrous effect which this would have upon his fleet. If he escaped all else, his ships, baffled by calms and catspaws while the British had a breeze, must lose the weather-gage, and with it the hope of evading pursuit, hitherto his chief preoccupation. Twice he signalled to wear,—first, all together, then in succession,—but, although the signals were seen, they could not be obeyed with the enemy close under the lee. "The French fleet," comments Chevalier justly, "had freedom of movement no longer. A fleet cannot wear with an enemy's fleet within musket-range to leeward."

The movement therefore continued as described, the opposing ships slowly "sliding by" each other until about 9.15, when the wind suddenly shifted back to south-east again. The necessity of keeping the sails full forced the bows of each French vessel towards the enemy (Fig. 8), destroying the order in column, and throwing the fleet into *échelon,* or, as the phrase then was, into bow and quarter line.[15] The British, on the contrary, were free either to hold their course or to head towards the enemy. Rodney's flagship (Fig. 8, a) luffed, and led through the French line just astern of the *Glorieux,* 74 (g), which was the nineteenth in their order. She was followed by five ships; and her next ahead also, the *Duke* (d), seeing her chief's movement, imitated it, breaking through the line astern of the twenty-third French. The *Glorieux,* on the starboard hand of Rodney's little column, received its successive broadsides. Her main and mizzen masts went overboard at 9.28, when the *Canada,* third astern of the *Formidable,* had just passed her; and a few moments later her foremast and bowsprit fell. At 9.33 the *Canada* was to windward of the French line. The flagship *Formidable* was using both broadsides as she broke through the enemy's order. On her port hand, between her and the *Duke,* were four French ships huddled together (c), one of which had paid off the wrong way; that is, after the shift of wind took her aback, her sails had filled on the opposite tack from that of the rest of her fleet.[16] These four, receiving the repeated broadsides, at close quarters, of the *Formidable, Duke,* and *Namur,* and having undergone besides the fire of the British van, were very severely mauled. While these things were happening, the *Bedford,* the sixth astern of the *Formidable,* perhaps unable to see her next ahead in the smoke, had luffed independently (b), and was followed by the twelve rearmost British ships, whom she led through the French order astern of the Cesar, 74 (k), twelfth from the van. This ship and her next ahead, the *Hector,* 74 (h), suffered as did the *Glorieux.* The *Barfleur,* which was in the centre of this column of thirteen, opened fire at 9.25. At 10.45 she "ceased firing, having passed the enemy's van ships;" that is, she was well on the weather side of the French fleet. Some of the rearmost of Hood's division, however, were still engaged at noon; but probably all were then to windward of the enemy.

The British ships ahead of the *Duke,* the van and part of the centre, in all sixteen sail, had continued to stand to the northward. At the time Rodney broke the line, several of them must have passed beyond the French rear, and out of action. One, the *America,* the twelfth from the van, wore without signals, to pursue the enemy, and her example was followed

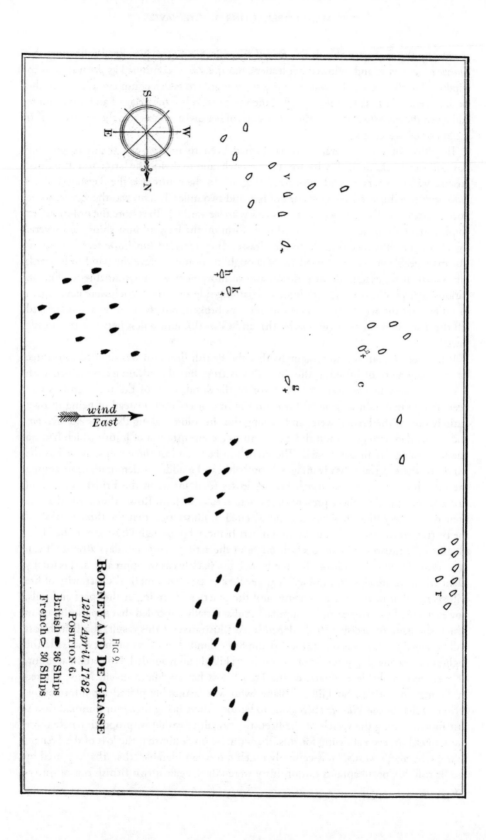

FIG 9.

RODNEY AND DE GRASSE

12th April, 1782

POSITION 6.

British ■ 36 Ships

French ⊘ 30 Ships

at once by the ship next ahead, the *Russell*, Captain Saumarez. No signal following, the *America* again wore and followed her leaders, but the *Russell* continued as she was, now to windward of the French; by which course she was able to take a conspicuous share in the closing scenes. At 11.33 Rodney signalled the van to tack, but the delay of an hour or more had given the *Russell* a start over the other ships of her division "towards the enemy" which could not be overcome.

The effect of these several occurrences had been to transfer the weather-gage, the position for attack, to the British from the French, and to divide the latter also into three groups, widely separated and disordered (Fig. 9). In the centre was the flagship *Ville de Paris* with five ships (c). To windward of her, and two miles distant, was the van, of some dozen vessels (v). The rear was four miles away to leeward (r). To restore the order, and to connect the fleet again, it was decided to re-form on the leewardmost ships; and several signals to this effect were made by de Grasse. They received but imperfect execution. The manageable vessels succeeded easily enough in running before the wind to leeward, but, when there, exactitude of position and of movement was unattainable to ships in various degrees of disability, with light and baffling side airs. The French were never again in order after the wind shifted and the line was broken; but the movement to leeward left the dismasted *Glorieux* (g), *Hector* (h), and *César* (k), motionless between the hostile lines.

It has been remarked, disparagingly, that the British fleet also was divided into three by the manœuvre of breaking the line. This is true; but the advantage remained with it incontestably, in two respects. By favor of the wind, each of the three groups had been able to maintain its general formation in line or column, instead of being thrown entirely out, as the French were; and passing thus in column along the *Glorieux, Hector,* and *César,* they wrought upon these three ships a concentration of injury which had no parallel among the British vessels. The French in fact had lost three ships, as well as the wind. To these certain disadvantages is probably to be added a demoralisation among the French crews, from the much heavier losses resultant upon the British practice of firing at the hull. An officer present in the action told Sir John Ross[17] afterwards that the French fired very high throughout; and he cited in illustration that the three trucks[18] of the British *Princesa* were shot away. Sir Gilbert Blane, who, though Physician to the Fleet, obtained permission to be on deck throughout the action, wrote ten days after it, "I can aver from my own observation that the French fire slackens as we approach, and is totally silent when we are close alongside." It is needless to say that a marked superiority of fire will silence that of the bravest enemy; and the practice of aiming at the spars and sails, however suited for frustrating an approach, substantially conceded that superiority upon which the issue of decisive battle depends. As illustrative of this result, the British loss will be stated here. It was but 243 killed and 816 wounded in a fleet of thirty-six sail. The highest in any one ship was that of the *Duke,* 73 killed and wounded. No certain account, or even very probable estimate, of the French loss has ever been given. None is cited by French authorities. Sir Gilbert Blane, who was favourably placed for information, reckoned that of the *Ville de Paris* alone to be 300. There being fifty-four hundred troops distributed among the vessels of the fleet, the casualties would be proportionately more numerous; but, even allowing for this, there can be no doubt that the loss of the French, to use Chevalier's words, "was certainly much more considerable" than that reported by the British. Six post-captains out of thirty were killed, against two British out of thirty-six.

Rodney did not make adequate use of the great opportunity, which accident rather than design had given him at noon of April 12th. He did allow a certain liberty of manœuvre, by discontinuing the order for the line of battle; but the signal for close action, hoisted at 1 P.M., was hauled down a half-hour later. Hood, who realised the conditions plainly visible, as well as the reasonable inferences there-from, wished the order given for a general chase, which would have applied the spur of emulation to every captain present, without surrendering the hold that particular signals afford upon indiscreet movements. He bitterly censured the Admiral's failure to issue this command. Had it been done, he said:—

> I am very confident we should have had twenty sail of the enemy's ships before dark. Instead of that, he pursued only under his topsails (sometimes his foresail was set and at others his mizzen topsail aback) the greatest part of the afternoon, though the *flying* enemy had all the sail set their very shattered state would allow.[19]

To make signal for a general chase was beyond the competence of a junior admiral; but Hood did what he could, by repeated signals to individual ships of his own division to make more sail, by setting all he could on the *Barfleur*, and by getting out his boats to tow her head round. Sir Gilbert Blane unintentionally gives a similar impression of laxity.

> After cutting the French line, the action during the rest of the day was partial and desultory, the enemy never being able to form, and several of the [our] ships being obliged to lie by and repair their damages. As the signal for the line was now hauled down, every ship annoyed the enemy as their respective commanders judged best.[20]

For this indolent abandonment of the captains to their own devices, the correctest remedy was, as Hood indicated, the order for a general chase, supplemented by a watchful supervision, which should check the over-rash and stimulate the over-cautious. If Hood's account of the sail carried by Rodney be correct, the Commander-in-Chief did not even set the best example. In this languid pursuit, the three crippled French ships were overhauled, and of course had to strike; and a fourth, the *Ardent*, 64, was taken, owing to her indifferent sailing. Towards sunset the flagship *Ville de Paris*, 110,[21] the finest ship of war afloat, having been valiantly defended against a host of enemies throughout great part of the afternoon, and having expended all her ammunition, hauled down her colours. The two British vessels then immediately engaged with her were the *Russell* and the *Barfleur*, Hood's flagship, to the latter of which she formally surrendered; the exact moment, noted in Hood's journal, being 6.29 P.M.

At 6.45 Rodney made the signal for the fleet to bring-to (form line and stop) on the port tack, and he remained lying-to during the night, while the French continued to retreat under the orders of the Marquis de Vaudreuil, who by de Grasse's capture had become commander-in-chief. For this easy-going deliberation also Hood had strong words of condemnation.

> Why he should bring the fleet to because the *Ville de Paris* was taken, I cannot reconcile. He did not pursue under easy sail, so as never to have lost sight of the enemy in the night, which would clearly and most undoubtedly have enabled him to have taken almost every ship the next day. . . . Had I had the honour

of commanding his Majesty's noble fleet on the 12th, I may, without much imputation of vanity, say the flag of England should now have graced the sterns of upwards of twenty sail of the enemy's ships of the line.[22]

Such criticisms by those not responsible are to be received generally with caution; but Hood was, in thought and in deed, a man so much above the common that these cannot be dismissed lightly. His opinion is known to have been shared by Sir Charles Douglas, Rodney's Captain of the Fleet;[23] and their conclusion is supported by the inferences to be drawn from Rodney's own assumptions as to the condition of the French, contrasted with the known facts. The enemy, he wrote, in assigning his reasons for not pursuing, "went off in a *close connected body*, and might have defeated, by rotation, the ships that had come up with them." "The enemy *who went off in a body of twenty-six ships of the line*, might, by ordering two or three of their best sailing ships or frigates to have shown lights at times, and by changing their course, have induced the British fleet to have followed them, while the main of their fleet, by hiding their lights, might have hauled their wind, and have been far to windward by daylight, and intercepted the captured ships, and the most crippled ships of the English;"[24] and he adds that the Windward Islands even might have been endangered. That such action was in a remote degree possible to a well-conditioned fleet may be guardedly conceded; but it was wildly improbable to a fleet staggering under such a blow as the day had seen, which had changed its commander just as dark came on, and was widely scattered and disordered up to the moment when signals by flags became invisible.

The facts, however, were utterly at variance with these ingenious suppositions. Instead of being connected, as Rodney represents, de Vaudreuil had with him next morning but ten ships; and no others during the whole of the 13th. He made sail for Cap François, and was joined on the way by five more, so that at no time were there upwards of fifteen[25] French ships of the line together, prior to his arrival at that port on April 25th. He there found four others of the fleet. The tale of twenty-five survivors, from the thirty engaged on April 12th, was completed by six which had gone to Curacao, and which did not rejoin until May. So much for the close connected body of the French. It is clear, therefore, that Rodney's reasons illustrate the frame of mind against which Napoleon used to caution his generals as "making to themselves a picture" of possibilities; and that his conclusion at best was based upon the ruinous idea, which a vivid imagination or slothful temper is prone to present to itself, that war may be made decisive without running risks. That Jamaica even was saved was not due to this fine, but indecisive battle, but to the hesitation of the allies. When de Vaudreuil reached Cap François, he found there the French convoy safely arrived from Guadeloupe, and also a body of fifteen Spanish ships of the line. The troops available for the descent upon Jamaica were from fifteen to twenty thousand. Well might Hood write: "Had Sir George Rodney's judgment, after the enemy had been so totally put to flight, borne any proportion to the high courage, zeal and exertion, so very manifestly shown by every captain, all difficulty would now have been at an end. We might have done just as we pleased, instead of being at this hour upon the defensive."[26]

The allies, however, though superior in numbers, did not venture to assume the offensive. After the battle, Rodney remained near Guadeloupe until the 17th of April, refitting, and searching the neighbouring islands, in case the French fleet might have entered some one of them. For most of this time the British were becalmed, but Hood remarks that there had been wind enough to get twenty leagues to the westward; and there, more wind probably would have been found. On the 17th Hood was detached in pursuit with ten sail of the line; and a day or two later Rodney himself started for Jamaica. Left to his own discretion, Hood pushed for the Mona Passage, between Puerto Rico and Santo Domingo, carrying studding-sails below and aloft in his haste. At daybreak of the 19th he sighted the west end of Puerto Rico; and soon afterwards a small French squadron was seen. A general chase resulted in the capture of the *Jason* and *Caton*, sixty-fours, which had parted from their, fleet before the battle and were on their way to Cap François. A frigate, the *Aimable*, 32, and a sloop, the *Cérès*, 18, also were taken. In reporting this affair to Rodney, Hood got a thrust into his superior. "It is a very mortifying circumstance to relate to you, Sir, that the French fleet which you put to flight on the 12th went through the Mona Channel on the 18th, only the day before I was in it."[27] A further proof of the utility of pursuit, here hinted at, is to be found in the fact that Rodney, starting six days later than de Vaudreuil, reached Jamaica, April 28th, only three days after the French got into Cap François. He had therefore gained three days in a fortnight's run. What might not have been done by an untiring chase! But a remark recorded by Hood summed up the frame of mind which dominated Rodney: "I lamented to Sir George on the 13th that the signal for a general chase was not made when that for the line was hauled down and that he did not continue to pursue so as to keep sight of the enemy all night, to which he only answered, 'Come, we have done very handsomely as it is.'"[28]

Rodney stayed at Jamaica until the 10th of July, when Admiral Hugh Pigot arrived from England to supersede him. This change was consequent upon the fall of Lord North's ministry, in March, 1782, and had been decided before the news of the victory could reach England. Admiral Keppel now became the head of the Admiralty. Rodney sailed for home from Port Royal on the 22d of July; and with his departure the war in the West Indies and North America may be said to have ended. Pigot started almost immediately for New York, and remained in North American waters until the end of October, when he returned to Barbados, first having detached Hood with thirteen ships of the line from the main fleet, to cruise off Cap François. It is of interest to note that at this time Hood took with him from New York the frigate *Albemarle*, 28, then commanded by Nelson, who had been serving on the North American station. These various movements were dictated by those of the enemy, either actually made or supposed to be in contemplation; for it was an inevitable part of the ill-effects of Rodney's most imperfect success, that the British fleet was thenceforth on the defensive purely, with all the perplexities of him who waits upon the initiative of an opponent. Nothing came of them all, however, for the war now was but lingering in its death stupor. The defeat of de Grasse, partial though it was; the abandonment of the enterprise upon Jamaica; the failure of the attack upon Gibraltar; and the success of Howe in re-victualling that fortress,—these had taken all heart out of the French and Spaniards; while the numerical superiority of the allies, inefficiently though it had been used heretofore, weighed heavily upon the imagination of the British Government, which now had abandoned all hope of subduing its American Colonies. Upon the conclusion of peace, in 1783, Pigot and Hood returned to England, leaving the Leeward Islands' Station under the command of Rear-Admiral Sir Richard Hughes, an officer remembered by history only through Nelson's refusing to obey his orders not to enforce the Navigation Acts, in 1785.

1. James Saumarez, Lord de Saumarez, G.C.B. Born, 1757. Commander, 1781. Captain, 1782. Captain of *Russell* in Rodney's action, 1782. Knighted for capture of frigate *Réunion*, 1793. Captain of *Orion* in Bridport's action, at St. Vincent, and at the Nile (when he was second in command). Rear-Admiral and Baronet, 1801. Defeated French and Spaniards off Cadiz, July 12th, 1801. Vice-Admiral, 1805. Vice-Admiral of England and a peer, 1831. Died, 1836.

2. *Ante*, p. 127.

3. Probably *Prudent*, 64. There was no *President* in the fleet.

4. The times and general movements are put together from Hood's Journal and the Log of the *Canada*, published by the Navy Records Society. "Letters of Lord Hood," pp. 64, 86.

5. When ships were in order of battle, or column, close to the wind, if they all tacked at the same time they would still be ranged on the same line but steering at an angle to it, on the opposite tack. This formation was called bow and quarter line, because each vessel had a comrade off its bow—to one side and ahead–and one off its quarter—to one side but astern. The advantage of this, if heading towards the enemy, was that by tacking again together they would be at once again in column, or line ahead, the customary order of battle.

6. Illustrations of other phases of this battle can be found in Mahan's "Influence of Sea Power upon History," pp. 470, 472.

7. White, "Naval Researches."

8. Sharp up by the starboard braces, the wind being on the starboard quarter. This emptied the aftersails of wind, neutralizing their effect, and, by causing the ship to move more slowly, kept her longer abreast an anchored opponent.

9. White, "Naval Researches."

10. *Ante*, p. 114.

11. Seven hundred and twenty feet. For ships of the line of that day this would make the interval between each two about four ships' length. At five knots speed this distance would be covered in something over a minute.

12. Probably not over one or two hundred yards from the enemy.

13. The position, in the French order, of the ships taken in the battle, is shown by the crosses in Positions 4, 5, 6.

14. *Canada's* log, 8.15; reduced to Hood's times, which are generally followed.

15. *Ante*, note 5.

16. This mishap occurred to three French vessels.

17. Ross, "Life of Saumarez," i. 71.

18. Circular pieces of wood which cap the top of the masts.

19. Letters of Lord Hood, p. 103. Navy Records Society.

20. Mundy, "Life of Rodney," ii. 234.

21. She is thus rated in the British Navy Lists published between the time of her capture and the receipt of news of her loss; but she seems to have carried 120 guns.

22. Letters of Lord Hood, pp. 103, 104.

23. See letter of Sir Howard Douglas, son to Sir Charles; "United Service Journal," 1834, Part II, p. 97.

24. Author's italics; Mundy, "Life of Rodney," ii. 248.

25. Troude. Chevalier says sixteen, differing with Troude as to the whereabouts of the *Brave*.

26. Letters of Lord Hood, p. 136.

27. *Ibid.*, p. 134.

28. *Ibid.*, p. 104.

XIII

THE FINAL RELIEF OF GIBRALTAR

T HE FALL OF LORD NORTH's Ministry, besides occasioning the recall of Rodney, drew Lord Howe out of his long retirement, to command the Channel Fleet. He hoisted his flag on the 20th of April, 1782, on board the *Victory*, 100. Owing to the various directions in which the efforts of Great Britain had to be made, either to defend her own interests or to crush the movements of the many enemies now combined against her, the operations of the Channel fleet were for some months carried on by detached squadrons,—in the North Sea, in the Bay of Biscay, and at the entrance of the Channel; Howe having under him several distinguished subordinates, at the head of whom, in professional reputation, were Vice-Admiral Barrington, the captor of Santa Lucia, and Rear-Admiral Kempenfelt. In the North Sea, the Dutch were kept in their ports; and a convoy of near 400 merchant ships from the Baltic reached England unmolested. In the Bay of Biscay, Barrington, having with him twelve of the line, discovered and chased a convoy laden with stores for the fleet in the East Indies. One of the ships of the line accompanying it, the *Pégase*, 74, surrendered, after a night action of three hours with the *Foudroyant*, 80, Captain John Jervis, afterwards Earl St. Vincent. Of nineteen transports, thirteen, one of which, the *Actionnaire*, was a 64-gun ship armed *en flûte*,[1] were taken; a weighty blow to the great Suffren, whose chief difficulty in India was inadequate material of war, and especially of spars, of which the *Actionnaire* carried an outfit for four ships of the line. After Barrington's return, Kempenfelt made a similar but uneventful cruise of a month in the Bay.

Howe himself went first to the North Sea in the month of May. Having there held the Dutch in check during a critical moment, he was directed next to go to the entrance of the Channel, leaving only a division in the Downs. Information had been received that an allied fleet of thirty-two ships of the line, five only of which were French, had sailed from Cadiz early in June, to cruise between Ushant and Scilly. It was expected that they would be joined there by a reinforcement from Brest, and by the Dutch squadron in the Texel, making a total of about fifty of the line, under the command of the Spanish Admiral, Don Luis de Cordova. The Dutch did not appear, owing probably to Howe's demonstration before their ports; but eight ships from Brest raised the allied fleet to forty. To oppose these Howe sailed on the 2d of July with twenty-two sail, of which eight were three-deckers. Before his return, in the 7th of August, he was joined by eight others; mostly, however, sixty-fours. With this inferiority of numbers the British Admiral could expect only to act on the defensive, unless some specially favourable opportunity should offer. The matter of most immediate concern was the arrival of the Jamaica convoy, then daily expected; with which, it may be mentioned, de Grasse also was returning to England, a prisoner of war on board the *Sandwich*.

On its voyage north, the allied fleet captured on June 25th eighteen ships of a British convoy bound for Canada. A few days later it was fixed in the chops of the Channel, covering the ground from Ushant to Scilly. On the evening of July 7th it was sighted off Scilly by Howe, who then had with him twenty-five sail. The allies prepared for action; but the British Admiral, possessing a thorough knowledge of the neighbouring coasts, either in his own person or in some of his officers, led the fleet by night to the westward through the passage between Scilly and Land's End. On the following morning he was no more to be seen, and the enemy, ignorant of the manner of his evasion, was thrown wholly off his track.[2] Howe met the convoy; and a strong gale of wind afterwards forcing the allies to the southward, both it and the fleet slipped by successfully, and reached England.

Howe was ordered now to prepare to throw reinforcements and supplies into Gibraltar, which had not received relief since Darby's visit, in April, 1781. For this urgent and critical service it was determined to concentrate the whole Channel Fleet at Spithead, where also the transports and supply-ships were directed to rendezvous. It was while thus assembling for the relief of Gibraltar that there occurred the celebrated incident of the *Royal George*, a 100-gun ship, while being heeled for under-water repairs, oversetting and sinking at her anchors, carrying down with her Rear-Admiral Kempenfelt and about nine hundred souls, including many women and children. This was on the 29th of August, 1782. On the 11th of September the expedition started, one hundred and eighty-three sail in all; thirty-four being ships of the line, with a dozen smaller cruisers, the rest unarmed vessels. Of the latter, thirty-one were destined for Gibraltar, the remainder being trading ships for different parts of the world. With so extensive a charge, the danger to which had been emphasised by numerous captures from convoys during the war, Howe's progress was slow. It is told that shortly before reaching Cape Finisterre, but after a violent gale of wind, the full tally of one hundred eighty-three sail was counted. After passing Finisterre, the several "trades" probably parted from the grand fleet.

On the 8th of October, off Cape St. Vincent, a frigate was sent ahead for information. It was known that a great combined force of ships of war lay in Algeciras Bay,—opposite Gibraltar,—and that an attack upon the works was in contemplation; but much might have happened meantime. Much, in fact, had happened. A violent gale of wind on the 10th of September had driven some of the allied fleet from their moorings, one vessel, the *San Miguel,* 72, being forced under the batteries of Gibraltar, where she had to surrender; but there still remained the formidable number of forty-eight ships of the line, anchored only four miles from the point which the relief ships must reach. This was the problem which Howe had to solve. More important still, though of less bearing upon his mission, was the cheering news brought by the frigate, when she rejoined on October 10th, that the long-intended attack had been made on the 13th of September, and had been repelled gloriously and decisively. The heavily protected Spanish floating batteries, from which success had been expected confidently, one and all had been set on fire and destroyed. If Howe could introduce his succours, the fortress was saved.

The admiral at once summoned his subordinate officers, gave them full and particular instructions for the momentous undertaking, and issued at the same time, to the masters of the supply-ships, precise information as to local conditions of wind and currents at Gibraltar, to enable them more surely to reach their anchorage. On the 11th of October, being now close to its destination, the fleet bore up for the Straits, which it entered at noon with a fair westerly wind. The convoy went first,—sailing before the wind it was thus to leeward of the fleet, in a position to be defended,—and the ships of war followed at some distance in three divisions, one of which was led by Howe himself. At 6 P.M. the supply-ships were off the mouth of the Bay, with a wind fair for the mole; but, through neglect of the instructions given, all but four missed the entrance, and were swept to the eastward of the Rock, whither the fleet of course had to follow them.

On the 13th the allied fleets came out, being induced to quit their commanding position at Algeciras by fears for two of their number, which shortly before had been driven to the eastward. During the forenoon of the same day the British were off the Spanish coast, fifty miles east of Gibraltar. At sunset the allies were seen approaching, and Howe formed his fleet, but sent the supply-ships to anchor at the Zaffarine Islands, on the coast of Barbary, to await events. Next morning the enemy was close to land northward, but visible only from the mastheads; the British apparently having headed south during the night. On the 15th the wind came east, fair for Gibraltar, towards which all the British began cautiously to move. By the evening of the 16th, eighteen of the convoy were safe at the mole; and on the 18th all had arrived, besides a fireship with 1,500 barrels of powder, sent in by the Admiral upon the governor's requisition. Throughout these critical hours, the combined fleets seem to have been out of sight. Either intentionally or carelessly, they had got to the eastward and there remained; having rallied their separated ships, but allowed Gibraltar to be replenished for a year. On the morning of the 19th they appeared in the north-east, but the relief was then accomplished and Howe put out to sea. He was not willing to fight in mid-Straits, embarrassed by currents and the land; but when outside he brought-to,—stopped, by backing some of the sails,—to allow the enemy to attack if they would, they having the weather-gage. On the following day, the 20th, towards sunset they bore down, and a partial engagement ensued; but it was wholly indecisive, and next day was not renewed. The British loss was 68 killed and 208 wounded; that of the allies 60 killed and 320 wounded. On the 14th of November the fleet regained Spithead.

The services rendered to his country by Howe on this occasion were eminently characteristic of the special qualities of that great officer, in whom was illustrated to the highest degree the solid strength attainable by a man not brilliant, but most able, who gives himself heart and soul to professional acquirement. In him, profound and extensive professional knowledge, which is not inborn but gained, was joined to great natural staying powers; and the combination eminently fitted him for the part we have seen him play in Delaware Bay, at New York, before Rhode Island, in the Channel, and now at Gibraltar. The utmost of skill, the utmost of patience, the utmost of persistence, such had Howe; and having these, he was particularly apt for the defensive operations, upon the conduct of which chiefly must rest his well-deserved renown. A true and noble tribute has been paid by a French officer[3] to this relief of Gibraltar:—

> The qualities displayed by Lord Howe during this short campaign rose to the full height of the mission which he had to fulfil. This operation, one of the finest in the War of American Independence, merits a praise equal to that of a victory. If the English fleet was favoured by circumstances,—and it is rare that in such enterprises one can succeed without the aid of fortune—it was above all the Commander-in-Chief's quickness of perception, the accuracy of his judgment, and the rapidity of his decisions, that assured success.

To this well-weighed, yet lofty praise of the Admiral, the same writer has added words that the British Navy may remember long with pride, as sealing the record of this war, of which the relief of Gibraltar marked the close in European and American waters. After according credit to the Admiralty for the uniform high speed of the British vessels, and to Howe for his comprehension and use of this advantage, Captain Chevalier goes on:—

> Finally, if we may judge by the results, the Commander-in-Chief of the English fleet could not but think himself most happy in his captains. There were neither separations, nor collisions, nor casualties; and there occurred none of those events, so frequent in the experiences of a squadron, which often oblige admirals to take a course wholly contrary to the end they have in view. In contemplation of this unvexed navigation of Admiral Howe, it is impossible not to recall the unhappy incidents which from the 9th to the 12th of April befell the squadron of the Count de Grasse. . . . If it is just to admit that Lord Howe displayed the highest talent it should be added that he had in his hands excellent instruments.

To quote another French writer: "Quantity disappeared before quality."

1. That is, with a great part of her guns dismounted, and below as cargo.
2. Chevalier, following La Motte-Picquet's report, ascribes Howe's escape to greater speed. ("Mar. Fran. en 1778," p. 335.) It must be noted that Howe's object was not merely to escape eastward, up Channel, by better sailing, but to get to the westward, *past* the allies, a feat impracticable save by a stratagem such as is mentioned.
3. Chevalier, "Mar. Fran. dans la Guerre de 1778," p. 358.

XIV

THE NAVAL OPERATIONS
IN THE EAST INDIES

T HE OPERATIONS IN INDIA, BOTH naval and military, stand by themselves, without direct influence upon transactions elsewhere, and unaffected also by these, except in so far as necessary succours were intercepted sometimes in European waters. The cause of this isolation was the distance of India from Europe; from four to six months being required by a fleet for the voyage.

Certain intelligence of the war between Great Britain and France reached Calcutta July 7th, 1778. On the same day the Governor-General ordered immediate preparations to attack Pondicherry, the principal seaport of the French. The army arrived before the place on the 8th of August, and on the same day Commodore Sir Edward Vernon anchored in the roads to blockade by sea. A French squadron, under Captain Tronjoly, soon after appearing in the offing, Vernon gave chase, and on the 10th an action ensued. The forces engaged were about equal, the French, if anything, slightly superior; a 60-gun ship and four smaller vessels being on each side. As the French then went into Pondicherry, the immediate advantage may be conceded to them; but, Vernon returning on the 20th, Tronjoly soon after quitted the roads, and returned to the Ile de France.[1] From that day the British squadron blockaded closely, and on the 17th of October Pondicherry capitulated.

On the 7th of March, 1779, Rear-Admiral Sir Edward Hughes sailed for the East Indies with a small squadron. The French also sent out occasional ships; but in 1779 and 1780 these went no further than the Ile de France, their naval station in the Indian Ocean. Hughes's force remained unopposed during those years. The period was critical, for the British were at war with Hyder Ali, Sultan of Mysore, and with the Mahrattas; and all depended upon command of the sea. In January, 1781, when Hughes was wintering at Bombay, the French squadron under Comte d'Orves appeared off the Coromandel coast, but, despite Hyder Ali's entreaties, it refused to cooperate with him. The different spirit of the two commanders may be illustrated from contemporary documents.

> We have advices from Fort St. George of a French squadron which appeared off that place on January 25, 26, and 27, consisting of 1 seventy-four, 4 sixty-fours, and 2 fifties. They proceeded south without making any attempt on five Indiamen then in the roads, with a number of vessels laden with grain and provisions; the destroying of which might have been easily accomplished, and would have been severely felt.
>
> "On December 8th, off Mangalore,"[2] writes Hughes, "I saw two ships, a large snow, three ketches, and many smaller vessels at anchor in the road with Hyder's flag, flying; and, standing close, found them vessels of force and all armed for war. I anchored as close as possible, sent in all armed boats, under

cover of three smaller ships of war, which anchored in four fathoms water, close to the enemy's ships. In two hours took and burned the two ships, one of 28 and one of 26 guns, and took or destroyed all the others, save one which, by throwing everything overboard, escaped over the bar into the port. Lost 1 lieutenant and 10 men killed, 2 lieutenants and 51 wounded.

It is interesting to note these evidences of Hughes's conceptions of naval warfare and enterprise, common though they were to the British service; for their positive character brings into strong relief the qualities of his next antagonist, Suffren, and his great superiority in these respects over the average run of French officers of that day.

D'Orves returned to the Ile de France.

When war with Holland began, the British government decided to attempt the capture of the Cape of Good Hope. For that object a squadron of one 74, one 64, and three 50s, with numerous smaller vessels, under Commodore George Johnstone, convoying a considerable body of troops, sailed from England on the 13th of March, 1781, in company with the Channel fleet under Vice-Admiral George Darby, then on its way to relieve Gibraltar. The French government, having timely notice of the expedition, undertook to frustrate it; detailing for that purpose a division of two 74s, and three 64s, under the since celebrated Suffren.[3] These ships left Brest on the 22d of March, with the fleet of de Grasse. They also carried some battalions of troops.

On April 11th the British squadron reached Porto Praya, Cape de Verde Islands. This bay is open to the southward, extending from east to west about a mile and a half, and is within the limits of the north-east trade-winds. Although aware that a French division was on his track, and conscious, by the admissions of his report, that protection could not be expected from the neutrality of the place, Johnstone permitted his vessels to anchor without reference to attack. His own flagship, the *Romney*, 50, was so surrounded by others that she could fire only with great caution through intervals. On the 16th of April, at 9.30 A.M., the *Isis*, 50, which was the outermost of the British squadron, signalled eleven sail in the north-east. Fifteen hundred persons were then ashore engaged in watering, fishing, embarking cattle, and amusing themselves. The strangers were Suffren's division. The meeting was not expected by the French commander, whose object in entering was simply to complete the water of the ships; but he determined at once to attack, and hauled round the east point of the bay in column, the two seventy-fours at the head, his own ship, the *Héros*, leading with the signal for battle (Fig. 1, line ab). Passing through, or along, the disordered enemy until he reached the only seventy-four among them, he there luffed to the wind, anchoring five hundred feet from the starboard beam of this vessel (f) which by an odd coincidence bore the same name—*Hero*. From this position he at once opened fire from both broadsides. His next astern, the *Annibal* (b), brought up immediately ahead of him, but so close that the *Héros* had to veer cable and drop astern (a), which brought her on the beam of the *Monmouth*, 64 (m).[4] The captain of the *Annibal* had thought the order for battle merely precautionary, and had not cleared for action. He was therefore taken unawares, and his ship did no service proportionate to her force. The third French vessel (c) reached her station, but her captain was struck dead just when about to anchor, and in the confusion the anchor was not let go. The ship drifted foul of a British East Indiaman, which she carried out to sea (c'c''). The two remaining French (d, e) simply cannonaded as they passed across the bay's mouth, failing through mishap or awkwardness to reach an effective position.

The attack thus became a mere rough and tumble, in which the two seventy-fours alone sustained the French side. After three quarters of an hour, Suffren, seeing that the attempt had failed, slipped his cable and put to sea. The *Annibal* followed, but she had been so damaged that all her masts went overboard; fortunately, not until her head was pointed out of the harbour. Johnstone, thus luckily escaping the consequences of his neglect, now called his captains together to learn the condition of their ships, and then ordered them to cut their cables and pursue. All obeyed except Captain Sutton of the *Isis*, who represented that the spars and rigging of his ship could not bear sail at once. Johnstone then ordered him to come out anyhow, which he did, and his fore topmast shortly went overboard. The disability of this ship so weighed upon the Commodore that his pursuit was exceedingly sluggish; and the French kept drawing him away to leeward, the *Annibal* having got a bit of canvas on a jury foremast. Night, therefore, was falling as Johnstone came near them; the *Isis* and *Monmouth* were two or three miles astern; the sea was increasing; if he got much further to leeward, he could not get back; he had forgotten to appoint a rendezvous where the convoy might rejoin; a night action, he considered, was not to be thought of. Yet, if he let the enemy go, they might anticipate him at the Cape. In short, Johnstone underwent the "anguish" of an undecided man in a "cruel situation,"[5] and of course decided to run no risks. He returned therefore to Porto Praya, put the captain of the *Isis* under arrest, and remained in port for a fortnight. Suffren hurried on to the Cape, got there first, landed his troops, and secured the colony against attack. Johnstone arrived in the neighbourhood some time later, and, finding himself anticipated, turned aside to Saldanha Bay, where he captured five Dutch East Indiamen.

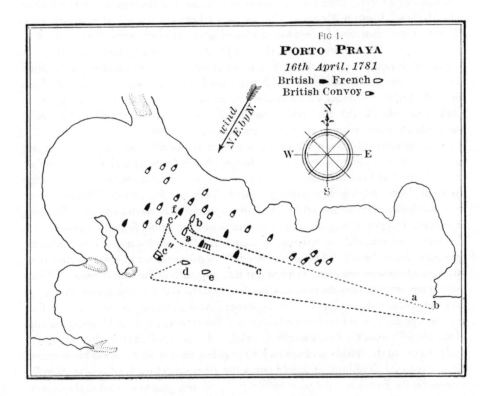

FIG 1.

PORTO PRAYA

16th April, 1781

British ● French ○
British Convoy ⊃

He then sent the *Hero, Monmouth*, and *Isis* on to India, to reinforce Hughes, and himself went back to England.

No accusation of misbehavior lies against any of the British subordinates in this affair of Porto Praya. The captain of the *Isis* was brought to a court-martial, and honourably acquitted of all the charges. The discredit of the surprise was not redeemed by any exhibition of intelligence, energy, or professional capacity, on the part of the officer in charge. It has been said that he never had commanded a post-ship[6] before he was intrusted with this very important mission, and it is reasonably sure that his selection for it was due to attacks made by him upon the professional conduct of Keppel and Howe, when those admirals were at variance with the administration.[7] His preposterous mismanagement, therefore, was probably not wholly bitter to the Navy at large. In the British ships of war, the entire loss in men, as reported, was only 9 killed, 47 wounded. Several casualties from chance shots occurred on board the convoy, bringing up the total to 36 killed and 130 wounded. The French admit 105 killed and 204 wounded, all but 19 being in the *Héros* and *Annibal*. Although precipitated by Suffren, the affair clearly was as great a surprise to his squadron as to the British. Therefore, the latter, being already at anchor and more numerous as engaged, had a distinct advantage; to which also contributed musketry fire from the transports. Nevertheless, the result cannot be deemed creditable to the French captains or gunnery.

Suffren remained in the neighbourhood of the Cape for two months. Then, having seen the colony secure, independent of his squadron, he departed for the Ile de France arriving there October 25th. On the 17th of December the whole French force, under the command of d'Orves, sailed for the Coromandel coast. On the way the British 50-gun ship *Hannibal*, Captain Alexander Christie, was taken. On the 9th of February, 1782, Comte d'Orves died, and Suffren found himself at the head of twelve ships of the line: three 74s, seven 64s and two 50s.[8] On the 15th Hughes's fleet was sighted, under the guns of Madras. It numbered nine of the line: two 74s, one 68, five 64s, and one 50. Suffren stood south towards Pondicherry, which had passed into the power of Hyder Ali. After nightfall Hughes got under way, and also steered south. He feared for Trincomalee, in Ceylon, recently a Dutch port, which the British had captured on the 5th of January. It was a valuable naval position, as yet most imperfectly defended.

At daylight the British saw the French squadron twelve miles east (Fig. 2, A, A) and its transports nine miles south-west (c). Hughes chased the latter and took six. Suffren pursued, but could not overtake before sunset, and both fleets steered south-east during the night. Next morning there were light north-north-east airs, and the French were six miles north-east of the British (B,B). The latter formed line on the port tack (a), "heading to seaward; Hughes hoping that thus the usual sea-breeze would find him to windward. The breeze, however, did not make as expected; and, as the north-east puffs were bringing the enemy down, he kept off before the wind (b) to gain time for his ships to close their intervals, which were too great. At 4 P.M. the near approach of the French compelled him to form line again (C), on the port tack, heading easterly. The rear ship, *Exeter*, 64 (e), was left separated, out of due support from those ahead. Suffren, leading one section of his fleet in person, passed to windward of the British line, from the rear, as far as Hughes's flagship, which was fifth from the van. There he stopped, and kept at half cannon-shot, to prevent the four ships in the British van from tacking to relieve their consorts. It was his intention that the second half of his fleet should attack the other side of the English rear. Actually, only two of the French rear did what Suffren expected, engaging to leeward of the extreme

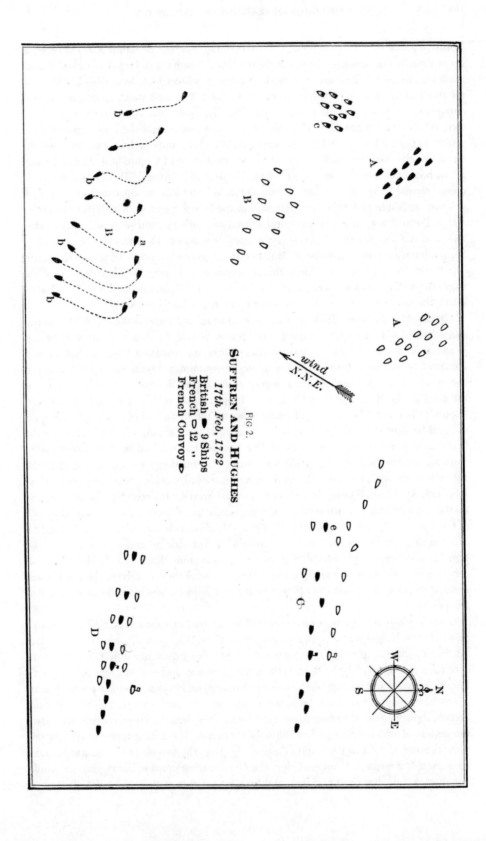

Fig 2.

SUFFREN AND HUGHES

17th Feb, 1782

British ● 9 Ships
French ◗ 12 "
French Convoy ◗

wind
N.N.E.

British rear; the others of the French rear remaining long out of action (C). However, as the position of Suffren's flagship prevented the British van from tacking into action, the net result was, to use Hughes's own words, that "the enemy brought eight of their best ships to the attack of five of ours." It will be noted with interest that these were exactly the numbers engaged in the first act of the battle of the Nile. The *Exeter* (like the *Guerrier* at the Nile) received the fresh broadsides of the first five of the enemy, and then remained in close action on both sides, assailed by two, and at last by three, opponents,—two 50s, and one 64. When the third approached, the master of the ship asked Commodore Richard King, whose broad pennant flew at her masthead, "What is to be done?" "There is nothing to be done," replied King, "but to fight her till she sinks." Her loss, 10 killed and 45 wounded, was not creditable under the circumstances to the French gunnery, which had been poor also at Porto Praya. At 6 P.M. the wind shifted to south-east, throwing all on the other tack, and enabling the British van at last to come into action. Darkness now approaching, Suffren hauled off and anchored at Pondicherry. Hughes went on to Trincomalee to refit. The British loss had been 32 killed, among whom were Captain William Stevens of the flagship, and Captain Henry Reynolds, of the *Exeter*, and 83 wounded. The French had 30 killed; the number of their wounded is put by Professor Laughton at 100.

On the 12th of March Hughes returned to Madras, and towards the end of the month sailed again for Trincomalee carrying reinforcements and supplies. On the 30th he was joined at sea by the *Sultan*, 74, and the *Magnanime*, 64, just from England. Suffren had remained on the coast from reasons of policy, to encourage Hyder Ali in his leaning to the French; but, after landing a contingent of troops on the 22d of March, to assist at the siege of the British port of Cuddalore, he put to sea on the 23d, and went south, hoping to intercept the *Sultan* and *Magnanime* off the south end of Ceylon. On the 9th of April he sighted the British fleet to the south and west of him. Hughes, attaching the first importance to the strengthening of Trincomalee, had resolved neither to seek nor to shun action. He therefore continued his course, light northerly airs prevailing, until the 11th, when, being about fifty miles to the north-east of his port, he bore away for it. Next morning, April 12th, finding that the enemy could overtake his rear ships, he formed line on the starboard tack, at two cables' intervals, heading to the westward, towards the coast of Ceylon, wind north by east, and the French dead to windward (Fig. 3, A, A). Suffren drew up his line (a) on the same tack, parallel to the British, and at 11 A.M. gave the signal to steer west-south-west all together; his vessels going down in a slanting direction (bb′), each to steer for one of the enemy. Having twelve ships to eleven, the twelfth was ordered to place herself on the off side of the rear British, which would thus have two antagonists.

In such simultaneous approach it commonly occurred that the attacking line ceased to be parallel with the foe's, its van becoming nearer and rear more distant. So it was here. Further, the British opening fire as soon as the leading French were within range, the latter at once hauled up to reply. Suffren, in the centre, wishing closest action, signalled them to keep away again, and himself bore down wrathfully upon Hughes to within pistol-shot; in which he was supported closely by his next ahead and the two next astern. The rear of the French, though engaged, remained too far distant. Their line, therefore, resembled a curve, the middle of which—four or five ships—was tangent to the British centre (B). At this point the heat of the attack fell upon Hughes's flagship, the *Superb*, 74 (C, d), and her next ahead, the *Monmouth*, 64. Suffren's ship, the *Héros*, having much of her rigging cut, could not shorten sail, shot by the *Superb*, and brought up abreast the *Monmouth*. The latter,

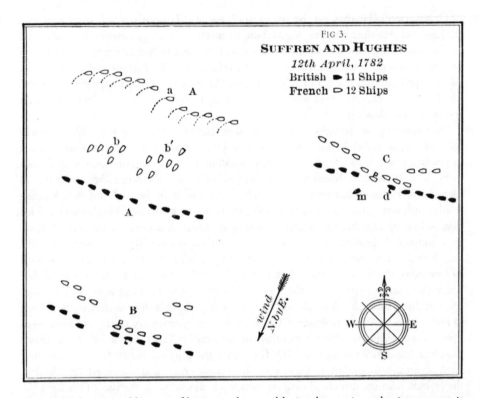

FIG 3.

SUFFREN AND HUGHES
12th April, 1782
British ● 11 Ships
French ◗ 12 Ships

already hotly engaged by one of her own class, and losing her main and mizzen masts in this unequal new contest, was forced at 3 P.M. to bear up out of the line (m). The place of the *Héros* alongside the *Superb* was taken by the *Orient*, 74, supported by the *Brillant*, 64; and when the *Monmouth* kept off, the attack of these two ships was reinforced by the half-dozen stern chasers of the *Héros*, which had drifted into the British line, and now fired into the *Superb*'s bows. The conflict between these five ships, two British and three French, was one of the bloodiest in naval annals; the loss of the *Superb*, 59 killed and 96 wounded, and of the *Monmouth*, 45 killed and 102 wounded, equalling that of the much larger vessels which bore the flags of Nelson and Collingwood at Trafalgar. The loss of the three French was 52 killed and 142 wounded; but to this should be added properly that of the *Sphinx*, 64, the *Monmouth*'s first adversary: 22 killed and 74 wounded. At 3.40 P.M., fearing that if he continued steering west he would get entangled with the shore, Hughes wore his ships, forming line on the port tack, heading off shore. The French also wore, and Suffren hoped to secure the *Monmouth*, which was left between the two lines; but the quickness of a British captain. Hawker, of the *Hero*, ran a tow-rope to her in time, and she was thus dragged out of danger. At 5.40 Hughes anchored, and Suffren did the same at 8 P.M. The total British loss in men on this occasion was 137 killed and 430 wounded; that of the French 137 killed, and 357 wounded.

The exhausted enemies remained at anchor in the open sea, two miles apart, for a week, repairing. On the 19th of April the French got under way and made a demonstration before the British, inviting battle, yet not attacking; but the condition of the *Monmouth* forbade Hughes from moving. Suffren therefore departed to Batacalo, in Ceylon, south of Trincomalee, where he covered his own convoys from Europe, and flanked the approach of his adversary's. Hughes, on the 22d of April, got into Trincomalee, where he remained till June 23d. He then went to Negapatam, formerly a Dutch possession, but then held by the British. There he learned that Suffren, who meanwhile had captured several British transports, was a few miles north of him, at Cuddalore, which had surrendered to Hyder Ali on April 4th. On the 5th of July, at 1 P.M., the French squadron appeared. At 3 P.M. Hughes put to sea, and stood south during the night to gain the wind,—the south-west monsoon now blowing.

Next morning, at daylight, the French were seen at anchor, seven or eight miles to leeward. At 6 A.M. they began to get under way. One of their sixty-fours, the *Ajax*, had lost her main and mizzen topmasts in a violent squall on the previous afternoon, and was not in the line. There were therefore eleven ships on each side. The action, known as that of Negapatam, began shortly before 11, when both fleets were on the starboard tack, heading south-south-east, wind southwest. The British being to windward, Hughes ordered his fleet to bear up together to the attack, exactly as Suffren had done on the 12th of April. As commonly happened, the rear got less close than the van (Fig. 4, Position I). The fourth ship in the French order, the *Brillant*, 64 (a), losing her mainmast early, dropped to leeward of the line (a′), and astern of her place (a″). At half-past noon the wind flew suddenly to south-south-east,—the sea-breeze,—taking the ships a little on the port bow. Most of them, on both sides, paid off from the enemy, the British to starboard, the French to port; but between the main lines, which were in the momentary confusion consequent upon such an incident, were left six ships—four British and two French—that had turned the other way (Positions II and III).[9] These were the *Burford, Sultan* (s), *Worcester*, and *Eagle*, fourth, fifth, eighth and tenth, in the British order; and the *Sévère* (b), third in the French, with the dismasted *Brillant*, which was now towards the rear of the fight (a). Under these conditions, the *Sévère*, 64, underwent a short but close action with the *Sultan*, 74; and with two other British ships, according to the report of the *Sévère's* captain. The remainder of the incident shall be given in the latter's own words.

> Seeing the French squadron drawing off,—for all the ships except the *Brillant* had fallen off on the other tack,—Captain de Cillart thought it useless to prolong his defence, and had the flag hauled down. The ships engaged with him immediately ceased their fire, and the one on the starboard side moved away. At this moment the *Sévère* fell off to starboard, and her sails filled. Captain de Cillart then ordered the fire to be resumed by his lower-deck guns, the only ones which remained manned, and he rejoined his squadron.

When the *Sévère's* flag came down, Suffren was approaching with his flagship. The *Sultan* wore to rejoin her fleet, and was raked by the *Sévère* in so doing. The *Brillant*, whose mainmast had been shot away in conflict with either the *Sultan* or the *Burford*, both much heavier ships, had at this later phase of the fight fallen under the guns of the *Worcester* and the *Eagle*. Her captain, de Saint-Felix, was one of the most resolute of Suffren's officers. She was rescued by the flagship, but she had lost 47 killed and 136 wounded,—an almost incredible slaughter, being over a third of the usual complement of a sixty-four; and Suffren's ships were undermanned.

These spirited episodes, and the fact that his four separated ships were approaching the enemy, and being approached by them, caused Hughes to give the orders to wear, and for a general chase; the flag for the line being hauled down. These signals would bring all the

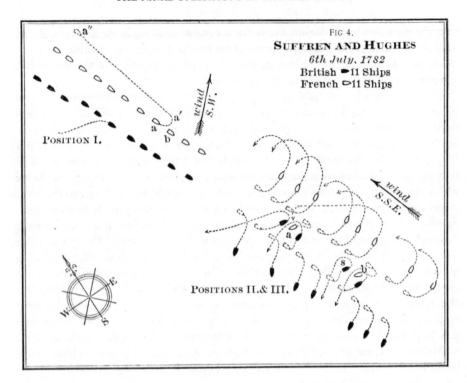

FIG 4.
SUFFREN AND HUGHES
6th July, 1782
British ●11 Ships
French ◗11 Ships

POSITION I.

POSITIONS II.& III.

main body to the support of the separated ships, without regard to their order in battle and therefore with the utmost expedition that their remaining sail power would admit. Two of the fleet, however, made signals of disability; so Hughes annulled the orders, and at 1.30 formed on the port tack, recalling the engaged vessels. Both squadrons now stood in shore, and anchored at about 6 P.M.; the British near Negapatam, the French some ten miles north. The loss in the action had been: British, 77 killed, 233 wounded; French, 178 killed, 601 wounded.

On the following day Suffren sailed for Cuddalore. There he received word that two ships of the line—the *Illustre*, 74, and *St. Michel*, 60, with a convoy of supplies and 600 troops—were to be expected shortly at Pointe de Galle, then a Dutch port, on the south-west side of Ceylon. It was essential to cover these, and on the 18th he was ready for sea; but the necessity of an interview with Hyder Ali delayed him until the 1st of August, when he started for Batacalo. On the 9th he arrived there, and on the 21st the reinforcement joined him. Within forty-eight hours the supply ships were cleared, and the squadron sailed again with the object of taking Trincomalee. On the 25th he was off the port, and, the operation being pushed energetically, the place capitulated on the 31st of August.

It is difficult to resist the impression that greater energy on Hughes's part might have brought him up in time to prevent this mishap. He reached Madras only on July 20th, a fortnight after the late action; and he did not sail thence until the 20th of August, notwithstanding that he apprehended an attempt upon Trincomalee. Hence, when he arrived there on the 2d of September, not only had it passed into the hands of the enemy, but Suffren had reembarked already the men and the guns that had been landed from his fleet. When Hughes's approach was signalled, all preparations for sea were hastened, and the following morning, at daybreak, the French came out. Hughes had been joined since the last action by the *Sceptre*, 64, so that the respective forces in the action fought off Trincomalee on September 3d were twelve of the line to fourteen, viz.: British, three 74s, one 70, one 68, six 64s, one 50; French, four 74s, seven 64s, one 60, two 50s. Suffren had also put into the line a 36-gun ship, the *Consolante*.[10]

While the French were getting underway from Trincomalee, the British fleet was standing south-south-east towards the entrance, close-hauled on the starboard tack, a fresh southwest monsoon blowing. When Hughes made out the hostile flags on the works, he kept away four points,[11] and steered east-south-east, still in column, under short canvas (Fig. 5, A). Suffren pursued, being to windward yet astern, with his fleet on a line of bearing; that is, the line on which the ships were ranged was not the same as the course which they were steering. This formation (A), wherein the advance is oblique to the front, is very difficult to maintain. Wishing to make the action, whatever the immediate event, decisive in results, by drawing the French well to leeward of the port, Hughes, who was a thorough seaman and had good captains, played with his eager enemy. "He kept avoiding me without taking flight," wrote Suffren; "or rather, he fled in good order, regulating his canvas by his worst sailers; and, keeping off by degrees, he steered from first to last ten or twelve different courses." Hughes, on his part, while perfectly clear as to his own object, was somewhat perplexed by the seeming indecision of an adversary whose fighting purpose he knew by experience. "Sometimes they edged down," he wrote; "sometimes they brought-to; in no regular order, as if undetermined what to do." These apparent vacillations were due to the difficulty of maintaining the line of bearing, which was to be the line of battle; and this difficulty was the greater, because Hughes was continually altering his course and Suffren's ships were of unequal speed.

At length, at 2 P.M., being then twenty-five miles south-east of the port, the French drew near enough to bear down. That this movement might be carried out with precision, and all the vessels come into action together, Suffren caused his fleet to haul to the wind, on the starboard tack, to rectify the order. This also being done poorly and slowly, he lost patience,—as Nelson afterwards said, "A day is soon lost in manœuvring,"—and at 2.30, to spur on the laggard ships, the French admiral gave the signal to attack, (a), specifying pistol-range. Even this not sufficing to fetch the delinquents promptly into line with the flagship, the latter fired a gun to enforce obedience. Her own side being still turned towards the British, as she waited, the report was taken by the flagship's men below decks to be the signal for opening fire, and her whole broadside was discharged. This example was followed by the other ships, so that the engagement, instead of being close, was begun at half cannon-shot.

Owing to his measured and deliberate retreat, Hughes had his fleet now in thoroughly good shape, well aligned and closed-up. The French, starting from a poor formation to perform a difficult evolution, under fire, engaged in utter disorder (B). Seven ships, prematurely rounding-to to bring their broadsides to the enemy, and fore-reaching, formed a confused group (v), much to windward and somewhat ahead of the British van. Imperfectly deployed, they interfered with one another and their fire consequently could not be adequately developed. In the rear a somewhat similar condition existed. Suffren, expecting the bulk of his line to fight the British to windward, had directed the *Vengeur*, 64, and the *Consolante*, 36, to double to leeward on the extreme rear; but they, finding that the weather sides of the enemy were not occupied, feared to go to leeward, lest they should be cut off. They attacked the rear British ship, the *Worcester*, 64 (w), to windward; but the *Monmouth*, 64 (m), dropping down to her support, and the *Vengeur* catching fire in the mizzen top, they were compelled to haul off. Only Suffren's own ship, the *Héros*, 74 (a), and her next astern, the *Illustre*, 74 (i), came at once to close action with the British centre; but subsequently the *Ajax*, 64, succeeding in clearing herself from the snarl in the rear, took station ahead (j) of the *Héros*. Upon these three fell the brunt of the fight. They not only received the broadsides of the ships immediately opposed to them, but, the wind having now become light yet free, the British vessels ahead and astern (h,s), by luffing or keeping off, played also upon them. "The enemy formed a semicircle around us," wrote Suffren's chief of staff, "and raked us ahead and astern, as the ship came up and fell off with the helm to leeward." The two seventy-fours were crushed under this fire. Both lost their main and mizzen masts in the course of the day, and the foretopmast of the flagship also fell. The *Ajax*, arriving later, and probably drawing less attention, had only a topmast shot away.

The British total of killed and wounded was very evenly distributed throughout the fleet. Only the rear ship lost an important spar,—the main topmast. It was upon her, as already mentioned, and upon the two leading ships, the *Exeter* and *Isis*, that fell the heaviest fire, proportionately, of the French. From the position of the seven van ships of the latter, such fire as they could make must needs be upon the extreme British van, and the *Exeter* was forced to leave the line. The loss of the French that day was 82 killed and 255 wounded; of which 64 killed and 178 wounded belonged to the *Héros*, *Illustre*, and *Ajax*. The British had 51 killed and 283 wounded; the greatest number of casualties in one ship being 56. Singularly enough, in such a small list of deaths, three were commanding officers: Captains Watt of the *Sultan*, Wood of the *Worcester*, and Lumley of the *Isis*.

At 5.30 P.M. the wind shifted suddenly from south-west to east-south-east (C). The British wore together, formed on the other tack, and continued the fight. It was during

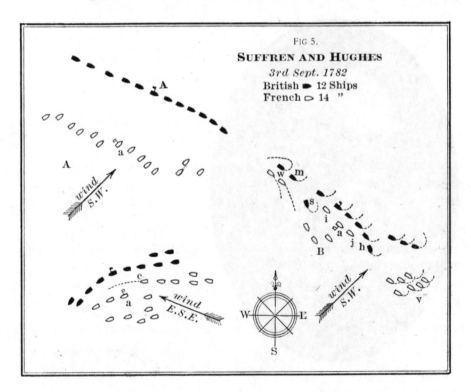

FIG 5.

SUFFREN AND HUGHES

3rd Sept. 1782

British ● 12 Ships
French ○ 14 "

this final act, and at 6 P.M., that the mainmast of the French flagship came down. The van ships of the French had towed their heads round with boats before 4, in order to come to the support of the centre, in obedience to a signal from Suffren; but the light airs and calms had retarded them. With the shift they approached, and passed in column (c) between their crippled vessels and the enemy. This manœuvre, and the failure of daylight, brought the battle to an end. According to Hughes's report, several of his fleet "were making much water from shot-holes so very low down in the bottom as not to be come at to be effectually stopped; and the whole had suffered severely in their masts and rigging." Trincomalee being in the enemy's possession, and the east coast of Ceylon an unsafe anchorage now, at the change of the monsoon, he felt compelled to return to Madras, where he anchored on the 9th of September. Suffren regained Trincomalee on the 7th of the month, but the *Orient*, 74, running ashore at the entrance and being lost, he remained outside until the 17th, saving material from the wreck.

The break-up of the south-west monsoon, then at hand, is apt to be accompanied by violent hurricanes, and is succeeded by the north-east monsoon, during which the east coasts of the peninsula and of Ceylon give a lee shore, with heavy surf. Naval operations, therefore, were suspended for the winter. During that season Trincomalee is the only secure port. Deprived of it, Hughes determined to go to Bombay, and for that purpose left Madras on the 17th of October. Four days later a reinforcement of five ships of the line arrived from England, under Commodore Sir Richard Bickerton, who at once followed the Commander-in-Chief to the west coast. In the course of December the entire British force was united at Bombay.

In Trincomalee Suffren had a good anchorage; but the insufficiency of its resources, with other military considerations, decided him to winter at Acheen, at the west end of

SIR EDWARD HUGHES, K.B.

PIERRE ANDRÉ DE SUFFREN
DE SAINT TROPEZ

Sumatra. He arrived there on the 2d of November, having first paid a visit to Cuddalore, where the *Bizarre*, 64, was wrecked by carelessness. On the 20th of December he left Acheen for the Coromandel coast, having shortened his stay to the eastward for reasons of policy. On the 8th of January, 1783, he was off Ganjam, on the Orissa coast, and thence reached Trincomalee again on the 23d of February. There he was joined on the 10th of March by three ships of the line from Europe: two 74s and one 64. Under their convoy came General de Bussy, with twenty-five hundred troops, which were at once despatched to Cuddalore.

On the 10th of April Vice-Admiral Hughes, returning from Bombay, passed Trincomalee on the way to Madras, The various maritime occurrences, wrecks and reinforcements, since the battle of September 3d had reversed the naval odds, and Hughes now had eighteen ships of the line, one of which was an eighty, opposed to fifteen under Suffren. Another important event in the affairs of India was the death of Hyder Ali, on the 7th of December, 1782. Although his policy was continued by his son, Tippoo Saib, the blow to the French was serious. Under all the conditions, the British authorities were emboldened to attempt the reduction of Cuddalore. The army destined to this enterprise marched from Madras, passed round Cuddalore, and encamped south of it by the shore. The supply-ships and lighter cruisers anchored near, while the fleet cruised to the southward. Being there to windward, for the south-west monsoon had then set in, it covered the operations against disturbance from the sea.

Towards the beginning of June the investment of the place was complete by land and by water. Intelligence of this state of things was brought on the 10th of June to Suffren, who by Bussey's direction was keeping his inferior fleet in Trincomalee until its services should be absolutely indispensable. Immediately upon receiving the news he left port, and on the 13th sighted the British fleet, then at anchor off Porto Novo, a little south of Cuddalore. Upon his approach Hughes moved off, and anchored again five miles from the besieged place. For the next two days the French were baffled by the winds; but on the 17th the south-west monsoon resumed, and Suffren again drew near. The British Vice-Admiral, not caring to accept action at anchor, got under way, and from that time till the 20th remained outside, trying to obtain the weather-gage, in which he was frustrated by the variableness of the winds. Meanwhile Suffren had anchored near the town, communicated with the general, and, being very short of men at the guns, had embarked twelve hundred troops for his expected battle; for it was evident that the issue of the siege would turn upon the control of the sea. On the 18th he weighed again, and the two fleets manœuvred for the advantage, with light baffling airs, the British furthest from shore.

On the 20th of June, the wind holding at west with unexpected constancy, Hughes decided to accept the attack which Suffren evidently intended. The latter, being distinctly inferior in force,—fifteen to eighteen,—probably contemplated an action that should be decisive only as regarded the fate of Cuddalore; that is, one which, while not resulting in the capture or destruction of ships, should compel his opponent to leave the neighbourhood to repair damages. The British formed line on the port tack, heading to the northward. Suffren ranged his fleet in the same manner, parallel to the enemy, and was careful to see the order exact before bearing down. When the signal to attack was given, the French kept away together, and brought-to again on the weather beam of the British, just within point-blank range. The action lasted from shortly after 4 P.M. to nearly 7, and was general throughout both lines; but, as always experienced, the rears were less engaged than the centres and vans. No ship was taken; no very important spars seem to have been shot away. The loss of the British was 99 killed, 434 wounded; of the French, 102 killed, 386 wounded.

As the ships' heads were north, the course of the action carried them in that direction. Suffren anchored next morning twenty-five miles north of Cuddalore. There he was sighted on the 22d by Hughes, who had remained lying-to the day after the fight. The British Vice-Admiral reported several ships much disabled, a great number of his men—1,121— down with scurvy, and the water of the fleet very short. He therefore thought it necessary to go to Madras, where he anchored on the 25th. Suffren regained Cuddalore on the afternoon of the 23d. His return and Hughes' departure completely changed the military situation. The supply-ships upon which the British scheme of operations depended, had been forced to take flight when Suffren first approached, and of course could not come back now. "My mind is on the rack without a moment's rest since the departure of the fleet," wrote the commanding general on the 25th, "considering the character of M. de Suffren, and the infinite superiority on the part of the French now that we are left to ourselves."

The battle of June 20th, 1783, off Cuddalore, was the last of the maritime war of 1778. It was fought, actually, exactly five months after the preliminaries of peace had been signed on January 20th, 1783. Although the relative force of the two fleets remained unchanged, it was a French victory, both tactically and strategically: tactically, because the inferior fleet held its ground, and remained in possession of the field; strategically, because it decided the object immediately at stake, the fate of Cuddalore, and with it, momentarily at least, the issue of the campaign. It was, however, the triumph of one commander-in-chief over another; of the greater man over the lesser. Hughes's reasons for quitting the field involve the admission of his opponent's greater skill. "Short of water,"—with eighteen ships to fifteen, able therefore to spare ships by detachments for watering, that should not have happened; "injury to spars,"—that resulted from the action; "1,121 men short,"—Suffren had embarked just that number—1,200—because Hughes let him communicate with the port without fighting. Notwithstanding the much better seamanship of the British subordinates, and their dogged tenacity, Suffren here, as throughout the campaign, demonstrated again the old experience that generalship is the supreme factor in war. With inferior resources, though not at first with inferior numbers, by a steady offensive, and by the attendant anxiety about Trincomalee impressed upon the British admiral, he reduced him to a fruitless defensive. By the seizure of that place as a base he planted himself firmly upon the scene of action. Able thus to remain, while the British had to retire to Bombay, he sustained the Sultan of Mysore in his embarrassing hostility to the British; and in the end he saved Cuddalore by readiness and dexterity despite the now superior numbers of the British fleet. He was a great sea-captain, Hughes was not; and with poorer instruments, both in men and ships, the former overcame the latter.

On the 29th of June a British frigate, the *Medea*, bearing a flag of truce, reached Cuddalore. She brought well-authenticated intelligence of the conclusion of peace; and hostilities ceased by common consent.

1. Now Mauritius.

2. On the Malabar—western—coast.

3. *Ante*, p. 114.

4. I infer, from the accounts, that the *Monmouth* was well east of the *Hero*, that the French had passed her first, and that the *Héros* was now on her port beam; but this point is not certain.

5. Expressions in Johnstone's Report.

6. Charnock, however, says that in 1762, immediately after receiving his post-commission, he commanded in succession the *Hind*, 20, and the *Wager*, 20. Moreover, before his appointment to the expedition of 1781, he had been Commodore on the Lisbon Station. But he had spent comparatively little time at sea as a captain.—W.L.C.

7. *Ante*, p. 58.

8. One being the captured British *Hannibal*, 50, which was commissioned by Captain Morard de Galles, retaining the English form of the name, Hannibal, to distinguish her from the *Annibal*, 74, already in the squadron.

9. In the plan. Positions II and III, the second position is indicated by ships with broken outlines. These show the two lines of battle in the engagement until the wind shifted to south-south-east. The results of the shift constituted a third position, consecutive with the second, and is indicated by ships in full outline.

10. Previously the British East Indiaman, *Elizabeth*.

11. Forty-five degrees.

GLOSSARY

ABACK. A sail is aback when the wind blows on the forward part tending to move the vessel astern.

ABAFT. Behind, towards the stern.

ABEAM.
ABREAST.
AFT.   } See "Bearing."
AHEAD.
ASTERN.

BEAM. The width of a vessel, so used because of the cross timbers, called beams.

BEAR, to. To be in a specified direction from a vessel.

BEAR, to. To change the direction of a vessel's movement. To bear *down*, to move towards; to bear *up*, or *away*, to move away, from the wind or from an enemy.

BEARING. The direction of an object from a vessel; either by compass, or with reference to the vessel itself. Thus, the lighthouse bears north; the enemy bears abeam, or two points off the port bow.

BEARING, Line of. The compass bearing on which the vessels of a fleet are ranged, whatever their bearings from one another.

BEARINGS, with reference to the vessel.

Abeam.
Abreast. } Perpendicular to the vessel's length.

Aft.
Astern.   } Directly behind.

Ahead. Directly before; forward.

Abaft the beam, starboard or port, weather or lee. To the rear of abeam, to the right or left, to windward or to lee-ward.

Before (or forward of) the beam (as above). Ahead of abeam, etc.

Broad. A large angle of bearing, used ordinarily of the bow. "Broad off the bow" approaches "before the beam."

On the bow, starboard or port, weather or lee. To one side of ahead, to right or left, to windward or to leeward.

On the quarter, starboard or port, weather or lee. To one side of astern; to right or left, to windward or to leeward.

BEARINGS, by compass. The full circle of the compass, 360 degrees, is divided into thirty-two *points*, each point being subdivided into fourths. From north to east, eight points, are thus named: North; north by east; north-northeast; northeast by north; northeast; northeast by east; east-northeast; east by north; East. From East to South, from South to West, and from West to North, a like naming is used.

BEAT, to. To gain ground to windward, by successive changes of direction, called tacks.

BOOM. See "Spars."

BOW, or head. The forward part of a vessel, which is foremost when in motion ahead. On the Bow. See "Bearing." To head "bows-on": to move directly towards.

BOW AND QUARTER LINE. See p. 158, note 5.

BOWSPRIT. See "Spars."

BRACES. Ropes by which the yards are turned, so that the wind may strike the sails in the manner desired.

BRING-TO. To bring a vessel's head as near as possible to the direction from which the wind blows; usually with a view to heaving-to, that is, stopping. See heave-to and luff.

BROADSIDE. The whole number of guns carried on one side of a vessel; starboard or port broadside, weather or lee broad-side.

CABLE. The heavy rope which was attached to the anchor, and held the ship to it. Cables are now chains, but in the period of this book were always hemp. To veer cable, to let more out, to let the ship go farther from the anchor. To slip the cable, to let it all go overboard, releasing the vessel. Cable's length: 120 fathoms.

CHASE, General. A chase by a fleet, in which, in order to more rapid advance, the places of the vessels in their usual order are not to be observed.

CLOSE-HAULED. See "Course."

COLUMN. See "Line Ahead."

COME UP. A ship comes up, when her bow comes more nearly to the direction of the wind. Used generally when the movement proceeds from some other cause than the movement of the helm. See "Luff."

CONVOY. A body of unarmed or weakly armed vessels, in company with ships of war.

CONVOY, to. To accompany a number of unarmed vessels, for their protection.

COURSE. The direction of a vessel's movement, with regard to the compass or to the wind.

Compass course. The point of the compass towards which the vessel heads.

Wind courses:

Close-hauled. As nearly in the direction from which the wind blows as is compatible with keeping the sails full; for square-rigged vessels six points. (See "Bearings by Compass."). For a north wind, the close-hauled courses are east-northeast and west-northwest.

Free. Not close-hauled.

Large. Very free.

Off the wind. Free.

On (or by) the wind. Close-hauled.

COURSES. The lowest sails on the fore and main masts.

CRUISE, to. To cover a certain portion of sea by movement back and forth over it.

CRUISER. A general term for armed ships, but applied more specifically to those not "of the line,"which therefore are more free and wider in their movements.

CURRENT

Lee Current. One the movement of which is away from the wind.

Weather Current. One which sets towards the wind.

EBB, ebb-tide. See "Tide."

FAIR, wind. A wind which allows a vessel to head her desired compass course.

FALL OFF. A vessel falls off, when, without the action of the helm, her head moves away from the wind. See "Come up."

FILL. ⎫ Sails are said to fill, or to be full, when the wind strikes the rear
FULL. ⎭ side, tending to move the vessel ahead.

FLOOD, flood tide. See "Tide."

FORE AND AFT. In classification of vessels, indicates those whose sails, when set, stretch from forward aft; more nearly lengthwise than across. Opposite to square-rigged.

FOREMAST, fore-topmast, etc. See "Spars."

FORESAIL, fore-topsail, etc. See "Sails."

FOUL, to. To entangle, to collide. A foul anchor, when the cable gets round the anchor.

FOUL, wind. A wind which prevents the vessel heading the desired compass course, compelling her to beat.

FREE, wind. A wind which allows the vessel to head the course desired. The amount to spare from the close-hauled course is sometimes designated. *E.g.*, the wind four points free; the wind would allow the vessel to come four points nearer the wind than her course requires.

FRIGATE. See "Vessel."

GAGE, weather and lee. A vessel, or fleet, is said to have the weather gage, when it is to windward of its opponent. Lee is opposite to weather.

HAUL, to. To haul (to) the wind is to change the course to that nearest the direction whence the wind comes.

To haul down the colors: to strike, to surrender.

HEAVE DOWN. To incline a vessel on one side, by purchases at the lower mastheads.

HEAVE-TO (HOVE-TO). To bring-to, (which see), and then to lay some sails aback, in order to keep the ship without movement ahead or astern.

HEEL, to. To incline a vessel on one side by shifting the weights on board, such as guns. "On the heel": to be thus inclined.

HELM. The tiller, or bar, which like a handle turns the rudder, and thus changes the course of the vessel.

Port the helm. To put the tiller to port, which turns the vessel's head to the right; to starboard the helm is the reverse.

Helm down. Tiller to leeward, vessel's head to windward; helm up, the reverse. See "Rudder."

HULL. The body of a vessel, as distinguished from the spars, or engines.

HULL, to (HULLED). A cannon ball striking the hull of a vessel is said to hull her.

JIB. See "Sails"
JIB-BOOM. See "Spars."

KEEP, to. To keep off, or away, is to change course away from the wind or from an enemy. See "To bear up."

LARGE. See "Course."

LEE. The direction toward which the wind blows. "Under the lee of," protected from
     wind and sea by land, or by a vessel, interposed.
   Lee Tide. See "Tide."

LEECH. The vertical side of a square sail. The upper and lower sides, horizontal, are
     called head and foot.

LEEWARD (pronounced looard). Direction of movement, or of bearing, opposite to
     the wind.

LIE-TO, to. To bring the vessels head on, or near, the wind, and remain nearly stopped.
     Usually in heavy weather, but not always.

LINE OF BATTLE. In the line of battle the vessels are ranged on the same straight line,
     steering the same course, one behind the others, so that all the broadsides are clear
     to bear upon an enemy. The line preferred is one of the close-hauled lines, because
     on them the movement of a vessel in the line is more easily regulated by backing, or
     shaking, some of the sails.

LINE, Ship of the. A vessel fitted by its force for the line of battle. Opposite generically
     to "cruiser." The modern term is "battleship."

LUFF, to. The movement of changing the course to nearer the direction whence the
     wind comes, by using the helm.

MAIN.   ⎫
MIZZEN.   ⎬   See "Spars" and "Sails."

MAST. See "Spars." "To the mast." A sail is said to be so when aback.

MONSOON. A trade wind, in the China and Indian seas, which blows uniformly from
     the northeast in winter, and from southwest in summer.

NEAP. See "Tide."

OFF—the wind. See "Course."
ON—the wind. See "Course."

PENNANT. A flag, indicating either the rank of the senior officer on board, or a signal
     applicable to a particular vessel.

POINT. See "Bearings, by Compass."

PORT. To the left hand, or on the left side, of a vessel, looking from aft forward.
     Opposite to Starboard.

PORT, to. Applied to steering. To move the tiller, or helm, to the left, which moves the
     rudder to the right and causes the vessel to change course towards the right hand.

QUARTER. Either side of the after part of a vessel;—starboard quarter, port quarter;
     weather quarter, lee quarter. Quarter deck: one side of the after upper deck, reserved
     for the officer exercising command, and for ceremonial purposes.

QUARTERS. A crew is at quarters when at the stations for battle.

RAKE, to. To fire the broadside from ahead or astern of an antagonist, so that the shot
     may sweep the length of the vessel, which at the period of this book was about four
     times the width.

RANDOM SHOT. The extreme range to which a gun could send its shot, giving very uncertain results.

REEF, to. To reduce the surface of a sail.

RUDDER. A solid framework, pivoted at the stern of a vessel, which being turned to one side deflects her course. See "Helm" and "Wheel."

SAILS. Sails are of two kinds: square, and fore and aft. Square sails spread more across the vessel, in the direction of her width. Fore and aft sails more in the direction of the length. Square sails are better for a free wind; and also for large vessels, because they can be more readily subdivided. Fore and aft sails trim nearer to the wind, and so are convenient for coasters, which generally are smaller.

Vessels carrying square sails are called square-rigged. They have always two masts, usually three; each carrying three or four sails, one above the other. These are named from the mast on which they are carried (see "Spars"); e.g., *main* sail, *fore* topsail, *mizzen* topgallant-sail; and also from their positions on the same mast. Thus, from lowest up, main sail, main topsail, main topgallantsail; and main royal, if there be a fourth. The fore and main sails are called also courses.

The topsails were the chief battle sails, because the largest, except the courses, and more manageable than the courses.

All square-rigged vessels carry fore and aft sails, three cornered, stretched between the bowsprit and jib-booms, and the fore topmast. These sails are called jibs.

Fore and aft vessels also carry jibs; but on each upright mast they have one great sail, the size of which makes it less easily handled in an emergency, therefore less fit for fighting. Above the big sail they have a small, light, three-cornered topsail, but this is merely a fair weather sail, useless in battle.

Vessels of war were almost all square-rigged, with three masts.

SAILS, STUDDING. Light square sails, for moderate weather, extended beyond the other square sails, to increase the normal spread of canvas. Set only with a free wind, and never in battle.

SCANTLING. The size, and consequent weight and strength, of the timbers of a vessel's hull.

SCHOONER. See "Vessel."

SHAKE, to. So to place a sail that the wind blows along it, neither filling nor backing. The sail is thus neutralized without taking in.

SHARP-UP. A yard is sharp-up, when turned by the braces as far as the rigging of the mast will allow. A close-hauled course requires the yards to be sharp-up, in order that the sails may be full.

SHIP. See "Vessel."

SLIP. See "Cable."

SLOOP. See "Vessel."

SPARS. A spar is a long piece of timber, cylindrical, tapering, in masts, towards one end, and in yards towards both. Spars serve for spreading the several sails of a vessel. The names of spars vary with their use and position. Chiefly, for ships of war, they divide into masts, yards, and booms.

A mast is an upright, and is in three connected pieces: the lower mast, the topmast, and the top-gallant-mast. Most ships of war had three such masts: fore, near the bow; main, near the centre; mizzen, near the stern.

The bowsprit is also a mast; not upright, but projecting straight ahead from the bow, approaching horizontal, but inclining upwards. Like the masts, it has three divisions: the lower, or bowsprit proper, the jib-boom, and the flying-jib-boom.

Across the masts, horizontal, are the yards, four in number, lower, topsail, topgallant, and royal. Yards are further designated by the name of the mast to which each belongs; *e.g.*, foreyard, main topsail yard, mizzen topgallant yard, main royal yard.

The bowsprit formerly had one yard, called the spritsail yard. This has disappeared. Otherwise it serves to spread the three-cornered sails called jibs. These sails were useful for turning a vessel, because their projection before the centre gave them great leverage.

Fore and aft vessels had no yards. See "Sails."

SPRING. See page 59, note 4.

SQUARE-RIGGED. See "Sails" and "Spars."

STAND, to. Used, nautically, to express movement and direction, e.g., "to stand toward the enemy," "to stand out of harbor," "to stand down," "to stand south." The underlying idea seems to be that of sustained, decided movement.

STARBOARD. To the right hand, or on the right side, of a vessel, looking from aft forward. Opposite to Port.

STEER, to. To control the course by the use of the helm and rudder.

STERN. The extreme rear, or after, part of a vessel.

STRATEGY. That department of the Art of War which decides the distribution and movements of armies, or of fleets, with reference to the objects of a campaign as a whole.

STRIKE, to. Applied to the flag. To haul down the flag in token of surrender.

TACK. A vessel is on the starboard tack, or port tack, according as the wind comes from the starboard or port hand.

TACK, to. When a vessel is close-hauled, with the wind on one side, to tack is to turn round towards the wind, in order to be again close-hauled, with the wind on the other side.

To wear is to attain the same object by turning away from the wind. Wearing is surer than tacking, but loses ground to leeward.

To tack, or wear, in succession, the leading vessel tacks, and those which follow tack, each, as it arrives at the same point; the order thus remaining the same. To tack, or wear together, all tack at the same moment, which reverses the order.

TACTICS. That department of the Art of War which decides the disposition and movements of an army, or of a fleet, on a particular field of battle, in presence of an enemy.

TIDAL CURRENTS.

Ebb tide, the outflow of the water due to the tides.

Flood tide, the inflow of the water due to the tides.

Lee tide, the set of the current to leeward.

Weather tide, the set of the current to windward.

TIDE. The rise and fall of the water of the oceans under the influence of the moon. Used customarily, but inaccurately, to express the currents produced by the changes of level.

High tide, or high water, the two highest levels of the day.

Low tide, or low water, the two lowest.

Neap tide: the least rise and fall during the lunar month.

Spring tide: the greatest rise and fall during the same, being soon after full and change of moon.

TRADE, the. A term applied to a body of merchant vessels, to or from a particular destination.

TRADE WIND. A wind which blows uniformly from the same general direction throughout a fixed period. In the West Indies, from the northeast the year round. See also "Monsoon."

VEER. See "Cable."

VESSEL. A general term for all constructions intended to float upon and move through the water. Specific definitions applicable to this book:

Ship, a square-rigged vessel with three masts.

Brig, a square-rigged vessel with two masts.

Schooner, a fore and aft rigged vessel with two or more masts.

Sloop, a fore and aft rigged vessel with one mast.

VESSELS OF WAR.

Ship of the Line. A ship with three or more tiers of guns, of which two are on covered decks; that is, have a deck above them. See "Line of Battle Ship."

Frigate. A ship with one tier of guns on a covered deck.

Sloop of War. A ship, the guns of which are not covered, being on the upper (spar) deck.

Sloops of war were sometimes brigs, but then were usually so styled.

WAKE. The track left by a vessel's passage through the water. "In the wake of": directly astern of.

WAY. Movement through the water. "To get underway": to pass from stand-still to movement.

WEAR, to. See under "Tack."

WEATHER. Relative position to windward of another object. Opposite to Lee. Weather side, lee side, of a vessel; weather fleet, lee fleet; weather gage, lee gage (see "Gage"); weather shore, lee shore.

WEATHER, to. To pass to windward of a vessel, or of any other object.

WEATHERLY. The quality of a vessel which favors her getting, or keeping, to windward.

WEIGH, to. To raise the anchor from the bottom. Used alone; *e.g.*, "the fleet weighed."

WHEEL. So called from its form. The mechanical appliance, a wheel, with several handles for turning it, by which power is increased, and also transmitted from the steersman on deck to the tiller below, in order to steer the vessel.

WIND AND WATER, between. That part of a vessel's side which comes out of water when she inclines to a strong side wind, but otherwise is under water.

WINDWARD. Direction from which the wind blows.

YARD. See "Spars."

INDEX

A

Algeciras 87, 160, 161
Arbuthnot, Marriott, British Vice-Admiral
60, 81, 102, 103, 104, 119, 120,
122, 123, 128
Arethusa 48, 61
Armed Neutrality, the 12, 108
Arnold, Benedict 12, 15, 16, 19, 20, 21, 22,
23, 24, 25, 26, 28, 34, 35, 39, 43,
104, 105, 119, 122, 123, 132
Asiatic Immigration 12

B

Barbados 71, 72, 99, 101, 102, 111, 116,
128, 137, 138, 143, 144, 157
Barrington, Samuel, British Admiral 71, 72,
74, 76, 77, 78, 81, 107, 144, 159
Basse Terre 137, 138
Belle Poule 48, 61
Blane, Sir Gilbert 88, 154, 155
Burgoyne, Sir John 12, 15, 20, 21, 25, 27,
43, 44, 45, 49
Byng, John, British Admiral 68, 97, 101,
128
Byron, John, British Vice-Admiral 47, 48,
49, 54, 56, 57, 59, 72, 76, 77, 78,
80, 81, 83, 85, 91, 95, 105

C

Canada 15, 16, 18, 20, 27, 35, 138, 139,
140, 141, 142, 152, 158, 160
Cap François 102, 103, 105, 116, 124, 143,
156, 157
Carkett, Robert, British Naval Captain 96,
101, 108, 109
Carleton, Sir Guy 16, 18, 19, 20, 22, 23,
24, 25, 26, 27, 30, 39, 43
Carolinas, North and South 30, 71, 81, 82,
103, 104, 119, 123
Champlain, Lake 12, 15, 16, 18, 19, 20, 21,
22, 26, 30, 34, 35, 38, 39, 43
Charleston, South Carolina 30, 34, 36, 81,
103, 104, 119

Charleston Harbour 30, 34
Chesapeake Bay 27, 82, 104, 119, 122,
127, 137
Clinton, Sir Henry, General 30, 34, 36, 40,
41, 44, 45, 46, 49, 81, 82, 103, 104,
119, 122, 123, 124
Commerce 47, 48, 107, 111, 131
Convoys 44, 47, 48, 49, 72, 76, 77, 78, 85,
86, 88, 89, 91, 92, 101, 102, 103,
105, 106, 107, 111, 112, 114, 115,
119, 123, 124, 131, 132, 134, 137,
143, 144, 145, 148, 156, 159, 160,
161, 165, 166, 171, 175
Cornwallis, Charles, Earl, General 30, 40,
54, 82, 104, 116, 119, 123, 124,
127, 128, 137, 147
Cornwallis, Sir William 80, 105, 106, 139,
140
Crown Point 16, 19, 25, 26, 27, 30, 35
Cuddalore 168, 170, 171, 175, 176, 177

D

D'Estaing, Comte, French Admiral 47, 48,
49, 51, 52, 54, 55, 57, 58, 59, 60,
61, 72, 74, 76, 80, 81, 82, 85, 104,
144
D'Orves, Comte, French Admiral 163, 164,
166
D'Orvilliers, Comte, French Admiral 61,
62, 64, 66, 67, 85, 86
Darby, George, British Vice-Admiral 107,
131, 132, 160, 164
Delaware 39, 40, 44, 45, 47, 48, 49, 51, 60,
124, 161
Des Touches, French Commodore 119,
120, 122
De Barras, French Commodore 122, 124,
125, 127, 128
De Bouillé, French General 92, 97, 138
De Cordova, Spanish Admiral 86, 89, 132,
159
De Grasse, Comte, French Admiral 26, 38,
82, 112, 114, 115, 116, 123, 124,

127, 128, 137, 138, 140, 142, 143, 144, 146, 147, 148, 150, 151, 154, 155, 157, 159, 162, 164

De Guichen, Comte de 82, 83, 92, 93, 94, 96, 97, 98, 99, 102, 103, 108, 112, 116, 132, 137

De Langara, Spanish Admiral 88, 89

De Suffren, Bailli, French Captain 12, 52, 80, 83, 89, 93, 114, 134, 159, 164, 165, 166, 168, 169, 170, 171, 172, 173, 174, 175, 176, 177

De Ternay, French Commodore 103, 106, 119

De Vaudreuil, Marquis, French Admiral 146, 150, 151, 155, 156, 157

Doggers-bank 132

Dominica 71, 92, 143, 145, 146, 148, 150, 152

Douglas, Sir Charles, British naval captain 18, 21, 22, 24, 25, 26, 28, 95, 156, 158

F

Farragut 60

Fighting Instructions 93, 96, 97, 108

France 12, 15, 26, 28, 40, 46, 47, 48, 58, 59, 71, 82, 85, 87, 108, 116, 122, 123, 124, 131, 132, 143, 151, 163

France, Ile de 90, 163, 164, 166

G

Gardiner's Bay 104, 119

Gates, Horatio, American General 23, 104

George, Lake 15, 16, 28, 43

Gibraltar 5, 12, 47, 87, 88, 89, 102, 107, 131, 132, 157, 159, 160, 161, 162, 164

Grant, James, British General 74, 76

Graves, Sir Thomas, British Admiral 103, 123, 124, 125, 127, 128, 134, 137, 139

Great Britain 12, 15, 18, 28, 29, 46, 47, 71, 85, 87, 102, 108, 112, 132, 133, 159, 163

Grenada 76, 80, 81, 82, 105, 116

H

Haïti 102, 103, 105, 116, 123, 124

Hardy, Sir Charles 85, 86, 87

Holland 12, 108, 164

Hood, Sir Samuel 26, 70, 111, 112, 114, 115, 116, 117, 123, 124, 125, 126, 127, 128, 129, 137, 138, 139, 140, 141, 142, 143, 144, 145, 146, 147, 148, 150, 152, 155, 156, 157, 158

Hotham, William, British naval captain 36, 38, 72, 102

Howe, Richard, Earl, British Admiral 24, 29, 34, 35, 40, 44, 45, 46, 47, 48, 49, 50, 51, 52, 54, 55, 56, 57, 58, 59, 60, 61, 69, 72, 104, 157, 159, 160, 161, 162, 166

Howe, Sir William, British General 20, 21, 27, 34, 35, 36, 38, 39, 40, 41, 43, 49, 82

Hudson River 15, 21, 27, 29, 35, 38, 39, 40, 43, 44, 45

Hughes, Sir Edward, British Admiral 83, 134, 163, 164, 166, 168, 169, 170, 171, 172, 174, 175, 176, 177

Hughes, Sir Richard 157

Hyder, Ali, Sultan of Mysore 163, 166, 168, 170, 171, 175

I

Inflexible 22, 23, 24, 25, 26, 28

J

Jamaica 34, 80, 85, 103, 105, 111, 123, 124, 128, 143, 156, 157, 159

Japan 13

Johnstone, George, British Commadore 164, 165, 177

Jones, John Paul, American naval captain 148

K

Kempenfelt, Richard, British Admiral 83, 137, 143, 159, 160

Keppel, Augustus, British Admiral 48, 59, 61, 62, 64, 65, 66, 67, 68, 69, 70, 71, 78, 81, 82, 83, 85, 97, 134, 157, 166

L

La Motte Picquet, French Commodore 82, 91, 105, 132, 162

Leeward Islands Station 71, 81, 87

Les Saintes 145, 147, 148

M

Manners. Lord Robert, British naval captain 141, 143
Martinique 71, 72, 76, 91, 92, 97, 98, 99, 102, 103, 105, 112, 114, 115, 116, 123, 138, 139, 143, 144
Mathews, Thomas, British Admiral 68, 97
Minorca 68, 87, 89, 90, 131, 132
Mobile 60
Monroe Doctrine 12, 29
Montgomery, Richard, American General 16, 18
Moultrie, Fort 30, 32, 34, 35
Moultrie, William, American officer 32, 33

N

Narragansett Bay 35, 40, 45, 48, 51, 54, 56, 76, 82, 103, 106
Nelson 30, 34, 35, 36, 43, 60, 78, 83, 89, 92, 97, 105, 111, 138, 141, 157, 169, 172
Newport, Rhode Island 40, 51, 52, 56, 57, 72, 103, 119, 122, 123, 124, 125
New Jersey 30, 39, 40, 43, 45, 49, 50
New York 15, 16, 20, 29, 30, 34, 35, 36, 38, 39, 40, 43, 44, 45, 46, 47, 48, 49, 50, 51, 52, 54, 55, 56, 57, 58, 59, 60, 72, 81, 82, 102, 103, 104, 111, 116, 119, 123, 124, 128, 157, 161

O

Order of Battle 68, 70

P

Palliser, Sir Hugh, British Admiral 62, 64, 65, 66, 68, 69, 70, 82, 97
Parker, Hyde, British Naval Captain 35, 38, 39, 81
Parker, Sir Hyde, British Admiral 78, 81, 91, 95, 108, 132, 133, 134, 135
Parker, Sir Peter, British Admiral 30, 36, 40, 103, 105, 111, 123, 124, 128
Pellew, Edward, British midshipman 24, 28, 34, 43
Philadelphia 27, 40, 43, 44, 45, 46, 48, 52, 104

Q

Quebec 16, 18, 19, 22, 25, 26

R

Rhode Island 40, 51, 52, 54, 55, 57, 58, 82, 103, 104, 106, 161
Riedesel, Baron 20, 24, 25, 26
Rochambeau, French general 116, 119, 124, 128
Rodney, Sir George 28, 40, 46, 55, 69, 76, 81, 82, 83, 87, 88, 89, 90, 91, 92, 93, 94, 95, 96, 97, 98, 99, 100, 101, 102, 103, 104, 107, 108, 109, 111, 112, 114, 115, 116, 117, 123, 124, 128, 131, 132, 133, 134, 143, 144, 145, 146, 147, 148, 150, 151, 152, 154, 155, 156, 157, 158, 159
Rowley, Joshua, Rear-Admiral 77, 78, 91, 95

S

Sandy Hook 35, 44, 49, 50, 52, 56, 81, 103, 124, 128
Santa Lucia 71, 72, 74, 76, 82, 91, 97, 98, 99, 102, 111, 112, 114, 115, 116, 138, 143, 144, 159
Saratoga 15, 27, 44
Saumarez, James 33, 34, 135, 137, 154, 158
Savannah 81, 82, 104
Schuyler, Philip, General 19, 25
Spain 12, 15, 40, 85, 87, 131, 132
St. Eustatius 111, 112, 115, 132
St. Kitts 26, 76, 81, 102, 111, 115, 127, 137, 138, 139, 143, 144
St. Lawrence, river 15, 16, 18, 19, 21, 28

T

Ticonderoga 16, 20, 23, 26, 27, 39, 43
Tippoo Saib, Sultan of Mysore 175
Tobago 116, 144
Trenton 40
Trincomalee 166, 168, 169, 170, 171, 172, 174, 175, 177

U

Ushant 61–70, 83, 85, 99, 137, 159, 160

V

Valcour Island 21, 23

W

Washington, Fort 39
Washington, George 12, 25, 29, 36, 38, 39, 40, 44, 45, 49, 51, 54, 102, 103, 104, 116, 119, 124, 128
West Indies 5, 12, 15, 48, 52, 71, 72, 76, 81, 82, 83, 87, 88, 89, 90, 102, 103, 108, 111, 112, 119, 123, 124, 128, 132, 133, 137, 157, 185
White, Thomas 78, 128, 129, 158

Y

Yorktown 12, 54, 82, 104, 116, 119, 123, 128

Z

Zoutman, Johan A., Dutch Admiral 132, 134

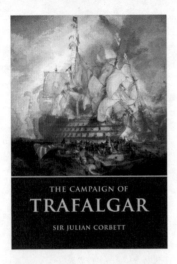

In 1910 Sir Julian Corbett published *The Campaign of Trafalgar* with the intent of providing the first 'staff account' of the celebrated battle. Beautifully written and meticulous in detail, Corbett examines the various relations of the events of the campaign, from Nelson's remarkable chase of Villeneuve, to Bonaparte's seemingly reckless unreadiness, while also evaluating the political manœuvres and negotiations carried on between Britain and her allies.

1 84588 059 5
£18
320 pages, 12 Maps and Diagrams

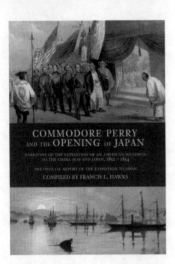

On 31 March 1854, Commodore Matthew Perry signed the Treaty of Kanagawa on behalf of the United States' government. This moment signalled the end of the ruling Japanese Shogunate's policy of isolationism, which had been in place since the sixteenth century. This is the official account of Perry's expedition which led to this historic moment. Written in a fluent and engaging style, this first-hand report provides a fascinating insight into both the details, as well as the wider social and cultural context, of this important expedition.

1 84588 026 9
£25
512 pages, 86 illustrations

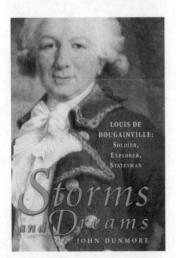

Louis de Bougainville is best known for his circumnavigation of the globe from 1766–1769. Throughout his distinguished career, however, he participated in many turning points of world history, including the birth of the United States and the French Revolution. One of Napoleon's senators, he was gifted in navigation, seamanship, soldiering, mathematics and the science of longtitude and latitude. John Dunmore brings the man and his era to life in this vivid and elegantly written biography.

1 84588 076 5
£20
296 pages, 15 illustrations

For further information please see www.nonsuch-publishing.com